THE CHALLENGE

SOVEREIGNTY, DEVOLUTION AND INDEPENDENCE

THE CHALLENGE TO WESTMINSTER

Sovereignty, Devolution and Independence

edited by

H.T. DICKINSON and **MICHAEL LYNCH**

TUCKWELL PRESS

First published in Great Britain in 2000 by
Tuckwell Press Ltd
The Mill House, Phantassie, East Linton, East Lothian, EH40 3DG
Scotland

ISBN 1 86323 152 3

British Library Cataloguing-in-Publication Data. A catalogue
record for this book is available on request from the British Library

Typeset in 12/14 Times
Printed and bound in Great Britain by
The Cromwell Press, Trowbridge, Wiltshire.

Contents

Contributors   vii
Preface   ix

1 Introduction   1
Michael Lynch and *H.T. Dickinson*

2 The Development of Parliamentary Sovereignty   12
Jeffrey Goldsworthy

3 Scotland's Parliament in its British context, 1603-1707   22
Julian Goodare

4 The Idea of Sovereignty and the Act of Union   33
John Robertson

5 Scottish Sovereignty in the Eighteenth Century   42
Alex Murdoch

6 Sovereignty in the American Revolution   50
H.T. Dickinson

7 Ireland: From Legislative Independence to Legislative Union,   61
    1782-1800
Thomas Bartlett

8 Church-State Relations in Scotland after the Union   71
Stewart J. Brown

9 Cultural Independence and Political Devolution in Wales   81
Keith Robbins

10 Sovereignty and Independence in the Dominions   91
Ged Martin

11 The Home Rule Campaign in Ireland   102
Charles Townshend

12 The First Home Rule Movement in Scotland, 1886-1918   113
Graeme Morton

13 Civil Society, Protest and Parliament: Housing and Land   123
     in Modern Scotland
Ewen A. Cameron

14 Legislative and Executive Autonomy in Modern Scotland   133
I.G.C. Hutchison

15 Home Rule and Devolution in Ulster   143
     Paul Arthur

16 From National Identity to Nationalism, 1945-1999   154
     James Mitchell

     Index   165

Contributors

PAUL ARTHUR is a Professor of Politics at the University of Ulster at Londonderry.

THOMAS BARTLETT is Professor of Modern Irish History at University College, Dublin.

STEWART J. BROWN is Professor of Ecclesiastical History and Dean of the Faculty of Divinity at the University of Edinburgh.

EWEN A. CAMERON is a Senior Lecturer in Scottish History at the University of Edinburgh.

H.T. DICKINSON is Richard Lodge Professor of British History at the University of Edinburgh.

JEFFREY GOLDSWORTHY is a Professor of Law at Monash University, Australia.

JULIAN GOODARE is a Lecturer in Scottish History at the University of Edinburgh.

I.G.C. HUTCHISON is a Senior Lecturer in History at the University of Stirling.

MICHAEL LYNCH is Sir William Fraser Professor of Scottish History at the University of Edinburgh.

GED MARTIN is Professor of Canadian Studies at the University of Edinburgh.

JAMES MITCHELL is a Professor of Politics at the University of Strathclyde.

GRAEME MORTON is a Lecturer in Economic and Social History at the University of Edinburgh.

ALEX MURDOCH is a Senior Lecturer in Scottish History at the University of Edinburgh.

KEITH ROBBINS is Senior Vice-Chancellor at the University of Wales, Lampeter.

JOHN ROBERTSON is a Fellow of St Hugh's College, Oxford.

CHARLES TOWNSEND is a Professor of Modern History at the University of Keele.

Preface

The restoration of a Scottish parliament in Edinburgh is a major political and constitutional development in the life of the nation. Its opening in 1999 caused great excitement in Scotland and very considerable interest across the world. It also inspired the historians in the various departments of history at the University of Edinburgh to come together to mark this auspicious occasion by hosting an international conference at the university in March 2000. While undoubtedly wishing well to this important experiment in devolution, these historians not unnaturally recognised that the new Scottish parliament was bound to face difficulties in establishing effective working relations with the Westminster parliament. The doctrine and practice of parliamentary sovereignty is so powerful and so entrenched that historians recognise that it will be difficult for the Westminster parliament to sacrifice some of its powers and to concede real influence to the legislative bodies it has established in Edinburgh, and also in Cardiff and Belfast. It was therefore decided that the focus of the conference in Edinburgh should be on the historical evidence that indicates the likely challenge that Westminster will face from these rival legislative bodies. One theme of the conference therefore focused on the earlier challenges posed by the desire for legislative devolution or even independence in Wales, Ireland, the American colonies and the white-settled Dominions of the empire. The other theme focused in more detail on the Scottish context. It concentrated on relations between the Edinburgh and Westminster parliaments before the Act of Union, on the discussions about sovereignty during the Union debates, on the extent to which Scotland did retain a measure of self-government after the Union, and on the long and tortuous campaigns for devolution or independence since the later nineteenth century.

A number of historians at the University of Edinburgh contributed papers to this conference (and essays to this book) and the various departments of history combined to plan and organise the conference. Katie Stevenson and other postgraduates in the Scottish History department played a major role in promoting and organising the conference. The conference and this book would not have been possible without generous financial support from the Scottish History Society, the departments of History and Scottish History at Edinburgh, and the Faculty Group of Arts, Divinity and Music at the university. The staunch backing of the Provost, Dr Frances Dow, and the Head of the History Department, Professor Robert Anderson, is particularly appreciated. We are also grateful to John Tuckwell for producing this volume so speedily and we are very appreciative of the efforts of Sir David Steel, the Presiding Officer of the new Scottish parliament, who opened the conference with a most appropriate introductory talk.

Harry Dickinson
Michael Lynch

1

Introduction

MICHAEL LYNCH and H.T. DICKINSON

For two centuries Westminster politicians and constitutional lawyers have stressed the importance of the doctrine of parliamentary sovereignty as the essential principle of Britain's unwritten constitution. This doctrine holds that the Westminster parliament's legislative authority is absolute, omnicompetent and legally unlimited. This creates problems for any other legislative body or political agency dealing with the Westminster parliament because the power of the latter is not limited by any norms that are legally enforceable by the courts or any other human agency. Parliament in this doctrine means its three component parts of monarch, House of Lords and House of Commons which, when acting in concert, possess unlimited legislative authority. This does not mean that parliament's authority is not limited by such norms as divine or natural law, by principles of justice and morality, or by long-established constitutional conventions, but it does mean that the Westminster parliament's authority cannot be limited by legally enforceable decisions taken by the courts or any other legislative body or human agency. The voters can, of course, change the composition of the House of Commons, but they cannot appeal to a written constitution or legally employ some other institution (such as a supreme court) in order to challenge and reject the legislative decisions taken by parliament.

It was generally accepted for centuries that there had to be in any polity a single, absolute, arbitrary and unlimited authority. It was widely accepted in England that it was far too dangerous to place this authority in the hands of the king alone or in the people at large. The propertied and ruling elite preferred to locate this authority in the king-in-parliament. The doctrine of parliamentary sovereignty developed over several centuries as king-in-parliament established itself as the most authoritative law-making institution in England. The supporters of this constitutional doctrine sought to promote the sovereignty of king-in-parliament in order to limit the power of the crown, to assert parliament's authority in matters of religion and to reject popular sovereignty and the natural rights of the subject. Parliament gradually achieved omnicompetent authority in all administrative, legislative and judicial matters and the power to make, repeal and amend any law. From the 1530s onwards parliament extended its omnicompetent authority in temporal matters into the spiritual sphere as the authority of the pope was rejected. Parliament assumed the power to interfere in the government of the church and even to decide such constitutional issues as the succession to the crown and the extent of the royal prerogative. Authority of this extent was not gained without a long struggle with the monarch and the staunch adherents of the divine right of kings, but, after the Glorious revolution of 1688-89, a growing majority of the political elite accepted that the sovereign authority in the state rested with the king-in-parliament. It appeared to the propertied elite that liberty and stability could be best achieved if the sovereign parliament could restrict the powers of arbitrary monarch and restrain the rights of an unruly people.

This interpretation of parliamentary sovereignty was essentially aristocratic since parliament was not really representative of the whole people. From the later eighteenth century its aristocratic nature was challenged by reformers who wished to make parliament more representative and accountable. Those who sought constitutional reform rarely desired to establish and certainly did not succeed in establishing a written constitution to limit the authority of parliament. Their goal was not to limit the power of parliament, but to make it more accountable to the people at large. From the late eighteenth century onwards the ability of the crown to influence the composition of parliament was slowly but steadily eroded, while a series of reforms from 1832 onwards greatly expanded the electorate and made the House of Commons much more representative of the people. The House of Commons also steadily increased its power in relation to both the crown and the House of Lords. While these changes made parliament a more democratic institution, they did not destroy the doctrine of parliamentary sovereignty and certainly did not make the people the sovereign authority in the state. The people achieved a greater role in deciding the composition of parliament, but they did not secure any constitutional authority or agency that could legally limit parliament's sovereign authority. There might now be conventions on how parliament may act and even moral restraints restricting in practice what parliament can do, but parliament's authority remains sovereign, omnicompetent and uncontrolled by any other agency. Parliament can legally limit its authority only by its own decisions, but these decisions can never be regarded as permanent and for all time. The doctrine of parliamentary sovereignty means that a subsequent parliament can always repeal or amend a legislative act passed by a previous parliament.

The doctrine of parliamentary sovereignty has become deeply entrenched in English (and to a significant, though lesser, extent in British) constitutional thought and practice since at least the mid-eighteenth century. It can reasonably be argued that this doctrine has helped to produce a political system that has achieved a combination of liberty and stability that has not been matched by any other nation over the last two centuries and more. This political success has made the doctrine of parliamentary sovereignty virtually sacrosanct in many circles. It certainly helps to explain why there is still a clear majority in the United Kingdom in favour of maintaining the union and the authority of the Westminster parliament and why there has been so much difficulty in surrendering authority to the European Union. It also means that the recent decision to devolve legislative authority to elected bodies in Edinburgh, Cardiff and Stormont is bound to raise constitutional difficulties both for the Westminster parliament and for these devolved legislative bodies. In the late 1990s Westminster took a constitutional leap in the dark with the creation of a new parliament in Scotland and new legislative assemblies in Wales and Northern Ireland. These devolved legislatures may not remain satisfied with the limited powers conceded to them by Westminster and there is clearly the potential for a sustained political challenge to the sovereign authority still claimed by the Westminster parliament. It is not at all clear at this stage whether this new constitutional arrangement will improve or ultimately destroy the unity of the United Kingdom.

The aim of this collection of essays is to explore what the historical record can tell us of the constitutional problems that may arise and can reasonably be expected to develop between Westminster and these new legislative bodies. After all, Westminster's authority has not always been unlimited or unchallenged, and the peoples of these islands have considerable historical experience of seeking to establish local legislative bodies more representative of their interests - at least in their opinion - than the parliament meeting at Westminster. Westminster's claim of sovereign authority has created political problems in England's relations with Scotland ever since the union of the crown in 1603. The first essay in this collection examines how the doctrine of parliamentary sovereignty developed over many centuries. Eight of the other essays in this volume examine important aspects of Scotland's relations with the Westminster parliament. These essays explore the authority of the Scottish parliament before it was dissolved by the Act of Union, rehearse the debates on sovereignty during the discussions on the Act of Union, assess how far Scotland escaped the influence of Westminster and governed itself after the Union, and trace the long and convoluted campaigns to establish devolved administrative and legislative bodies in Edinburgh. The other six essays explore the historical record of other British peoples - in these islands and in overseas colonies - who also have had experience of either accommodating themselves to, or challenging the authority of, the Westminster parliament.

I

Different traditions of the uniqueness of the Westminster parliament, both before and after 1707, and of the distinctive 'democratic' character of Scottish politics have served to obscure the similarities between the two institutions. As is consistently argued in this volume, both the English and Scottish parliaments claimed and exercised sovereign power; their similarities (in the aggregation and exercise of power and their broad composition as representative of a largely landed elite) outweighed their differences (of being bi-cameral and unicameral legislatures respectively). The notion, readily and somewhat uncritically accepted in the later 1980s by both the Scottish Constitutional Convention and the General Assembly, that Scotland enjoyed a political tradition which was markedly more 'democratic' than that of both England or post-1707 Britain is largely based on a myth.

It is an extraordinary tribute to the power of populist notions of history that the Scottish Constitutional Convention based its historical arguments and its Claim of Right (1988) on seriously flawed assumptions - both about an alleged distinctive notion of sovereignty in the Scottish political tradition and the workings of the pre-1707 Scottish parliament. These assumptions seemed to have worked at three levels. Like much else in modern populist thinking, there were echoes in the Claim of Right of the ringing tones of certain passages in the Declaration of Arbroath (1320) which emphasised the rights of the Scottish people to rid themselves of kings who did not come up to the mark prescribed for them. Yet, the Declaration did not enjoy the popularity in the sixteenth or seventeenth centuries which it has had in the twentieth and it played little or no part in the pre-1707 debates. Neither the advocates nor the opponents of a union in 1706-7 appealed to the sovereignty of the 'people'. Alternatively, it is largely from George Buchanan that the notion of the historicity of a Scottish democratic 'tradition' derives. Yet by 1700, the Buchanan tradition, based on his *Rerum Scoticarum Historia* which had gone through a large number of editions in printing presses throughout Europe during the century after its first publication in 1582, had largely lapsed. The sting in his arguments about the right of the 'people' to depose kings, originally targeted on Mary, Queen of Scots, had been drawn after the unseating of James VII in 1689. It is a striking example, both of the resonance of an historical source across the centuries and of the capacity for it to be misunderstood. For Buchanan, *populus* meant the people who mattered, as distinct from *universus populus*, who did not. Even then, he had to make a further distinction because, in the civil war which followed Mary's deposition in 1567 the majority of the nobility had taken the wrong side: he drew a line between those who were right and those who disenfranchised themselves by wilful error. It is a view of politics which would not be out of place in Pinochet's Chile. Yet, retranslated as the will of the people as a whole, it has, as a result of Lord Cooper's celebrated ruling in 1950 - that the unlimited sovereignty of parliament was a 'distinctively English principle' with 'no counterpart in Scottish constitutional law' - become almost an article of faith in a new Scottish political tradition.

The third level of misunderstanding is more straight-forward. The workings and legislation of the pre-1707 parliament are not well known and the sources for many aspects of its work are poor. The last sizeable work of any authority on the Scottish parliament was written by Robert Rait in 1924. Scotland's equivalent of England's celebrated *History of Parliament* details only burgh and shire commissioners, the least powerful element in the Scottish house. Little is available to tell us of debates in the pre-1707 parliament, except for stray gleanings from private correspondence, and only a little less of how members voted; apart from an isolated case in 1621, there are no division lists before 1689, and half of those which survive belong to the Union debate of 1706-07 itself. Fines were imposed for non-attendance, although the parliament sat, even after 1689, only seven or eight weeks of the year, with business confined to two days a week. More is available, of course, to tell us about its legislation. Increasingly in the later seventeenth century it engaged in a remarkable amount of economic interventionism, stimulating agricultural change, small industries and colonial ventures, not all of which ended, like the well-known Darien adventure, in disaster. The greatest contrast between the two institutions lay in their working practices. Yet otherwise, the increasingly wide agenda on which the Scottish parliament legislated serves to underline the fact that it claimed untrammelled sovereignty. How else, one might ask, did it think that it had the authority to legislate itself out of existence?

In the pre-Union debates, the nearest anyone involved in this controversy came to a more radical position was probably George Ridpath, who argued for a linkage between sovereignty and 'freehold'. This, however, fell considerably short of a Locke-style position. Freeholders in Scotland, although a relatively new phenomenon, were only a tiny addition to the traditional landed elite in parliament: they had one or two representatives per shire and, after 1660, were subject to annual election; each noble, by contrast, was entitled to represent himself. The often-quoted admission by Sir John Clerk of Penicuik, that the Union had been carried 'contrary to the inclinations of at least three-fourths of the kingdom', was less an admission of its unpopularity than a pointer to how much the post-Union government had to guard against popular unrest. The more broadly accepted view saw Scotland's sovereignty in terms of its utility. Viewed in that perspective, the economic difficulties which had become manifest from the mid-1690s onwards focused for proponents of incorporating union such as William Seton of Pitmedden on the 'advantages' which such a union would bring. The profound worries of other sectors of the Scottish economy resulted in a series of splits amongst the burgh commissioners in 1706-07 on the disadvantages likely to be brought about by free trade.

How did power and sovereignty operate in pre-Union Scotland? The experience of the sixteenth and seventeenth centuries leaves seemingly conflicting impressions. The age of what is often called 'state formation' produced in Scotland, as it did in England, a parliament sitting by authority of the crown which claimed supreme authority in all matters. These included religion, as happened in the so-called 'Black Acts' parliament of 1584 and also in the 'Golden Acts' parliament of 1592, when the privileges of the church were granted and confirmed by parliament. The general assembly, despite generations of Presbyterian claims to the contrary, was a subordinate body, which clearly after 1592 sat by authority of parliament. This status was confirmed both in 1689-90, when the church was 'by the law established', and after 1707, when its privileges were guaranteed by the Act of Union. The result in the United Kingdom produced by the Act of Union of 1707 was, as S.J. Brown terms it, a 'religiously schizophrenic state', with Anglican and Presbyterian churches each recognised as state churches. It is another example of parallel development between England and Scotland as well as convergence.

On the other hand, how Scotland was actually governed after 1603, when a multiple kingdom came into being and, after 1707, when a state emerged which was 'united' but not unitary, defies easy explanation. In the immediate circumstances following the union of the crowns, it is too simple a solution to think merely in terms of 'absentee kingship' for the first king of what he insisted on calling 'Great Britain' was too closely in touch with the politics of the northernmost of his three kingdoms to alter the course of the creation of a monarchical state, with the focus of its power invested in privy council and parliament. It has been claimed that what James VI and I did was to buy time for the unpopular notion of a union. Yet also, his close links with Scotland prevented the device of a viceroy, which was the solution for Ireland, despite - or because of - its parliament. That contrast, with Ireland, repeatedly came into the mind of contemporaries. After 1603, the avoidance of a viceroy guaranteed Scotland a degree of autonomy which Ireland lacked. Scotland had the means to avoid what its own privy council warned of in 1607: that the union of the crowns should not be allowed to reduce it to the status of a 'slavish and conquered province' - like Ireland, it might be added. Although the guarantor of its existence fluctuated, Scotland enjoyed an administrative autonomy.

This brings us to the second set of definitions of how Scottish and British politics worked. The Cromwellian regime of the 1650s had, for the first time, produced a parliament for the three kingdoms, even if it deliberately eschewed the idea of Britain: it was called the parliament of the 'Commonwealth of England, Scotland and Ireland'. That experience of direct rule was not repeated, either after 1660 or after 1707. The restored monarchy, after 1660, produced a different solution, in which there was a nostalgic and calculated calling up of the past. Even so, the restored Scottish parliament was part of a new solution in the partnership between crown and political elites. With what was now genuinely an absentee monarchy, the secretary of state increasingly acted as the king's representative. Lauderdale in the 1660s and 1670s began very much to look like a viceroy, using the previously largely ceremonial office of royal commissioner to parliament as the linkage between the crown, firmly ensconced in England, and political elites in Scotland. In this sense, the role of Lauderdale before the union of parliaments is reminiscent of the roles played by both the Campbell dukes, Argyll and Islay, in the four decades after that union. They were virtual viceroys. But they were also part of the practical guarantees that made Scotland, both before and after 1707, a distinctively separate part of the British archipelago. The pre-1707 parliament produced large amounts of legislation relating to Scotland. The post-1707 Westminster parliament, praised by a leading authority on eighteenth-century England for passing an impressive, growing amount of legislation, virtually ignored Scotland, passing only nine acts specifically relating to it between 1707 and the last Jacobite rising in 1745.

This point can provoke both optimistic and pessimistic interpretations of what was going on. Was Scotland after 1707 run as a colony characterised both by neglect and heavy-handed interference or as a province which enjoyed virtual autonomy or 'semi-independence'? In the latter view, Scotland, after 1707 as before, was not treated as a 'naked province', subject to England or to English viceroys, as was Ireland. Westminster interfered only rarely in Scottish affairs, largely because of the successful buffer of the Scottish managers, who produced a relatively reliable phalanx of support for the government in the Commons and, in return, were largely left to their own devices in Scotland. Even in the aftermath of the '45 rising, the 3rd duke of Argyll succeeded in protecting Scotland - and the Campbell interest - from English-framed legislation which targeted Highland society, the episcopalian church and what was seen as a primitive legal system. The worst teeth of the Disarming Acts were pulled, schemes to introduce Irish-style plantations in the Highlands averted, and the annexation of Jacobite estates transformed from a punitive exercise into a scheme for economic regeneration. Sovereignty, in the sense of the continuation of a distinctive and largely autonomous system of governance, continued and expanded after the 1740s. The foundations were laid for the emergence of the 'parish state' in the eighteenth century, the civic society of nineteenth-century Scotland and the eventual wholesale devolution of executive powers to the Scottish Office in the twentieth century.

In describing the relationships forged between Scotland and the new British state, which as before, claimed unlimited sovereignty, the main features involved ambiguity or potential self-contradiction. The new parliamentary union underwrote the fiction, established by the Scottish parliament in 1689-90, that presbyterianism was established because its rival, episcopacy, was 'contrary to the inclinations of the generality of the people'. Yet equally, the passing by the Westminster parliament in 1712 of both a Patronage Act and a Toleration Act in effect underwrote schism and dissent. In one sense, the history of Scottish religion in the century after 1707 was of the official endorsement afforded to a Presbyterian 'parish state', in which education and poor relief as well as religious discipline were controlled by the courts of the state church, and the encouragement afforded to the growth in the general assembly of a 'Moderate' party, sympathetic to establishment aims of preserving order and the existing fabric of society. In another perspective, the same period was increasingly dominated by the growth of what was in effect licensed dissent: between 1790 and the 1830s, the numbers of Dissenters increased from about ten per cent of the Scottish population to over 30 per cent. Consistently, from the 1830s to the 1930s the state church turned to the British state for support in a programme of church extension to maintain religious uniformity in a fast-changing society. And persistently, the British state declined to help halt the pressures which were producing a religiously pluralistic society. Episcopalians, Protestant dissenters and Roman Catholics, in turn, were offered a measure of protection by the British state from the ambitions of the state church to restore a Presbyterian commonwealth. In short, the whole period since the Union of 1707 has seen a tension between the British state and a pro-Union Scottish established church. In the new arrangements since 1999 of a Scottish parliament, that tension has taken a new form: a largely pro-devolution Church of Scotland, which now numbers some 17 per cent of the population in its communion, persists in its aspirations as the 'national church', while the Holyrood parliament insists that, within its spheres of authority, it is the authentic representative of the people. Yet the voice of other churches, and particularly that of the Roman Catholic community, has never been louder.

The Union state which claimed unchallenged sovereignty nevertheless had growing difficulties in devoting enough time to the differing problems of the far-flung empire over which it exercised authority, not least because distinctive legislative solutions were needed for different parts of it. This was particularly the case with issues relating to local government. Two key issues in later nineteenth and early twentieth-century Scotland, Highland land legislation and urban housing, arguably held a more important place on the Scottish political stage from the 1870s onwards than did the home rule issue. The former produced crofting legislation which, although partly dependent on Irish land precedents, was carefully ring-fenced; the 1886 Act remained the basis for successive government approaches to the issue into the 1990s. The latter was instrumental in turning Scotland from the nineteenth-century parish state into the municipal state in which, as late as 1981, some 55 per cent of Scottish housing was provided by the public sector, more than double the figure which obtained in England and Wales.

In retrospect, with the setting up of a Scottish parliament secured, by means of the thirty-fifth of thirty-five Home Rule bills in the course of the twentieth century, it may be tempting to trace too firm a thread in the growth of demand for home rule. In the nineteenth century, as Graeme Morton emphasises, the desire was not for less Union but more - in the phenomenon of Unionist-Nationalism. The focus of much of the demands of Scottish 'nationalism', from the 1850s onwards, was on administrative reform. In this, the Scottish national movement contrasted sharply with parallel movements in Ireland and Wales, which were more broadly based in their make-up and aspirations. Such reform could well and often did mean a different kind of devolution, granting greater powers to the nineteenth-century version of the parish state, the town and county councils in a society which moved from being still largely rural in the 1770s to one of the most heavily urbanised societies in Europe three-quarters of a century later. The National Association for the Vindication of Scottish Rights (NAVSR), which sought merely a re-adjustment of details within the Union of 1707, was the dominant voice of the 1850s. It is common to assert that by the 1880s, with the emergence of the Scottish Home Rule Association (SHRA) , the age of home rule had arrived. It is argued here, by Graeme Morton, that the SHRA throughout its existence remained a marginalised body on the fringes of mainstream politics. The adoption by Gladstone, a late convert to home rule, in his Midlothian campaign of 1880 of the blunderbuss solution of home rule all round was an attempt to square the circle of preserving the sovereignty of an imperial parliament and addressing the obvious needs for better local government.

Similarly, the two essays below which consider twentieth-century Scotland emphasise the volatility and marginal nature of support for home rule. Political nationalism posed little or no electoral threat before the Hamilton by-election of 1967. The remarkable size of the Scottish Covenant campaign, with the government itself privately conceding that its petition had been signed by some 40 per cent of adult Scots, has to be set against the simple fact that the movement had evaporated by 1952. Home rule was afforded notional support by the Labour party, which blew alternately luke-warm and cold on the issue, reflecting an internal division within it of 'nationalist' and unionist tendencies.

Historians of modern Scotland, surveying the past century from the now secured redoubt of a restored Scottish parliament, are increasingly beginning to voice doubts about the inevitable victory of home rule. Yet there can be little doubt in their minds that the steady progression of 'corporatism' - the growth of administrative devolution - has indelibly marked the history of Scotland from the mid-1930s until 1979. Its main landmarks were fourfold: the abolition of most of the administrative boards, the remaining vestiges of the 'parish state' in 1928, with a consequent widening in the administrative responsibilities of the civil service and an increase in the authority of the Scottish secretary; the Gilmour Report of 1937, which transferred almost all the work of the Scottish Office to Edinburgh; the Balfour Commission report of 1953, which transferred further responsibilities, including electricity, roads and bridges, and control of food and health to the Scottish secretary; and the Kilbrandon Commission of 1969, which confirmed the extent of the transfer of the extent of administrative autonomy enjoyed by the Scottish Office and, in effect, doubted whether more devolution could be effected. It marked the fullest extent of what James Mitchell here terms the existence of 'Scottish national identity within British state nationalism'. It was a re-working, in the second and third quarters of the twentieth century, of the Unionist-Nationalism of the nineteenth century.

The lack of a clear-cut decision in the 1979 referendum and the securing of one in the referendum of 1997 can be explained in different ways, including their timing and the very different forms which they took - one was a vote of confidence on a messy compromise of an actual bill and the other took the form of a vote for a principle and also separated the issue of a parliament from that of its fiscal powers. Another interpretation is that the Union state, which had had a long history of protecting Scottish national identity, was just as much at issue in 1997, after the assaults on it during the long years of Thatcherism, as the umbrella solution of a Scottish parliament. That is why the ramifications of the 1997 referendum may in the future be just as much debated as the result of the referendum of 1979.

II

Wales has been directly subject to the Westminster parliament since the 1530s - longer than any other British territory - and yet its constitutional subordination to that parliament has produced relatively little resentment or resistance. There may be some obvious reasons for this: Wales is small in extent and population; it was never (like Scotland) a united polity with its own capital city and centralised administrative and legislative institutions; and it was never (like Scotland) a separate, independent nation. The sovereign authority of the Westminster parliament has never been seriously challenged in Wales in recent centuries and its efforts to secure either home rule or complete independence have never secured the level of local support of the kind found in Scotland or Ireland. And yet no one can doubt that Wales is 'different' and that the Welsh people have a very strong sense of their cultural identity and, for centuries, many of them spoke their own distinctive language.

In maintaining their cultural identity while acknowledging the authority of parliament, the Welsh have accomplished a significant balancing act. They have been prepared to live with a Westminster parliament, with an overwhelming English majority, while managing to retain a large measure of cultural independence. This has been achieved in large part because the ruling elite within Wales was composed of Welshmen. These men formed a partnership with the ruling elites in England and managed to establish themselves as an effective interest or pressure group at Westminster, while succeeding in preserving the cultural distinctiveness of the principality. They promoted or at least worked hard to preserve the continuing vitality of the Welsh language and culture. Westminster at times wisely recognised that Wales was different and that it needed separate legal provisions for religious, educational and tenurial issues in particular. This kind of recognition has kept Welsh resentment within bounds and has made it difficult to create from the later nineteenth century the kind of powerful home rule movement found in Ireland and Scotland. Home rule did come onto the Welsh political agenda, but only fitfully, erratically and unsuccessfully. The establishment of county councils and the consequent transfer of power at the local level blunted the appeal of the wider objective for home rule. A devolutionary strand was never entirely absent from the Liberal and Labour parties that have dominated Welsh politics since the mid-nineteenth century, but sectional, regional and class divisions have been more prominent than any appeal for home rule. Plaid Cymru, founded in 1925, did not win a parliamentary seat at Westminster until 1966. The proposal for a devolved assembly in Wales was heavily defeated in the referendum in 1979. The referendum in 1997 did not produce an overwhelming majority in favour of devolution and the legislative assembly established in Cardiff in 1999 lacks some of the powers conceded to the new Scottish parliament. Wales may show fewer signs than Scotland of wishing to end the union with England, but its experience does show that the Welsh have maintained distinctive characteristics and a measure of cultural independence despite the English predominance at Westminster. It does not appear likely that the Welsh assembly will pose the kind of challenge that might come from Edinburgh or Belfast in the coming years.

The constitutional history of the British-settled Dominions of the British empire does provide examples of the gradual evolution from devolved legislative assemblies to complete national independence. Their experiences may provide a model for the future constitutional development of Scotland but, as Ged Martin's essay shows, the Dominions do not provide an unambiguous historical example for Scotland. Canada, Australia and New Zealand, in turn, acquired first devolved legislative assemblies with limited legislative powers. They then each acquired a two-chamber legislative body described as a parliament and they later achieved Dominion status between 1926 and 1931, but these developments did not mean that these parliaments possessed the sovereign authority that had been exercised for so long over them by the Westminster parliament. Although they aped many of the procedures of the Westminster parliament, they could not exercise the same degree of authority as the latter. This meant that there were bound to be some disputes between these Dominion legislatures and the imperial parliament at Westminster, but the path from legislative devolution to full legislative independence was not rapid, smooth nor inevitable. Most colonials were satisfied to remain as overseas Britons and friction with Westminster was intermittent and usually at a low level. In 1931 the imperial parliament passed the Statute of Westminster, which promised that the Westminster parliament would never legislate for the dominions except at their express desire. Even this act however fell short of being an unambiguous charter of independence. It was not locally adopted in the Dominions for more than a decade. Ultimate control over some constitutional issues remained at Westminster for much longer. The slow and relatively peaceful evolution from devolution to full legislative independence in the Dominions however has not solved all the internal problems within these former colonies. The national legislatures have faced considerable problems from the centrifugal forces created by quite sharp divisions within the peoples and provinces making up these nations. The historical experience of the Dominions suggests that devolution can evolve into full independence, but this independence does not resolve all the strains and tensions affecting the internal affairs of these countries.

The British settlers in the American colonies were the first group to challenge and then forcibly reject the sovereign authority of the Westminster parliament. While cherishing their British liberties and while supporting the parliamentary efforts to limit the authority of the crown, these colonists were not prepared to accept that the Westminster parliament possessed unlimited authority over their lives, liberty and property. By the mid-eighteenth century, the American colonists had gained a considerable measure of internal self-government and they had established local legislative assemblies to levy local taxes, to pass local laws, and to represent their local interests. The Westminster parliament regarded these devolved legislatures as subordinate institutions with no constitutional right to challenge its own sovereign authority over all the affairs of the British empire. When, in the 1760s, the Westminster parliament set out to pass laws for and to levy taxes in the American colonies, this exertion of parliamentary authority was first resisted by economic boycotts and then defeated by armed rebellion. The majority of British politicians could not abandon their support for parliamentary sovereignty which they saw as their best defence against an arbitrary monarch and an unruly people. The American colonists, on the other hand, could not agree to obey the decisions of a parliament that clearly did not recognise their best interests or adequately represent their views. Having rejected parliamentary sovereignty by force of arms, the Americans then had to engage in profound and prolonged internal discussions on the nature and location of sovereignty in their new republic. One of the most impressive constitutional debates in human history finally led to a series of written constitutions and extensive bills of rights, at federal and state level, and at efforts to enshrine the more radical doctrine of the sovereignty of the people. Should devolution in Scotland evolve into independence, then the extent and quality of the constitutional debates held in the new United States of America could well serve as a model worth emulating.

Wales has produced the best example of accommodation to the Westminster parliament. The Dominions have shown an ability to evolve from devolution to full independence in a piecemeal and relatively peaceful fashion. The American colonies have provided the clearest example of a radical rejection of the sovereign authority of the Westminster parliament and a remarkable effort to write a very different constitution. The historical record of Ireland shows some features of all of these experiences and the relationship of Northern Ireland to the rest of the United Kingdom remains even more problematic in the immediate future than Scotland's relations with Westminster.

Ireland, like Scotland, had a separate parliament for several centuries before it was dissolved by a fully incorporating union with the Westminster parliament beginning in 1801. This Irish parliament however never possessed the legislative independence enjoyed by the Scottish parliament in the last years of its existence and the executive in Dublin was always more under English domination than the Scottish executive in Edinburgh before the Act of Union of 1707. Ireland might have claimed to be a separate kingdom sharing the same monarch as England, but it was an English colony for centuries in a way that Scotland never was. Poynings' Law in 1495 ensured that all legislation proposed by the Irish parliament had first to secure the prior approval of the Irish and the English privy councils. The Declaratory Act of 1720 went even further in denying the Irish parliament full legislative independence by asserting that the Westminster parliament could legislate for Ireland. The Irish viceroy, furthermore, was almost always an English aristocrat and his main supporters in the Irish government were either fellow-Englishmen or members of the Anglo-Irish elite who were the recipients of crown patronage.

The American revolution gave the patriot opposition in the Irish parliament (led by Henry Grattan and aided by the armed Irish Volunteers) an opportunity to challenge the English domination of the Dublin legislature. Poynings' Law was amended, the Declaratory Act was fully repealed and the Westminster parliament formally renounced its claim to legislate for Ireland. The new constitution of 1782, establishing what became known as Grattan's parliament, did not however give Ireland full legislative independence. The privy council in England could still amend or reject Irish legislation and sometimes did so. Irish Catholics - a clear majority of the population - were still denied seats in the Irish parliament even after the propertied minority among them gained the right to vote in 1793. And the Irish executive was still dominated by British appointments and British interests. The failure to solve the bitter sectarian divisions in Ireland or to make the Irish parliament representative even of all the propertied classes of Ireland helped provoke the bloody Irish rebellion of 1798. The British government's response to this disaster was to drive through the act of union in 1800, which dissolved the separate Irish parliament and gave Ireland representation in the Westminster parliament.

Until 1829 however the Irish Catholics were denied seats in the Westminster parliament and so the union got off to a disastrous start. Even when Catholic emancipation was conceded, the Catholic majority in Ireland faced continued religious and socio-economic grievances that meant they were never reconciled to the union. by the 1840s there were demands for the repeal of the union and from the 1870s home rule became the principal objective of a substantial body of Irish MPs at Westminster. Some home rulers argued that their objective would actually strengthen rather than destroy Ireland's links with Britain, but it is doubtful whether Ireland would have stayed long in this half-way house. A series of home rule bills were defeated in parliament and, when a home rule bill was eventually passed in 1914, its implementation was delayed because of the outbreak of the First World War. These delays encouraged both the growth of nationalism and republicanism in Ireland and the resort to armed resistance to British rule. Home rule no longer satisfied militant Irish opinion, while the Protestant majority in Ulster took a very different stance and was determined to fight to stay within the United Kingdom. The result of this polarisation of Irish opinion was that 26 counties secured their own parliament in Dublin and promptly sought to advance from devolution to complete independence, while six counties in Ulster stayed within the British state.

These six counties were granted a devolved legislative body at Stormont. From the outset this subordinate legislature failed to establish an effective working relationship with the Westminster parliament. The Protestant unionists in Ulster became an entrenched majority in the Stormont legislature and strove to defend their sectional interests at the expense of the large Catholic minority and at the risk of betraying the political principles which the Westminster parliament claimed to uphold. Devolution was deliberately designed to keep the Northern Ireland question out of British politics and to restrict British influence in the politics of Northern Ireland. Ulster affairs were not discussed at Westminster because Northern Ireland had its own subordinate legislature where such matters could be debated and decided. Despite the fact that Stormont had limited constitutional powers, in practice it was granted considerable autonomy as well as being given generous financial and economic assistance by the Westminster parliament. Westminster's supervisory role was decidedly limited and Northern Ireland developed many of the characteristics of an independent state. Stormont was able to pursue policies and to turn a blind eye to injustices that would not have been tolerated by the Westminster parliament. Stormont failed to satisfy the aspirations of the large Catholic minority because it dared not alienate the Protestant unionists. From the 1970s this alarming situation exploded into violence that polarised the community even more seriously than before. The Westminster parliament imposed direct rule in an effort to solve this bloody conflict, but even this failed top provide an answer to the Ulster question. After repeated efforts to reach an agreement, Northern Ireland was granted a devolved legislative assembly in Belfast that was elected in such a manner as to try to ensure it represented all major shades of opinion in Northern Ireland. This agreement has so far got off to a very hesitant start compared to the new Scottish parliament. It is not at all clear that this devolved legislature will reconcile the warring communities in Northern Ireland and even less clear how it will evolve constitutionally. The experiment of devolution in Northern Ireland since the 1920s can provide few positive examples, but many dire warnings, for the new Scottish parliament in Edinburgh.

It has variously been argued in this volume that the roots of the sovereignty of the Westminster parliament go deep. Such is the inbuilt conservatism and indeed inertia of British politics, in which, *pace* Harold Wilson's well-known saying that a 'week is a long time in politics', developments in constitutional matters are to be measured in decades rather than years, months or weeks, that the future of the new parliamentary institutions in Scotland and Wales seem secure. What remains deeply unclear, however, is not the role of Holyrood or Cardiff but of Westminster. In a thoughtful editorial on the day after the Scottish parliament opened, *The Times* argued that devolution was not merely the 'settled will of the Scottish people', in John Smith's celebrated phrase; 'the real business for the United Kingdom', it predicted, 'had only just started'. The dynamics of the Union itself, now almost 300 years old, and the nature of Britishness, a favourite theme of the administration of Tony Blair, are both at stake and in question. The most serious challenge to Westminster has, ironically, been posed, by Westminster itself.

2

The Development of Parliamentary Sovereignty

JEFFREY GOLDSWORTHY

The doctrine of parliamentary sovereignty holds that parliament's legislative authority is legally unlimited, meaning that it is not limited by any norms that are legally enforceable by the courts or any other human agency. This formulation of the doctrine is relatively modern. It depends on the development of agreement and clarity in legal terminology, and in particular, on distinguishing between matters of law and of morality. But the authority that the doctrine describes is much older, and has survived many changes in legal terminology, political thought, and the distribution of political power.

'Parliament' means the king in parliament, and the doctrine therefore asserts that the king and the two houses, when acting in concert, possess unlimited legislative authority. The doctrine is not concerned with the internal relationships, or the relative political powers, of parliament's three component parts. It is equally consistent with the pre-modern idea that parliament's authority belonged to the king, who chose to exercise it only with the consent of his subjects, and with the modern idea that it belongs to the community as a whole. That is why parliament's legislative authority was unaffected by the gradual shift of political predominance from the king to the two houses, and ultimately to the House of Commons alone.

The doctrine is also consistent with parliament's authority being limited by such norms as divine and natural laws, principles of justice and morality, and constitutional conventions and principles, provided that they are not legally enforceable against parliament by the courts or any other human agency. The doctrine is therefore consistent with the idea that those norms are enforceable by extra-legal means, such as divine retribution, and popular resistance or rebellion. It is consistent both with the ancient idea that all human authority is subject to 'higher law', and with enlightenment theories of social contract and legitimate revolution.

I

The development of parliamentary sovereignty within Britain
The historical development of parliament's authority within Britain can be divided into five stages:
1. the early evolution of parliament to the end of the fifteenth century, when it rose to pre-eminence in temporal matters among the various councils of the king;
2. its successful assertion of supreme authority in matters of religion during the sixteenth century, when it first became truly omnicompetent;
3. the contest between royalist and parliamentarian ideologies during the seventeenth century, culminating in parliament's successful assertion of authority to control both the royal succession, and royal prerogatives previously alleged to be inviolable;
4. the clarification of parliament's legal authority during the eighteenth century, when it was eventually realised that disagreements between advocates of parliamentary, and of popular, sovereignty, were confused by a failure to distinguish law from constitutional morality; and

5. the reconciliation of constitutional conservatives and democratic reformers during the nineteenth century, brought about by the extension of the right to vote and electoral reform.

In a nutshell, after the early evolution of parliament and its authority, the major questions that were successively resolved concerned the relationships between parliament and the church, parliament and the crown, and parliament and the people.

During the first period, the authority of parliament was unquestionably that of the medieval English king, fortified by the counsel and consent of his magnates. The king was said to be subject to law, but the law was mainly unwritten custom, and since he was the source of all temporal jurisdiction and judgment, he could not be legally compelled to observe it. The only available method of restraining a lawless king was political rather than legal. He was widely believed to be obligated to seek the advice and consent of his magnates, in matters affecting their interests. But if they failed to persuade him to obey the law, they could only resist, or, as a last resort, attempt to depose him. They knew that the common law offered them no remedy, because its judges were his judges. Since there were no judicial means of compelling the king to obey the law when he acted against his magnates' wishes, obviously there were no such means when he acted with their consent. There was no authority within the realm able to oppose the king and his magnates when they were united. The possibility of a legal challenge to the validity of whatever laws they might choose to make would have been unthinkable.

Parliament evolved from the medieval tradition of baronial counsel and consent. Participation in law-making was gradually extended from the magnates to representatives of counties and towns. By the late fourteenth century, parliament had become the most authoritative institution in the realm in temporal matters, apart from the monarchy itself. As the king's highest court, it was an instrument of royal government, but was also said to represent the entire community and to express its collective counsel and consent. Every subject was deemed to consent to its acts. For that reason, when affairs of the highest importance, including the deposition of kings, needed to be authoritatively settled, parliamentary validation was invariably sought. The Lords and Commons both looked to parliament, rather than inferior courts, to redress their most serious grievances. In temporal matters, it exercised omnicompetent authority, including what we now classify as administrative, legislative, and judicial powers. Its ability to change the law was obvious and frequently acknowledged. It was accepted that statutes could be repealed only by subsequent statutes, even when the former were believed to have been enacted by the parliament of a usurper. Its authority was agreed to be subordinate to the law of God, but inferior courts had no authority to invalidate its acts on that ground. The only human institution that claimed such an authority was the church, headed by the pope, with respect to purely spiritual matters.

In the 1530s, which ushered in the second stage of development, the Reformation parliament transferred ultimate authority over the church in England from the pope to the king. Consequently, the king, in parliament, could legislate with respect to spiritual as well as temporal matters, and was, in practice, fully sovereign. That sovereignty was demonstrated by the enactment of many statutes dealing with matters of fundamental constitutional and religious importance, such as the succession to the throne, the royal prerogative, property rights, and ecclesiastical government and doctrine. Whatever private reservations they may have held, judges and bishops dutifully enforced these statutes without questioning their validity. Even when Tudor monarchs regarded earlier statutes as contrary to God's law, they ensured that they were formally repealed by parliament, rather than simply ignored on the ground that they were null and void. Government officials, lawyers and learned authors frequently attested to parliament's omnicompetent and unchallengeable authority.

But the nature of parliament and its authority was the subject of disagreement. Was it 'the king, in parliament', or a composite institution, 'the king-in-parliament'? Royalist theories maintained that statutes were made by the king alone, exercising his God-given authority with the consent of his subjects. Parliamentarian theories held that the king, Lords and Commons exercised a shared legislative power on behalf of the whole community. These theories agreed on many points: for example, that every community needs a final decision-maker, entrusted with unchallengeable authority to make and declare law; that this decision-maker could not be bound by human laws, because they might have to be over-ridden in an emergency; and that everyone was obligated to obey its decisions, unless they were manifestly contrary to the law of God, in which case passive disobedience only was permitted. The question that divided them was whether this final, unchallengeable decision-maker was the king alone, or the king, Lords and Commons in parliament. That question was resolved during the third stage of development, as a consequence of the constitutional struggles of the seventeenth century.

Royalists maintained that supreme authority belonged to the king alone, who was appointed by God, and was more trustworthy than any other person or body, because he had been raised to a station above self-interest, and infused with special wisdom and love for his subjects. But they agreed that his authority was highest when he made laws with the consent of his subjects in parliament. The making of laws in parliament was the most absolute - the most unchallengeable - of his powers, standing at the pinnacle of his divinely ordained authority. His judges, whom he appointed to enforce his laws, had no authority to question their validity. Some royalists held that his legislative power was nevertheless limited: he could not alienate or restrict his God-given authority, or change the course of its descent after his death. But their view was not far removed from the idea of parliamentary sovereignty. The king was both fully sovereign, and 'at his highest' in parliament, and the only limits to his sovereignty were those inherent in its divine source and inalienable nature.

Parliamentarians believed that final, unchallengeable authority was shared by the king, Lords and Commons in parliament, who together represented the entire community. Parliament was often said to represent the church as well, because since the 1530s, the community and the church had been officially regarded as one and the same. Consequently, its authority extended to the interpretation of the word of God. Its decisions embodied not only the consent, but also the combined wisdom of the community; if not actually infallible, it was more trustworthy than any other decision-maker. As the highest court in the land, it was not subject to the laws that bound inferior courts, let alone to their interpretations of those laws. The authority of parliament and that of the common law had the same source: the reason of the community. As the voice of the community, parliament was the supreme interpreter of the common law, and could over-ride even fundamental legal principles if reason required. Since declaring law and making law were both matters of reason, they were ultimately indistinguishable. Parliament alone could be trusted never to violate the rights of the people: it was their foundation and chief protector. The judges of inferior courts were ineligible to play that role, because the king's powers of appointment and dismissal made them unduly susceptible to his influence.

The idea that judges had authority to declare acts of parliament invalid, for violating divine or natural law, or fundamental principles of the common law, was therefore inconsistent with the prevailing hierarchy of political authority, and with the principal theories - both royalist and parliamentarian - which sought to justify that hierarchy. That idea was therefore not widely accepted even within the legal profession. This fact later became obscured for two reasons. The first was the common habit of referring to hypothetical statutes contrary to divine or natural law as 'unlawful' or 'void', which is now generally regarded as a confusion of legal and moral terminology. This was rarely intended to mean that the judiciary had authority to declare such statutes legally invalid. James I, for example, could not have meant that when he said that a municipal law contrary to God's law would be 'unjust and unlawful'. What he and others meant is that such a law would not be morally binding, even though it could legally be repealed only by the proper authority. Judges, like other subjects, might justifiably disobey such a law, but it did not follow that they had legal authority to declare them invalid, any more than it followed that ordinary subjects had such authority.

The second reason why the legally unlimited authority of statute was subsequently obscured was the notoriety acquired by Sir Edward Coke's unrepresentative dictum in *Dr Bonham's* case (1610), that statutes contrary to 'common right and reason' would be 'controlled' by the common law and 'adjudged void' [44]. What Coke meant is unclear, but the dictum was included in the list of reasons for his dismissal in 1616 as chief justice of the king's bench. Many contemporary statesmen and eminent lawyers clearly disagreed with him, because they described parliament's authority as sovereign, absolute, unlimited, uncontrollable, and even arbitrary, and its laws as subject to correction only by itself.

During the civil war, royalist and parliamentarian theorists explicitly agreed on this score. When parliamentarians such as Henry Parker declared that parliament's authority was absolute and arbitrary, royalists agreed, but added that parliament included the king, and therefore its unlimited authority could not lawfully be exercised without his actual consent. What they vehemently denied was the parliamentarians' argument that sovereignty belonged to the entire community rather than a single person, and therefore could be exercised by the two houses alone, in an extreme emergency threatening the safety of the community.

During the Interregnum, the Levellers and the army proposed that legislative authority should be subjected to legal limits, to be ratified by an Agreement of the People. But influential republicans, such as Milton and Harrington, disagreed. Milton argued, as many would do in the following century, that every generation possesses the same unfettered right as its fallible predecessors to alter its laws and even its method of governance, a right necessarily exercised by its representatives in parliament. The failure of the various revolutionary regimes during the 1650s created a deep aversion within England to deliberate constitutional innovation and written constitutions, and a strong preference for pragmatic, incremental adaptation of customary institutions.

When the monarchy was restored in 1660, so was the sovereignty of the king in parliament. But the idea that its authority was limited by fundamental laws was probably more popular after the Restoration than it had been before. An understandable yearning for security and stability must have enhanced its appeal. Moreover, Sir Edward Coke's ambiguous dictum in *Dr Bonham's* case had gained some currency, after being invoked by some royalist lawyers who were punished by the two houses during the civil war.

After the Restoration, those who appealed to fundamental laws were mostly monarchists, seeking to protect the succession and prerogatives of the crown from statutory interference. But not all monarchists took that approach. Most of them adhered to the old royalist theory that the king's sovereign authority was absolute, and denied that it was limited by any laws other than God's. During the Exclusion Crisis, monarchists successfully resisted attempts to enact statutes excluding James, the Roman Catholic duke of York, from the throne. Some of them did so on the ground that such a statute would violate a fundamental and unalterable law of the land, which limited the authority of the king, even in parliament. But others did not agree that the king's legislative authority was limited by laws of the land; they argued, instead, that exclusion would be inconsistent with the divinely predestined descent of his sovereign power after his death. Others still - probably a majority -

accepted that an Act of Exclusion would be legally valid, but opposed it as a
dangerous incitement to civil war.

During this period some unpopular judicial decisions, widely condemned as
unduly partial towards the king's interests, discredited the idea that parliament's
authority might be limited by judicially enforceable laws. Parliament's sovereignty
was enthusiastically endorsed by Whig lawyers and members of parliament during
the Exclusion Crisis, on the ground that parliament needed unlimited power to be
able to defend the nation in unexpected emergencies - such as the duke of York's
impending accession to the throne. The influential Whig historian, William Petyt,
angrily dismissed the suggestion that judges could invalidate a statute as a
'monstrous conceit': the judges 'ought to be, and never were other than executors,
and not executioners, of the ... ordinances and establishments of Parliaments' [154].
The best known Whig theorist, John Locke, insisted that the legislature was
entrusted by the people with limited authority. But he held the limits to be enforceable
only by armed rebellion, leading to the dissolution of the constitution. No means of
legal enforcement were available because, while the constitution remained intact, the
legislature was superior to all other organs of government. The supremacy of the
legislature was the 'first and fundamental positive law of all commonwealths',
whereas the power of the community to resist tyranny was granted by 'a law
antecedent and paramount to all positive laws of men' [151-52]. This thesis, that the
supreme power recognised by the constitution, that of the legislature, was
subordinate to a power outside the constitution, that of the people, became very
popular during the next century.

Parliament's sovereign authority was consolidated during the fourth stage of
development, in the eighteenth century. The Revolution of 1688 vindicated the
parliamentarian theory of the Whigs, who held that sovereignty was vested in the
king in parliament rather than the king alone. Statute was used to control both the
royal succession and so-called inseparable prerogatives of the crown, which some
royalists had previously deemed sacrosanct. The sovereignty of parliament was
central to the ideology of Court Whigs, and by 1702, was endorsed by establishment
Tories as well. The ideologies of Court Whigs and Tories converged. The Tories
adopted the Whig theory that legislative sovereignty belonged to the king, Lords and
Commons in parliament, and the Whigs agreed with the Tories that 'the people' had
only an indirect and limited role in public decision-making.

Whigs and Tories alike described the British constitution as a well-balanced
combination of the best aspects of the monarchical, aristocratic, and democratic
forms of government, each of which checked the worst aspects of the others. While
the Commons protected the subject against any tendency towards tyranny, the
counter-weights of king and Lords prevented the excesses of unchecked democracy.
The checks and balances among the three component parts of parliament adequately
protected the rights of all sections of the community, leaving no need for anything
like judicial review of legislation. As Sir William Blackstone put it, 'there can no
inconvenience be attempted by either of the three branches, but will be withstood by
one of the other two' [201].

This idealised understanding of the constitution was not shared by everyone.
Disagreements about the relationship between parliament's authority and the crown
were replaced by disagreements about the relationship between parliament's authority
and the people it purported to represent. In the early decades of the century, members
of the so-called 'Country' party challenged the ancient fiction that parliament
faithfully represented all subjects, and was incapable of acting against their interests.
They warned that the court's use of manipulative and sometimes corrupt methods to
maintain majority support within parliament might undermine the independence of the
House of Commons, pervert its representative function, and destroy the
constitutional balance. They insisted that members of the house were delegates in the

strict sense of the term, bound to act according to the wishes of their constituents. They proposed a variety of electoral reforms to ensure that ultimate authority would be retained by the electors, and parliament's authority effectively restricted to the purposes for which it was conferred. In the second half of the century, their agenda was taken up and extended by agitators for democratic reforms, who argued that the people rather than parliament were sovereign.

But none of these advocates of electoral reform ever suggested that the limits to parliament's authority were judicially enforceable. They regarded them as enforceable only through the ballot box, or in an extreme case, by resistance. Daniel Defoe warned members of the House of Commons that they were not omnipotent, but conceded that 'there are no stated proceedings to bring you to your duty'; parliamentary tyranny would have to be 'reduced by extrajudicial methods', namely, 'that force which [the people] are very loath to make use of' [175]. As Viscount Bolingbroke put it, 'who has the right, and the means, to resist the supreme legislative power; I answer the whole nation has the right, and a people, who deserve to enjoy liberty, will find the means' [176]. Almost everyone agreed that parliament was governed both by natural law and fundamental customary principles, which in an extreme case were enforceable by resistance or even rebellion. But there was disagreement about whether those norms, and that method of enforcement, deserved to be called 'legal'.

Before the eighteenth century, people had often described human laws contrary to God's law as 'void' or 'unlawful'. They did not mean that there were judicial means of authoritatively declaring such laws to be invalid. Nevertheless, that mode of speech no doubt inspired those in the eighteenth century who declared that in the face of oppression, 'resistance becomes the law of the land'. If resistance could never be lawful, they argued, there would be no difference between the constitution of Britain and that of the most arbitrary tyranny. On the other hand, many prominent statesmen and lawyers developed Locke's insights into a sophisticated defence of the thesis that the people's right to resist tyranny was a moral and not a legal right. They thought that this was especially true of any right to resist parliament. In their view, it was unnecessary for the law to recognise any limits to parliament's authority, because the people had never needed, and would never need, any legal pretext to resist tyranny. And it was undesirable for the law to do so, because those limits were so abstract and vague, that if promulgated as law they would be much more likely to be interpreted too broadly, inciting unjustified resistance, than to be violated by parliament. That is why Blackstone denied that human laws contrary to natural law were valid, but also asserted that parliament's authority was sovereign, uncontrollable, absolute, and despotic [181, 202]. He was using 'valid' in a moral rather than a legal sense. The remedy for any tyrannical abuse of parliament's authority was resistance, and although in an extreme case this might be morally justified, it was not and in his opinion should not be authorised by law.

Disagreements about whether or not parliament's authority was 'sovereign' or 'omnipotent' seem to have been more apparent than real. Of course, the underlying moral and political disputes that generated those disagreements were only too real: for example, the dispute that lost Britain its American colonies. The point is that what seemed to be disagreement about the legal authority of parliament confused rather than clarified those underlying disputes, because on that issue substantial agreement was concealed by divergent use of terminology. Both sides agreed that parliament's authority was limited by higher norms, which both agreed were enforceable in a sufficiently extreme case by resistance. Disagreements concerned terminology and details: whether those norms were properly regarded as 'legal', whether resistance could ever be deemed 'lawful', and what an extreme case might be. The terminology that people preferred depended on whether they regarded parliamentary tyranny, or unjustified resistance, as the greater danger. Members and supporters of governments, who feared resistance more than tyranny, claimed that parliament's authority was legally unlimited, while their opponents, who were more fearful of tyranny, denied that claim in order to emphasise parliament's subjection to higher principles.

Some individuals shifted from one mode of speech to the other, to suit the occasion. In 1795, for example, Charles James Fox attacked the Treasonable Practices and Seditious Meetings Bills on the ground that 'neither Lords nor Commons nor King, no, nor the whole legislature together, were to be considered as possessing the power to enslave the people of this country'. But earlier during the same debate he stated that he 'could never consent to the proposition that there were some fundamental laws of the constitution which Parliament was incompetent to alter. They certainly were competent ... so far as their acts would necessarily be recognised in the decisions of the various courts of judicature in the kingdom. But though they might be competent in point of power ... [t]here were many laws of the constitution which never ought to be repealed' [187].

This kind of confusion inspired constitutional lawyers and legal philosophers to advocate a sharper distinction between legal and moral terminology. When Sir Robert Chambers, Blackstone's successor, ascribed unlimited and irresistible power to parliament, he cautioned that he was speaking only of juridical, and not moral, power [203]. Jeremy Bentham and his disciple John Austin taught generations of lawyers to think in these terms. Their success led to general acceptance of terminology that accommodated both sides of the issue. 'Law' came to be understood as norms enforceable by the courts. Customary limits to parliament's sovereignty, enforceable by political rather than judicial methods, could be described as 'constitutional', but not 'legal', limits. Legal authority was then distinguishable from moral authority, and the legal sovereignty of parliament from the political sovereignty of the electorate.

Claims that the British parliament does not have sovereign authority within Scotland should be assessed with these distinctions in mind. The Union of England and Scotland, in 1707, was brought about by statutes that included provisions declaring certain institutions to be permanently unalterable, but this had little noticeable impact on the English doctrine of parliamentary sovereignty, which eventually came to be accepted by most Scottish lawyers as well. Even those who originally described the provisions as legally unalterable - including Englishmen such as Defoe, as well as Scots - did not believe that they were judicially enforceable. Like Locke, they regarded them as enforceable only by resistance. As for recent claims, I am not aware of anyone who argues that those provisions can legally be altered only by first dissolving the Union and reinstating the original, independent parliament of Scotland. Instead, it is sometimes argued that the British parliament can legitimately alter them only with the consent of a majority of Scottish electors, obtained in a referendum. But that is a matter of political legitimacy, not legal validity. Any referendum would have to be initiated and organised by parliament, which would therefore be the author of any resulting alteration. And that presupposes that parliament does have the requisite legal authority.

Throughout the eighteenth century, most politicians, lawyers, and political theorists agreed that parliament possessed legally unlimited legislative authority within Britain. This was generally admitted even by the dissident Americans, who denied that it had unlimited authority over them. The theory of the necessity of legislative sovereignty was so influential that they cast it off only with great difficulty, inventing in the process a whole new system of government, in which their legislatures are limited by written constitutions, adopted by special conventions, and enforceable by the judiciary. But this novel method of controlling legislatures found little favour in Britain, even among those who advocated radical constitutional reform. The reformers pinned their hopes on universal suffrage, equal representation, and more frequent elections. They did not trust the common law or the judges to protect their freedoms, and rejected the very idea of immutable laws on the ground that no generation had any right to shackle its descendants. Their goal was not to limit parliament's powers, but to make it more accountable to the people. Joseph Priestley expressed confidence that, if the House of Commons were made a truly representative body, 'every other reform could be made without any difficulty whatever' [219]. And Richard Price affirmed that, provided the Commons truly represented the people, government by King, Lords, and Commons 'is the perfection of government' [219].

The reformers' goal was eventually realised during the fifth stage of development, in the nineteenth century, thereby reconciling, at least to the satisfaction of most Britons, the legal sovereignty of parliament and the political sovereignty of the people. The sovereignty of parliament was preserved, but given a new - or rather, a renewed - justification, in that electoral reforms made more plausible a claim that had been frequently made since the fourteenth century: that parliament represented the entire community.

The sovereignty of parliament became a rarely questioned assumption of British constitutional thought, an apparently necessary truth frequently reiterated on both sides of the political spectrum. Consequently, it is sometimes disparaged as a 'dogma'. But it was never a dogma in the sense of an unreasoned article of faith. Over the centuries, it has been defended for many different reasons, not all of them compatible with one another or acceptable today. These include the ideas that:
1. as a matter of either logical or practical necessity, there had to be a single, ultimate and unlimited law-making power in the kingdom;
2. with the consent of his subjects in parliament, the king exercised an absolute power to make law, conferred by and subject only to God;
3. parliament was the highest court in the land, the authority of last resort from which no appeal was possible, which could make new laws as well as interpret and apply old ones;
4. if its authority were limited, parliament might be unable to take extraordinary measures needed to protect the community in emergencies;
5. every generation must be equally free to make and change its laws, as contemporary circumstances might require;
6. all subjects were represented in parliament, and were therefore deemed to consent to its acts and to be estopped from disputing them;
7. parliament's decisions reflected the collective wisdom of the entire community, which, if not infallible, was far superior to that of any other agency in the state;
8. the ability of the king, Lords, and Commons to check and balance one another was the best possible safeguard against tyranny;
9. the judges, appointed by the crown, could not to be trusted with authority to nullify parliament's judgments; and
10. to limit parliament's powers to prevent it from abusing them would be to adopt a cure much more dangerous than the highly improbable disease of parliamentary tyranny.

II

Parliamentary sovereignty outside Britain
In discussing the extent of parliament's authority, it is useful to distinguish between the dimensions of 'depth' and 'breadth'. By 'breadth', I mean the territories in which its authority is acknowledged and obeyed, and by 'depth', the subject-matters on which it is legally competent to legislate.

The doctrine of parliamentary sovereignty is concerned with the dimension of depth rather than breadth. By asserting that parliament's legislative authority is unlimited, the doctrine does not foolishly claim that parliament's authority is acknowledged and obeyed in every corner of the globe, but rather, that where it is acknowledged and obeyed, it extends to everything that might possibly be a subject-matter of legislation. This includes everything everywhere in the world: the subject-matters on which parliament can legislate are not territorially limited. It can validly prohibit Americans from smoking in the streets of New York. But that is still a matter of depth rather than breadth. Such a law would be enforceable against recalcitrant Americans in the United Kingdom, but would not be recognised as valid or enforced in America. It would be a valid part of British, but not of American, law.

Legal, as distinct from moral, authority does not exist unless it can generally be exercised effectively. Whether or not parliament has legal authority to change the law of any given territory depends on whether its legislation is accepted as valid law by legal officials, and generally obeyed by the residents, in that territory. But that acceptance and obedience need not be voluntary: threats and force can be sufficient to establish and maintain effective legal authority.

This is just as true in Britain as anywhere else. Even there, parliament is sovereign only because its authority is accepted by legal officials, and generally obeyed by everyone else. Moreover, during some periods and with respect to some issues, that acceptance and obedience were secured partly by threats and force. For example, when parliament abolished papal jurisdiction and declared the king to be supreme head of the church in England, the Treasons Act (1534), and several exemplary executions, were needed to suppress dissent. But eventually, for the most part, parliament's sovereign authority came to be voluntarily accepted by both officials and subjects.

That acceptance of the constitution, and indeed the constitution itself, are mainly matters of custom. There was never a constitutive moment when popular consent to the British constitutional order was expressly given. England had, and Britain still has, a largely 'customary' constitution, rather than one deliberately planned and adopted at a particular time.

In the seventeenth and eighteenth centuries, the lack of an equivalent customary foundation for parliamentary sovereignty in some British colonies and dominions led to conflict between local residents and the British government. The American War of Independence is one example; but parliamentary authority had previously been resisted in Ireland and Barbados. The fundamental problem was that parliamentary sovereignty lacked the solid foundation in local custom that it enjoyed in Britain: it had not been clearly accepted by local officials, who included independent-minded members of local legislatures, or by the local populace.

To complicate matters, some of the main reasons believed to justify parliamentary sovereignty within Britain were inapplicable to these territories. Local residents insisted that parliament's claim to represent, and therefore to embody the wisdom and consent, of all subjects, was in their case simply false. The checks and balances among the king, Lords, and Commons therefore offered them no protection from oppression. British officials argued in reply that these territories were subject to British government, that in every government there was necessarily a sovereign power, and that in British government that power was parliament. But these normative and analytical arguments were inconclusive. Legal, as opposed to moral, authority, cannot be established by theoretical reasoning. It simply does not exist unless it has been, or can be, effectively exercised. To be effectively exercised within some territory it must be accepted by local officials, and generally obeyed by local residents, whether voluntarily or not. In the absence of voluntary acceptance and obedience, Britain resorted to force. It succeeded in Ireland and Barbados, but failed in North America.

From the time of the American revolution until today, there has been some confusion about the sense and significance of the fact that the British constitution is founded mainly on custom. It was claimed then, and is still claimed by American historians today, that in eighteenth-century Britain the legal authority of all governmental institutions, including parliament, was limited by custom. This ancient 'customary constitution' is supposed to have finally succumbed to the positivist theory of sovereignty only in the nineteenth century. These claims are erroneous, and a consequence of one or both of two possible confusions. The first confusion is between customary norms that are legal, in the sense of being somehow legally enforceable, and those that are extra-legal, and better described as norms of constitutional morality or convention. As we have seen, the eighteenth-century parliament was limited by norms of constitutional morality or convention, but not by law.

The second possible confusion is between the breadth and depth of parliament's authority. In terms of breadth, parliament's legal authority was and is limited by custom, and in some colonies and dependencies it lacked a secure foundation in local custom. But of course it does not follow that within Britain, parliament's legal authority was limited by custom. It is true that the British constitution was based on custom, but the constitution included the sovereignty of parliament. Within Britain, the sovereignty of parliament was therefore based on custom, but not limited by it. In some colonies and dependencies, equivalent customs were never clearly established. Parliamentary authority was successfully imposed on some of them by force, but in the American colonies, the attempt to do so failed.

References and Further Reading:
References in square brackets are to Jeffrey Goldsworthy, *The Sovereignty of Parliament, History and Philosophy* (Oxford, 1999). The first two sections of this essay are based on that book, and include some material first published in it. The subject-matter of the final section - parliamentary sovereignty outside Britain - is examined in Jack P. Greene, *Peripheries and Center: Constitutional Development in the Extended Polities of the British Empire and the United States, 1607-1788* (Athens, GA, 1986).

3

Scotland's Parliament in its British context
1603-1707

JULIAN GOODARE

Parliamentary history has always been a peculiarly English pursuit. Those who study it can never entirely forget the great tradition of constitutional history in which the story of medieval and early modern England was that of the rise of parliament as a great national institution. This was believed to be a *unique* institution, for in most other countries parliaments were phenomena of the middle ages, and were dispensed with in the age of absolute monarchy. Indeed, some Englishmen saw it thus at the time. Sir Dudley Carleton said in the House of Commons in 1626:

> In all Christian kingdoms you know that parliaments were in use
> anciently ... until the monarchs began to know their own strength,
> and, seeing the turbulent spirit of their parliaments, at length they
> little by little began to stand upon their prerogatives, and at last
> overthrew the parliaments throughout Christendom, except here
> only with us [Kenyon, 45].

In fact, Christendom still had several other parliaments, and one of them was in Scotland. The questions raised by Carleton - the 'turbulent spirit' of parliaments, and royal prerogatives as an alternative system of government - also apply to the Scottish parliament.

I

The tradition of English uniqueness has made the nature of the Scottish parliament difficult to grasp. The English and Scottish parliaments however were recognised at the time to be more or less equivalent. Both contained representatives of the propertied elite; both were formally royal councils and courts of law, while finding their main business in legislation and taxation. During the Jacobean union negotiations it was assumed that they had comparable powers and that their concurrence to union was required in similar ways. The Scottish parliament in 1607 found it natural to refer to its English counterpart as 'the estaittis of England', not an English phrase but the one it used to describe itself.

Mention of the term 'the estates' is a good moment at which to point out that there are two senses in which we can use the term 'parliament'. In one usage it could mean the estates - and the Scottish parliament, unlike the English, was very much a parliament of estates. These estates were bishops (when these existed, which broadly speaking they did 1600-38 and 1661-89), titled peers, commissioners of shires and commissioners of royal burghs. Unlike in England, all the estates sat and voted in a single chamber. Otherwise the bishops and peers were roughly equivalent to the English House of Lords, and the shire and burgh commissioners to the English Commons.

There was an even closer parallel with England in the second usage of the term 'parliament'. Acts of parliament ran in the name of the crown, 'with advice and consent of the estates of parliament'. When it came to legislation, the crown itself was very much a component of parliament. In our period the kings of Scotland lived in England and parliaments were held by royal commissioners, whose consent was necessary to the passage of an act. As in England, we can conceive of 'parliament' as something separate from the crown, but the assembly of a parliament was also an occasion when consensus was sought among a body of legislators who *included* the crown.

The seventeenth century was the paramount age of royal absolutism in Europe. Scottish kings, like many others, sought to make themselves the personal focus of government and to draw all estates and privileged groups into a direct dependence on the royal will. This was a controversial process. Some, particularly among the nobility, welcomed it as promoting strong, stable and orderly government; others opposed it as undermining their liberties and privileges. Seventeenth-century Scottish political history was largely about this controversy.

When those who opposed royal absolutism sought a platform for their views and activities, they found it in parliament. Parliament was prominent in two successful revolutions against an absolutist crown - those of 1638 and 1689. Perhaps if the revolution of 1638 had been more successful, that of 1689 would have been unnecessary. But the verdict of 1689 proved final, and the moment at which parliament declared James VII to have 'forfeited' the throne was the moment at which royal absolutism in Scotland ceased for good.

We should not, however, assume that the main function of parliament was to oppose an absolutist crown. The roots of that assumption lie in eighteenth-century Whig historiography. Colin Kidd, who has written in detail on this historiography, seems to endorse it when he calls the seventeenth-century parliament 'pliant' and 'emasculated' because it passed legislation to strengthen the crown in the 1680s (Kidd, 131). This raises several problems. First, there is the question of how far we interpret things as 'crown versus parliament'. Sometimes we do, of course. But plenty of people in the 1680s wanted to see a strong crown, and many of them sat in parliament.

The second problem with the idea of an 'emasculated' parliament is its assumption that when it did come to 'crown versus parliament', the crown would always win. The reason for the crown's dominant position is usually given as the existence of the Lords of the Articles. 'Articles' were legislative proposals which were to be formed into acts. (The Scots did not use the English term 'bill': a proposed act was an 'act'.) The Lords of the Articles were a drafting committee elected by parliament; all legislative proposals had first to be submitted to it. For most of the seventeenth century, the committee consisted of eight representatives from each of the four estates - bishops, nobles, shire commissioners and burgh commissioners. Crucially, bishops and nobles selected *each other*'s representatives, and these then selected the representatives of the other estates. Because all bishops were royal appointees, the crown could use them to nominate the entire committee. This monopoly control of the parliamentary agenda has been compared to Poynings' Law in Ireland. And the crown also had a veto on legislation. As Charles II's great minister, the duke of Lauderdale, summed up: 'Nothing can come to parliament but through the Articles, and nothing can pass in the Articles but what is warranted by his majesty, so that the king is absolute master in parliament both of the negative and the affirmative' [Rait, 78].

But historians who have taken this at face value have forgotten that crown control of the parliament. During a parliament, opposition could be very effective. Effective parliamentary opposition does not primarily mean being able to propose matters for debate, or getting legislation approved - the aspects that the crown controlled. The Scottish opposition in the parliaments of 1703 and 1704 did actually pass its own legislation in the teeth of the ministry - an unusually assertive episode with few parallels even in England. But what usually matters is effective *opposition* - being able to block unpopular legislation proposed by the government. Charles II could (in theory) make sure that only his proposals were debated by parliament: he could veto anything he did not like; but he could not actually make parliament pass his proposals. For this, he needed a majority of votes in the full parliament. The Lords of the Articles as such did not furnish a single extra vote to the government, and in the full parliament they were irrelevant.

Another problem with the traditional belief in parliament's subservience to the Lords of the Articles is that Scotland also had conventions of estates, which were parliaments in almost all but name and had much the same membership. They could not pass permanent legislation, but they could tax and issue temporary orders. Their procedure was simpler, and governments sometimes chose to hold conventions of estates instead of parliaments. Conventions of estates did not have Lords of the Articles; the traditional theory would expect them to be less subservient than parliaments. They were not.

Let us look at some of the instances of opposition to the crown in seventeenth-century parliaments and conventions of estates. In 1600 a convention of estates rejected the government's central policy - a scheme to revise the parliamentary tax assessments that seemed likely to triple direct taxation. In the parliament of 1617, the king's flagship proposal was a law to enable him to regulate the church by royal edict: he had to withdraw it after preliminary discussions, realising that it would never pass. In the parliament of 1621, ratification of the Five Articles of Perth (entailing more ceremonial church worship) proved enormously contentious, and the government had to put in huge efforts and grant many concessions to secure a majority. In the convention of estates of 1625, a large tax for military preparations was refused outright. In the parliament of 1633, with the king present, there was a huge fuss about an act on the royal prerogative; in the voting it was almost defeated. In 1639 the Covenanters seized control of parliament and used it to govern Scotland for over a decade in spite of the king. In 1669-73 there was vociferous parliamentary opposition, and parliament eventually had to be adjourned in 1673 as unmanageable. In 1686 James VII's main priority was an act for toleration of Catholicism. Although he offered free trade with England in return, which the Scots very much wanted, parliament rejected the royal proposal firmly. This was in the middle of the very decade in which Dr Kidd regards parliament as 'emasculated'.

And the Lords of the Articles were abolished in 1689. This allowed the Scottish parliament more freedom to chart its own course instead of merely saying yes or no to royal proposals. Often it was distinctly intractable in this. But Andrew Fletcher of Saltoun regarded the parliaments of this period as unusually *subservient*, claiming that the leading Scottish politicians had sold out to their English counterparts who pulled wires behind the scenes. We shall return to this point, but suffice it to say just now that in the Scottish parliament we are dealing not with an assembly of stooges but with a powerhouse.

II

Parliament in its full sense - that is, estates and crown - was very much a sovereign body. It had not always been one, but it became one in the course of the sixteenth century. Traditional accounts of the Scottish parliament have often said that it was not sovereign, but this is wrong. What I mean by sovereignty is the exercise of untrammelled power by a government. I leave to others the dignified trappings of power - the flags and crowns - or national identities - who was or was not a Scot, and the stories of how the Scots had got to be Scots - or the legalities of power - arguments about whether power was being exercised *de facto* or *de jure*. These are sometimes important questions, and parliament itself undoubtedly had both a symbolic and a functional significance. In this context however I am concerned purely with the functional question of who had the power to issue commands and get them obeyed.

Sovereignty in this sense - the exercise of untrammelled power by a government - did not exist in medieval Europe. Power was shared and diffused. All sorts of people, not only kings, had the power to issue commands and get them obeyed. Sovereign states emerged in the sixteenth century. The Reformation had a lot to do with this: national rulers chose their state's religion and regulated their churches. Like many other countries, Scotland in the sixteenth century gradually became a sovereign state. The power of the pope was abrogated by parliament in 1560, and the church's doctrine and organisation were thereafter supervised by parliament. The general assembly of the church, which used to be thought of as limiting parliamentary sovereignty, was a subordinate body that lobbied parliament for what it wanted. Meanwhile, the power of feudal barons was slowly subordinated to that of the crown. The crucial turning-point was the 'act anent feuding' of 1598, requiring feuds to be submitted to royal justice, and the curtailment of private military power was completed during the first quarter of the seventeenth century.

Sovereignty is not an all-or-nothing affair. The most useful definition of it (at least for this period) is that of John Austin, who relied on the idea of 'habitual obedience' to a government's commands. He pointed out that a weak government would have to defer to its stronger neighbours, and there was no clear point at which it would cease to be sovereign. A federal or confederal government could also share sovereignty with its constituent states. Still, a satellite state would normally be largely sovereign. The stronger neighbour might supervise certain aspects of its political life, but in its interventions it would usually negotiate from strength rather than issuing direct commands.

Scotland in the late sixteenth century became a satellite state of this kind. The process by which it acquired a dependence on England, the Reformation of 1560, was the same process by which Scottish sovereignty was enhanced by removing papal authority. Elizabethan England could be ruthless towards Scotland if it ever showed signs of stepping out of line, but so long as Scotland maintained its pro-English diplomatic stance it did not seek annexation or closer control. The English ambassador was always an important figure in the corridors of power when a parliament met, but parliament remained sovereign. This is noteworthy because as recently as the 1540s, England had tried to annex Scotland and had failed. After about 1550, the English seem quite suddenly to have lost the desire to conquer Scotland; they never really regained it.

In 1603 Scotland formally changed from being a satellite state to being part of a multiple kingdom. James VI and I tried to unite Scotland and England; although this failed, he did succeed in governing the kingdoms in parallel. The continuance of a separate Scottish parliament meant that sovereignty continued. The English were mainly concerned about Scotland in wartime, and there were fewer wars after the Anglo-Spanish peace of 1604. Unlike Ireland, Scotland presented few problems and few possibilities, so the norm for the English was to ignore it.

The abortive Jacobean union project left Scotland without a viceroy. Kings of multiple kingdoms usually appointed viceroys in the lesser kingdoms as local intermediaries. But because James in 1603 expected a full union shortly, he left the Scottish privy council collectively in charge, authorising them to sign the documents that he had previously signed. He still reached major decisions by consensus with the council, though the discussions were now by correspondence or by councillors' visits to Westminster. James was very much present in Scottish government after 1603 - a point which tends to be obscured by describing him as an 'absentee'. Because his system worked, he never set up the barrier of a viceroy between himself and the Scottish political classes. The Scots were pleased by this, believing that it gave them a higher status than Ireland which did have a viceroy.

The revolution of 1638 nullified royal authority, and placed Scottish government entirely in the hands of the estates. Until then, the crown had been the only constitutional link with England; with that gone, had Scotland suddenly become independent? The answer is no, for various reasons. The revolution was only provisional until a settlement was reached with the crown. This was never really achieved, but the story of the 1640s is the story of attempts to achieve it. The Covenanters sought to achieve security for their revolution by exporting it to England, exploiting their links with English parliamentarians who were as dissatisfied with Charles I as they were themselves.

How should we interpret conflict between the Scottish estates and the crown? Should we see the estates as basically Scottish, the crown as basically English or British? On the whole we should not. It depends how the crown acted at any given moment. For most purposes, the crown was happy to be Scottish in Scotland, English in England. So long as the two countries did not diverge, this dual approach was easy to maintain; it could even enhance the crown's freedom of manoeuvre. In the main examples of crown-parliament conflict, the issue was not simply Anglicisation. Even with the covenanting revolution, where the trigger was the introduction of a version of the English prayer book, the Covenanters' objection to the book was not that it was English, but that it was superstitious and crypto-Catholic. A strong movement in England itself felt much the same way.

There is also the question of whether the Scots even wanted independence. Nobody seriously advocated separation from England - the basis of most modern nationalism. The Covenanters could have separated easily enough. In June 1640 they assembled in a parliament which they had initially persuaded Charles I to summon but which he had subsequently tried to cancel. As a result he did not send a royal commissioner to it. The Covenanters could have used this as a pretext for declaring that he had abdicated, and doing what the Portuguese did later that very year: elevating a suitably-compliant junior member of the royal dynasty to the throne of an independent Scotland. Instead they pursued a single-mindedly British solution to their problems, a solution that in some ways entailed closer union. They soon found themselves in alliance with English parliamentarians in their opposition to the crown. In 1649, when an English republic was proclaimed, they had a second opportunity for separation that did not even need a junior royal; Charles II himself would have made an excellent king of a separate Scotland. Instead the Covenanters proclaimed him king of Scotland, England and Ireland, thus precipitating an Anglo-Scottish war. Their strategy was not nationalist in the modern separatist sense; it was British.

The result of the Anglo-Scottish war, in 1651, was an English conquest and assimilation of Scotland. Henry VIII had thirsted to conquer Scotland and had failed: Oliver Cromwell acted only to protect English security, but succeeded. The eventual result was an incorporating union, with a single parliament for the 'Commonwealth of England, Scotland and Ireland'. This perhaps set a precedent (if anyone chose to follow it), but at the Restoration of 1660 the union, and the English military occupation that had sustained it, were dissolved. Because the English had been reluctant conquerors, the Cromwellian union was an interlude rather than the turning-point that it became for Ireland. So the new regime of 1660 - and it was a *new* regime, however convenient the term 'restoration' - restored the separate Scottish parliament.

But it did not restore the whole governmental system, in particular not the partnership between crown and Scottish privy council. Instead, the leading minister for Scotland increasingly looked like a viceroy, in the sense of an intermediary between local elites and crown. The post which carried this role was that of royal commissioner to parliament - so we need to look carefully at this aspect of parliamentary politics.

The commission itself simply empowered the commissioner to represent the king in parliament. In practice this meant holding a temporary court in Holyrood, opening and closing parliament, and giving the royal assent to approved statutes. Before 1638 commissioners usually confined themselves to this ceremonial role, though they did sometimes (notably in 1621) take responsibility for piloting government measures through parliament. But after the Restoration, meetings of parliament were longer, and commissioners began to be leaders of a ministerial team managing parliament more actively. This was clear for the duke of Lauderdale, who was both commissioner and secretary of state.

This was developed further after the Glorious Revolution of 1689, by which the monarchy was subordinated more fully to the estates. Government was now dependent on a parliamentary majority, and the entire ministerial team was expected to enjoy parliament's confidence. The commissioner was usually the man who was expected to form a ministry, and to whom the king's instructions on how to govern were issued. As such his role differed little from that of a viceroy - except that he was a practising Scottish politician rather than an English envoy. The only commissioner resembling an English envoy was James, duke of Albany and York, in 1681-2. His situation was unusual, since it was his position as heir apparent to the throne that the parliament had been called to confirm. The appointment of an ordinary English politician as commissioner seems never to have been likely, though such men were often appointed as Irish viceroys.

III

Scotland's parliament, then, came a long way in the seventeenth century, but remained a sovereign body. The nature of its British context however needs further investigation. Was the Scottish parliament a British institution? If so, it was perhaps a provincial body, comparable to some of the French provincial estates or German *Landtage*. But perhaps Britain in the seventeenth century was merely a geographical expression, and the Scottish parliament rightly belongs only in a Scottish context? There are no simple answers to these questions, but they can at least be brought into more precise focus by asking: How far did the Scottish parliament act to foster Britishness, and how far did it maintain or foster distinctive Scottishness?

Fostering Britishness could take several forms. The most obvious would be the creation of explicitly British structures of authority. Various union schemes were discussed abortively in 1604-7, 1669-70 and 1702, while another such scheme succeeded in 1706-7. In 1640-41 the Treaty of London provided for Anglo-Scottish 'conservators', and the Committee of Both Kingdoms co-ordinated the Anglo-Scottish war effort against the king in 1644-7. In the 1650s the Cromwellian union was a central fact of British life. In the half-century after 1660, we shall see that the gradual creation of a common British army was important, though it was achieved without reference to the Scottish parliament.

Britishness of a kind could also be fostered through Anglicisation. After the failure of the Jacobean union project, this was an important theme, and much of it involved parliament. The revival of episcopacy between 1600 and 1612, the introduction of justices of the peace in 1609, and the introduction of ceremonies into Scottish worship after 1614, were consciously designed to make Scotland more like England. There was also Anglicisation of the Scottish parliament itself. The biggest single instance of this was the introduction of shire commissioners in 1587 (Anglicisation could occur before 1603). Impeachment of the crown's ministers, revived in England in 1621, was assumed to be competent to the Scottish parliament in 1673 and 1689, and in 1641-2 there were trials under parliamentary commission that looked similar. In 1640 came the introduction of English-style 'sessions' of parliament.

Maintaining Scottishness was more a matter of failing to do these things, or of doing things that went in a different direction from what England was doing. Acts that were *directly* un-British were rare. The Scottish parliament was hardly fostering Britishness when between 1639 and 1661 it repeatedly legislated against Scots marrying in England. But except during its tense and ambiguous final years, the Scottish parliament hardly ever displayed a spirit of separatism.

There were two reasons for this. First, parliament rarely needed to assert Scottish separateness: it was a daily reality. The vast bulk of what the Scottish parliament did related to internal Scottish affairs. In matters like the 'Act concerning probative witnesses in writs and executions' of 1681, no connection with or relation to England is apparent. Second, the men in the Scottish parliament were not necessarily thinking in national terms, either Scottish or British, when they legislated. The most deeply-felt issues were religious ones; theological thinking, though it drew on national traditions and indeed local ones (as with the conservative 'Aberdeen Doctors' of the 1630s), was basically universalist. When the Covenanters abolished episcopacy in 1638 as 'contrary to the law of God', they were partly throwing down a challenge to the English, but they were also stating the truth as they saw it. Such a truth was far easier for a theologian to justify than the pluralist arguments for the next abolition of episcopacy, in 1689: 'a great and insupportable greivance to this nation and contrair to the inclinationes of the generalitie of the people' [Dickinson and Donaldson, 205].

So when we have put together all the consciously 'Scottish' and deliberately 'British' aspects of seventeenth-century Scottish parliamentary activity, it does not add up to the story of the seventeenth-century Scottish parliament. One can of course label anything that happened north of Berwick as 'Scottish' (or indeed as 'British'), but this is not particularly helpful. Most of the things done in or by the Scottish parliament bore only indirectly, if at all, on the national question.

If this was true of Scotland, it was also true of England. But one can still ask whether England became more British in the seventeenth century. The explicitly British structures that embraced Scotland have already been mentioned: they embraced England too. Mirroring the Anglicisation of Scotland we might expect to see the Scotticisation of England ... or would we? Nevertheless, there were arguably some instances of it. The early seventeenth-century crown sought not only to change the Scottish church to introduce the kind of ceremonies found in England, but to change the English church to foster the kind of educated preaching clergy found in Scotland. The English Triennial Act of 1641 may well have owed something to the similar Scottish act of 1640. In 1667 the crown put the English treasurership into commission, launching what would become a dominant government department - the Treasury. This went parallel with, and was originally intended to be preceded by, a similar Scottish treasury commission. Some of these policy initiatives were royal rather than parliamentary, but they do at least illustrate the extent to which fostering Britishness was not entirely a one-way street along which Scotland was Anglicised.

So some of what we are seeing is not 'Anglicisation' or 'Scotticisation' but *parallel development* and *convergence* of the two countries, as similar issues evoked increasingly similar responses. This would be the best way of interpreting the two treasury commissions of 1667. The Scottish 'Act suspending public debts' of September 1672 had different roots from the English 'Stop of the Exchequer' in January, but may well have been inspired by it. Also in 1672, the Scottish act banning imports of Irish grain and livestock looks rather like England's Irish Wool Act of 1662.

Governmental diversification within England might also have the effect of making England more British. This is best explained through an analogy. Twentieth-century British governments were usually constituted by a cabinet of ministers: most were responsible for functionally-specialist departments but one took charge of a regionally-specialist department for Scotland. Some of the functionally-specialist departments covered both Scotland and England: others ceded responsibility to the Scottish Office; this did not prevent Britain having an integrated government, indeed it fostered it. If Britain had had an 'English Office' as well as a Scottish Office, it could hardly have been so well integrated.

The story of the departmentalisation of English government - the move away from an 'English Office' - is a long one and only part of it belongs to the seventeenth century, but we may note Charles I's tendency in the 1630s to give responsibility to a number of specialist ministers rather than a single favourite. The duke of Buckingham, assassinated in 1628, was the last royal adviser of the century (with the possible exception of Clarendon in the 1660s) to be actively involved in all aspects of policy-making. The treasury commission of 1667 is also part of this story; so is the Board of Trade of 1696, which incidentally was partly prompted by the launch of the Company of Scotland in the previous year. The rise of religious pluralism in late seventeenth-century England, though not a governmental development, also allowed the church of Scotland to fit comfortably into a British pattern of multiple Protestant denominations. By 1700 English government had a well-developed departmental structure into which responsibility for Scotland could be slotted.

IV

James VI and I in 1607 offered the English parliament a series of analogies as to how he saw Scotland's position in the projected union. Scotland would 'with time become but as Cumberland and Northumberland, and those other remote and northern shires'. Its local privileges would be comparable to those of Kent or Cheshire. The union would be like that with Wales. He mentioned that 'Irish, Scottish, Welsh, and English' all offered him allegiance - yet he had no comparison to offer with Ireland, although the dual Anglo-Scottish monarchy looked in some ways quite like the dual Anglo-Irish monarchy. James's reticence becomes more comprehensible when we see the context in which he had Ireland in mind. He warned against treating Scotland as a 'naked province' subject to England: 'I hope you meane not I should set garrisons over them, as the Spaniards doe over Sicily and Naples, or governe them by commissioners, which are seldome found succeedingly all wise and honest men' [Sommerville, 164, 169, 172-3]. Ireland *was* governed in this way. Whether or not viceroys of Ireland were 'wise and honest', they probably seemed not to be, because the difficulties of governing Ireland tended to make their tenure of office brief and their departure ignominious.

The Irish parliament was also subject to Poynings' Law, which required that proposed Irish legislation be remitted to England by the viceroy and authorised by the English monarch and council under the great seal. This explicitly subordinated the Irish parliament to the English government. One of the reasons Ireland was difficult to govern was that it was explicitly governed in English interests. Scotland was not. In Scotland, monarchs could choose to be guided by English, rather than Scottish, interests, and when dealing with the Scottish parliament they could take advice from their English ministers. But they did not have to. Usually they seem to have preferred making English and Scottish policy separately. The tradition of Scottish sovereignty made it the easiest thing to do.

In other respects, too, Ireland was more subservient than Scotland. From 1642 onwards, the English parliament itself periodically legislated for Ireland. A particularly drastic English statute of 1691 imposed a tough anti-Catholic oath on members of the Irish parliament. Then there was a large standing army in Ireland after 1649, with many Scottish and English officers. Irish revenues were used to reward English royal servants, and in the 1680s money was actually transferred from the Irish exchequer to England. This could not have happened in Scotland. The Irish administration in Dublin Castle was more subservient to Westminster than its Scottish counterpart. The crown in Scotland was generally Scottish: the crown in Ireland was generally English.

Nevertheless, towards the end of our period, Scots who were beginning to lose confidence in their own parliament began to ponder Irish comparisons. A paper circulated during the 1703 Scottish parliament lamented the 'wretched state' of Ireland, excluded from English trade: 'I desire to know, then, my lord, where lies the difference of our case, from that most deplorable state of Irish parliaments, save that in the one cases, the legislative is openly determined by command, and in the other by a no less operative influence of men' [Ferguson (1974), 30].

This brings us back to Andrew Fletcher, and to his famous assertion of 1703: 'It is not the prerogative of a king of Scotland I would diminish, but the prerogative of English ministers over this nation' [Fletcher, 80]. The first part of the great republican's claim need not detain us, but the second is significant and has been much quoted. What influence did English ministers have over Scotland? This question cannot be fully answered in a brief survey, but some suggestions may be made.

Accounts of seventeenth-century politics have not usually viewed English ministers in general as having much time for Scottish affairs or even knowledge of them. In 1667-73 there was intricate political intrigue among various Scottish politicians, attempting either to use or to subvert the authority of the commissioner, Lauderdale. Parliament met frequently and much of politics was parliamentary politics, but English politicians were not involved. They were not trying to influence Scotland. The English House of Commons petitioned repeatedly for the removal of Lauderdale in the late 1670s, but its complaint was that his fostering of Scottish military power was intended to furnish the means for altering the English constitution. In William's reign, only about half a dozen English politicians were even noticed north of the Border - and two of those (Portland and Albemarle) were Dutch, while another (Gilbert Burnet) was actually Scottish.

Things changed under Anne, because it was the job of English politicians to resolve the succession crisis that began in 1700 and became increasingly serious during her reign. The renewal of war with France in 1702 sharpened the question of Scottish allegiance. If the Scottish parliament had rejected the Hanoverian succession, as it threatened to do in 1703 and 1704, this would have affected England directly. Harley, Godolphin and Marlborough - the 'triumvirate' castigated in the union debate by Belhaven - were trying to solve this problem, and to maximise their party political advantage at Westminster in the process. They were not imperialists trying to extend English influence north of the Border.

V

So English ministers in 1706 had no more desire to conquer and annex Scotland than they had had in 1660, or indeed in 1560. Scottish sovereignty continued, and in some ways had been enhanced since 1689. The Glorious Revolution reduced the power of the crown, leaving more power with the separate English and Scottish parliaments. Because the crown now had to hesitate before vetoing legislation, the two parliaments could adopt divergent policies if they so wished. The Scottish politicians of the 1690s did not wish to separate from England any more than their predecessors of the 1640s; nationalism in a separatist sense was still absent. But issues had arisen since the 1640s that would not only unsettle Anglo-Scottish relations, but pose challenges for Scottish parliamentary sovereignty.

The main issue was economic. In 1651, when Cromwell was conquering Scotland so reluctantly, the English parliamentary government did two things in which it very much believed. The first was to propose political and economic union to the Netherlands, in the hope of converting Anglo-Dutch trade rivalry into peaceful co-operation. Then, when the Dutch refused the union, the English passed a Navigation Act restricting trade in English goods to English ships, an attack on the Dutch carrying trade. It soon led to war - England's first commercial war. It had become accepted that a government's leading responsibility was to foster economic growth.

The series of Navigation Acts, together with the rise of English colonies, created what later became known as the 'Old Colonial System'. Colonial trade was channelled through England and markets were opened for it by the English navy. Because of the Cromwellian union, Scotland was within the system during its first decade - but at the Restoration found itself outside it. The Scottish parliament immediately realised the significance of this, passing its own Navigation Act in 1661. But with a far smaller merchant fleet, no navy and no colonies, this was an empty gesture. Parliament was slightly more effective in promoting manufacturing industry, either to provide exports or to replace imports, by means of preferential tariffs. It authorised a large number of new market centres, facilitating the marketing of agricultural surpluses. In 1672, in the same spirit, it cancelled the royal burghs' overseas trading monopoly.

As commercial policy became a vehicle for national aspirations, parliaments thus became vehicles for commercial policy. The culmination of long and intense Scottish legislative effort came in 1695, when the Company of Scotland was established as an attempt to open some kind of colonial trade. It became the focus of national aspirations in the late 1690s. It was not a national concern instead of a profit-seeking one: it was a national concern because it was a profit-seeking one. Nor did it begin as an attempt to rival England - indeed it sought out English investment. The English East India Company however lobbied successfully to block this threat to its own position, and thereafter the Company of Scotland sought to foster the Scottish economy using only Scottish investment resources. The colony it founded at Darien (1698-1700) collapsed tragically.

The English parliament thus used statutes successfully to promote commercial growth and the building of a colonial empire. The Scottish parliament tried to copy it, and failed. It had nominal sovereignty over commercial policy, but could not make its orders effective in practice. One reason for English success was that it pursued integrated foreign, military and commercial policies. Scotland had commercial policies, developed for it in parliament, but not foreign policies. Traditionally, Scottish foreign policies had been made or at least endorsed by parliament, but from the 1590s onwards, monarchs ceased to consult it over such issues - and after 1603 there was little sense in which Scotland had a foreign policy at all. Instead it was caught up in English foreign policy. After 1651 this led to a series of wars, first with the Netherlands, then with France, which served no Scottish interests and merely harmed Scottish trade.

This then leads on to the other issue that undermined Scottish sovereignty: the changing nature of military power. Alongside the increased emphasis on commercial policy came an increased emphasis on military policy. After 1660 the English and Scottish governments maintained peacetime armies. This undermined parliamentary sovereignty in Scotland, because the crown was the supreme commander of the regular army and it never had to share that power with parliament. This was a notable change since the 1640s, when parliament had had armed forces under its direct control. The Restoration regime did also create a Scottish militia, a part-time military force based on propertied elites. Parliament had rather more control over this. The Act of Security (1703-4) ordered the militia to be mustered; but although musters were held, they did not produce a significant fighting force. And if the Scottish estates had fallen into conflict with the crown, the regular Scottish army would probably have been expected to fight for the crown. Scottish sovereignty in the military sphere was modest at best.

Scottish sovereignty at the end of the seventeenth century was thus a fragile thing. Parliament was very much sovereign in a Scottish context, and indeed had come to symbolise Scottish sovereignty. But its most important activity - the making of economic policy - no longer worked. It appeared to have the power to issue commands and get them obeyed, but it was failing in certain key functions. It could not command a Scottish army and navy into existence. Still less could it command a Scottish colony to prosper. As a result, the debate on the union of 1707 was essentially about whether a parliament was a symbolic or a functional thing. To the unionists, the question was not whether Scotland should have a parliament: it was whether it should have a symbolic Scottish parliament or a functional British one.

Further Reading:
The British Problem, 1534-1707, ed. Brendan Bradshaw and John Morrill (London, 1996); *A Source Book of Scottish History*, vol. iii (1567-1707), ed. William Croft Dickinson and Gordon Donaldson (2nd edn., Edinburgh, 1961); William Ferguson, 'Imperial crowns: a neglected facet of the background to the Treaty of Union of 1707', *Scottish Historical Review*, 53 (1974), 22-44; William Ferguson, *Scotland's Relations with England: a Survey to 1707* (Edinburgh, 1977); *Andrew Fletcher of Saltoun: Selected Political Writings and Speeches*, ed. David Daiches (Edinburgh, 1979); Julian Goodare, *State and Society in Early Modern Scotland* (Oxford, 1999); *The Scots and Parliament*, ed. Clyve Jones (Edinburgh, 1996); *The Stuart Constitution: Documents and Commentary*, ed. J.P Kenyon (2nd edn., Cambridge, 1986); Colin Kidd, *Subverting Scotland's Past: Scottish Whig Historians and the Creation of an Anglo-British Identity, 1689-1830* (Cambridge, 1993); Brian P. Levack, *The Formation of the British State: England, Scotland, and the Union, 1603-1707* (Oxford, 1987); *Scots and Britons: Scottish Political Thought and the Union of 1603*, ed. Roger A Mason (Cambridge, 1994); R.S. Rait, *The Parliaments of Scotland* (Glasgow, 1924); P.W.J. Riley, *The Union of England and Scotland* (Manchester, 1978); *A Union for Empire: Political Thought and the British Union of 1707*, ed. John Robertson (Cambridge, 1995); *James VI & I, Political Writings*, ed. J.P. Sommerville (Cambridge, 1994); Christopher A. Whatley, *'Bought and Sold for English Gold'? Explaining the Union of 1707* (Glasgow, 1994).

4

The Idea of Sovereignty and the Act of Union

JOHN ROBERTSON

By 1702, the year of William III's death, it was clear that Scotland was facing a crisis of sovereignty. Two events - two failures - had brought the crisis into the open. The first was the collapse of the Darien venture, which had become apparent in 1700. This was not simply a commercial and financial disaster; failure was directly due to the Scots' inability to defend the settlement with their own naval power, and to the ease with which the king of Scotland could be over-ruled by his other person, the king of England. As one observer, probably Lord Belhaven, put it, Scotland's sovereignty had been 'trampled underfoot'; to another, George Ridpath, the invasion of 'our sovereignty and freedom' was greater than any since our betrayal by Baliol [Belhaven (?), 42; Ridpath, *Scotland's Grievances* , Part I]. The second, even more critical failure was that of the Stewart succession in the Protestant line, when it became clear that Anne would have no surviving heirs. The crisis was precipitated by the unilateral action of the English parliament, determining by the Act of Settlement (1701) that the succession to its crown would pass to the Hanoverian heirs of James I's daughter Elizabeth. Since Elizabeth was no less the daughter of James VI, the proposed succession was equally legitimate from a Scottish point of view, but it underlined the much greater strength of dynastic continuity in the claim of the exiled, Roman Catholic James VII and his heirs. The need for the Scots to respond by vindicating their own sovereignty was accentuated by the confidence with which English antiquarian publicists had begun to revive old claims for the suzerainty of the English crown over Scotland. Although Ridpath had sought to head off the threat by publishing Sir Thomas Craig's treatise on homage as *Scotland's Sovereignty asserted* in 1695, the antiquaries were undeterred, their tendentious scholarship serving further to irritate Scottish sensibilities.

The twin failures of Darien and the succession precipitated the Anglo-Scottish union negotiations of 1702 and 1705-7. Throughout this fraught period, Scotland's sovereignty was necessarily at the centre of public debate. But it would be a mistake simply to proceed to examine the debate as if it developed *sui generis*. Since its starting-point was the Scots' existing understanding of their kingdom's sovereignty, we can begin by reviewing that understanding. But it would be surprising were the Scots ignorant of recent developments in thinking about sovereignty beyond Scotland itself: by identifying these developments, we will be better able to grasp the extent to which Scottish ideas of sovereignty were changed in the course of the Union debate.

I

At the outset, it is important to recognise that 'sovereignty' was not in the early modern period the settled, clear-cut concept we may imagine it to be now. On the contrary, the term carried a range of meanings and connotations. Fundamental to its instability was its development as a vernacular word, covering a range of Latin concepts: *majestas, dominium, imperium, summa potestas*. Not surprisingly, jurists who were accustomed to disputation over the several Latin concepts struggled to pin down the inclusive new vernacular term. The idea was most easily associated with the power of rulers, those who might exercise the 'marks' or 'rights' of sovereignty, the *jura majestatis*. Alternatively, it might describe the status of those from whom rulers originally derived their authority, especially if that authority might be revoked when abused or abandoned. But it was harder to apply the idea of sovereignty to kingdoms or commonwealths as entities independent of their rulers; insofar as it was, it tended to be as a general synonym for the kingdom's 'independence' or 'liberty'.

In the case of Scotland, for example, sovereignty was most readily attached to the monarchy itself. The sovereignty of the Scottish crown was closely associated with its dynastic antiquity, as the supposedly oldest continuous monarchy in Europe (the case afforced by the forty mythical kings and four hundred years of their rule added to the story by Hector Boece). In addition to the usual marks of sovereignty, Scottish kings also claimed to possess 'imperial' status, with a crown 'closed' over the king's head. Asserted in the late fifteenth century, the claim to such status had been consolidated by James V in the 1530s, the better to vindicate his independence from both the pope and the newly 'imperial' realm of Henry VIII of England. Later in the sixteenth century there emerged a rival historical account of sovereignty in Scotland, which identified it with the rights of the Scottish 'people' against their kings. This account did not deny the continuity of the monarchy; but it asserted that the 'people' had a right to resist kings whose rule degenerated into tyranny. The most radical exponent of this view was George Buchanan; in the seventeenth century the theory was reworked in the light of the covenants and the acts of the parliament of 1641 by Samuel Rutherford, and again, on behalf of the covenanting remnant in the 1660s, by James Steuart of Goodtrees.

By the last quarter of the seventeenth century, however, this 'monarchomach' tradition was in eclipse. Between 1660 and 1689 the crown's sovereignty was vindicated by Sir George Mackenzie and Bishop Andrew Honyman in the ultra-royalist terms of divine, hereditary and absolute right. The events of 1688-89 had checked these excesses; but while the Convention parliament boldly declared James VII to have 'forfeited' his throne, there was no revival of Buchananite argument. Defenders of the Revolution were careful to avoid suggesting that sovereignty had at any point reverted to the Scottish people.

II

Before 1700, therefore, Scottish discussions of sovereignty seem to have been preoccupied with traditional concerns. Outwith Scotland, by contrast, the concept had been undergoing radical development. Contributors to this process numbered French, Dutch and German jurists - Bodin, Grotius and Pufendorf are only the best-known names; but the most radical sovereignty theorist of them all was undoubtedly the Englishman, Thomas Hobbes. In two works, the Latin *De Cive* (1647) and the English *Leviathan* (1651), Hobbes articulated a three-fold transformation of the concept of 'sovereign power' (his preferred term).

First, he elaborated a concept of sovereign power which was both independent of the physical person or persons who ruled and superior to the 'multitude' of individuals who made up the citizens of the commonwealth. In insisting that it made no sense to ascribe sovereign power to the people, Hobbes was exemplary of a general determination among European jurists to associate it exclusively with government. But he was original in characterising the sovereign as an artificial, representative 'personation' of the commonwealth, implying that the state was an idea distinct from those who exercised power within it. The second radical feature of Hobbes's treatment of sovereignty was his willingness to accept sovereignty acquired by conquest. Again, the doctrine was not his invention; but his formulation of it was unusually clear-cut. Hobbes had in mind not simply internal conquest, as the regicide usurpation of power in England in 1649, but external, as by England over Ireland and Scotland in the 1650s. Towards each other, he reasoned, sovereigns were as in the state of nature: a sovereign power unable to defend its subjects was legitimately conquered.

The third and arguably most radical of Hobbes's transformations was in his account of sovereign power in matters ecclesiastical. In the third and fourth books of *Leviathan*, Hobbes explained that the civil sovereign's authority rightfully extended to the appointment of priests, the interpretation of scripture and the conduct of worship. So arguing, he refuted not only *jure divino* episcopacy but *jure divino* presbytry - and any claim that a Gentile people might imitate the Biblical Hebrews and make a covenant direct with God. (The extent to which Leviathan was, in context, an all-out attack on the pretensions of Scottish presbyterianism has, I think, been under-appreciated.)

Radical as Hobbes was in clarifying and extending the reach of sovereignty, however, it is no less important to note that he did not make sovereign power an end in itself. It was justified in so far as it secured the peace of the commonwealth, and the liberty of its subjects. The measure of sovereignty, in short, was its utility.

Hobbes's impact on Scottish political thinking after the Restoration is a subject still to be explored. (It is only now becoming clear how great it was in England, especially among Anglican clergymen.) There are signs that royalist lawyers such as Mackenzie and churchmen such as Archbishop Leighton preferred to evade rather than face his challenge; they clearly associated him with the dangers of Epicurean philosophy. Nor was his a name frequently referred to during the Union debate itself. Once that debate put Scotland's sovereignty under the spotlight, however, the transformations of sovereignty which I have associated with Hobbes could no longer be ignored. In critical respects they may be seen to have shaped the terms in which Scotland's sovereignty was discussed, enhancing the interest and significance of the debate.

III

The first phase of the Union debate was initiated by Andrew Fletcher in his *Speeches* to the parliament which met in May 1703. Seizing the opportunity offered by the crown's need to settle the succession, he proposed a series of limitations to accompany an Act of Security. These would require that any future monarch shared with England would be obliged to rule Scotland in conjunction with the Scottish parliament. Fletcher did not put the case for limitations in terms of Scotland's sovereignty, a concept he very rarely used. He preferred to talk of Scotland's 'liberties', and of the need to end its 'dependence' on the English court. But the clear implication of his proposals was that the Scots could not hope to vindicate their independence without reforming and strengthening their parliament. It has been observed that Fletcher's limitations reproduced the measures of the parliament of 1641; Fletcher, however, was careful to dissociate his proposals from the 'peevish, imprudent, and detestable conduct of the Presbyterians', and would rather appeal to the 'antient constitution' which existed before the union of the crowns. Even then he was unspecific, referring generally to laws for the liberty of the subject which had been 'industriously and designedly left out' of the last two editions of our acts [Fletcher, *Speeches*, in *Political Works*, 132, 135]. How effectively the Scottish parliament had ever exercised anything resembling sovereign powers he did not attempt to establish.

Simultaneously, however, an attempt to make up for Fletcher's vagueness was undertaken by George Ridpath, in his *Historical Account of the Ancient Rights and*

Power of the Parliament of Scotland (1703). There is no evidence that this was written in collusion with Fletcher; but it is not surprising that the editor of Craig's treatise on homage should have seen the opportunity - or the danger - in Fletcher's unsubstantiated claims. Ridpath set out to show that before the union of the crowns the estates assembled in parliament had held 'a commanding share in all the rights of sovereignty' [*Historical Account*, 3]. He acknowledged the difficulties he faced: the loss of the nation's records, the nobility's greater reputation for fighting it out. Nevertheless, he set about adapting Buchanan's story to his purposes, demonstrating thereby that the estates had possessed the right to resist the crown when it invaded the constitution, to determine their own meetings, to exercise a share of the *jura majestatis*, and to settle the succession. He also identified the laws which had been omitted from recent editions of Scottish Acts.

Ridpath's efforts, however, were to little avail: his claims were echoed by few other contributors to the debate. The fundamental problem, it would seem, was their lack of a credible basis in fact, or at least record. All 'ancient constitutions', the English as well as the Scottish, were myths; but to be viable politically, a myth needed a foundation of accepted fact, of remembered events, and it was very difficult to construct such a myth for the Scottish parliament for the time before the union of the crowns. There existed a much more recent foundation for the claims of parliament in the events of 1641; but as Fletcher pointed out, their credibility was undermined by the religious enthusiasm which had inspired them.

No one, indeed, was quicker to acknowledge the failure of the case he had made for the Scottish parliament than Andrew Fletcher himself. He admitted it within months of the end of the parliamentary session, in the *Account of a Conversation Concerning a Right Regulation of Governments for the common Good of Mankind*. In the course of his vivid, but probably imaginary, conversation with the earl of Cromarty, Sir Christopher Musgrave and Sir Edward Seymour, Fletcher defended his conduct in the recent session, and subjected the arguments of those who favoured incorporating union (some of which had yet to appear in print) to withering criticism. But he also acknowledged that the real problem of Scotland's relation to England was the disproportion of their resources, and the economic, cultural and political preponderance of London in particular. When the problem was seen in this enlarged perspective, the only solution which Fletcher could envisage was one requiring a re-drawing of the entire political map of Europe. This would be divided into ten to twelve geographical areas, each of which would in turn be subdivided among ten or twelve cities and their surrounding territories: constituting 'distinct sovereignties' - for once Fletcher used the term - these would be united only on a confederal basis [*Account of a Conversation*, in *Political Works*, 207-8]. The three kingdoms of the British Isles would themselves be divided into twelve separate sovereignties, two of them within Scotland. To achieve a lasting balance between the parts of Britain, in other words, the sovereign kingdom of Scotland (along with those of England and Ireland) would have to cease to exist.

A year later Fletcher completed his demolition of the ancient constitution of Scotland when he casually proposed to parliament that the succession be offered to the prince of Prussia, on the grounds that he was at least a Calvinist. Since the Hohenzollerns had only had their royal title accepted since 1700, Fletcher was in effect offering to transfer the crown of the oldest continuous dynasty in Europe to the youngest. Contempt for the historical shibboleths of Scottish sovereignty could hardly be more clearly expressed.

IV

Once Fletcher had shot his bolt on behalf of parliament, non-Jacobite defenders of Scotland's independent sovereignty were hard put to it to find an alternative basis for its vindication. Politically, moreover, they were placed on the defensive by the passing of the Alien Act in 1705, and the subsequent decision of the Scottish parliament to treat for union. Nevertheless Ridpath and his fellow London-Scot James Hodges demonstrated both resilience and ingenuity in arguing their corner. They pointed out that by threatening to deprive Scots of their naturalised status in England, the Alien Act recognised that the Scots actually enjoyed the status, and were therefore already within an 'incorporating' union. This being so, there was no need to abolish the Scottish parliament to achieve such a union, and there were two good reasons to keep it.

The first was that in a united parliament the Scots would have no guarantee that their interests, and in particular their Presbyterian church, would be respected, since their representatives would easily be outvoted by English members. Second, in any case, the estates of Scotland did not possess the authority to dissolve themselves without consulting their constituents in the shires and burghs. On this point much was made of the opinion of the royalist Sir George Mackenzie, whose *Observations on the Acts of Parliament* (1687) had commented on the limited powers of the estates in relation to earlier union negotiations. The opinion was reprinted in a pamphlet by the Reverend Robert Wylie (who had previously distinguished himself as leader of the clerical chorus calling for the execution of Thomas Aikenhead, the young Edinburgh student accused of atheism in 1697), and it was referred to approvingly by many of the treaty's opponents. Ridpath insisted that what was held by freehold could not be transferred to another nation, especially 'legislature, and decisive judicature, which are rights of sovereignty' [*Considerations upon the Union* (1706), 54]. The argument impressed the English unionist pamphleteer Daniel Defoe, who assumed that Scottish freeholders were akin to their English counterparts. But this was a fallacy. The Scottish freeholders were a tiny group of direct vassals of the crown, who had been granted the privilege of sending only one or two of their number to parliament, while the great nobility continued to be required to attend in person. The argument that the dissolution of the Scottish parliament needed the consent of the freeholders thus fell far short of calling for a popular mandate. Little better than special pleading, it was not the best ground from which to conduct the final defence of Scotland's independent sovereignty.

V

Each of these arguments in defence of Scottish sovereignty was challenged by those who believed that the best outcome of the crisis would be an incorporating, parliamentary union with England. From 1700 onwards the leading proponents of this case were William Seton of Pitmedden and George Mackenzie, Viscount Tarbat and earl of Cromarty (also the nephew of the royalist lawyer of the same name). Confidently they rebutted the successive arguments of Fletcher, Ridpath and Hodges. The Scottish parliament itself, they pointed out, had never been the independent, sovereign institution it was claimed; on the contrary, it was part of the 'Gothic constitution of government', when an unruly and oppressive nobility destroyed the peace of the country by their quarrels [Seton, speech on the Union, in Defoe, *History of the Union* (1786), 313-14]. (In his critique of the nobility, and of its responsibility for the backwardness of Scottish agriculture, Seton shared much common ground with Fletcher.) Insofar as parliament had exercised sovereignty, it had been in conjunction with the crown.

The later arguments of Ridpath, Hodges and others received equally short shrift. Responding to the claims made on behalf of the freeholders, Seton distinguished Scotland's form of government from a 'Polish aristocracy', in which the gentry prescribed rules to their representatives [speech on the Union, in Defoe, *History*, 360]. In Scotland, Cromarty explained, the 'supreme sovereign power is (not delegate) but devolved' upon the crown and parliament [Cromarty, *A Friendly Return* (1706), 29]. As for a guarantee of Scottish interests after the Union, none was needed, since the proposed Union would involve no surrender of sovereignty, but a mutual communication of rights, as Grotius had explained in Book II, chapter 9, section ix of his *Laws of War and Peace* [Seton, speech on the Union, in Defoe, *History*, 362]. The authority of Grotius was invoked by the Union's supporters only a little less than Mackenzie's was by their opponents, but arguably with no more satisfactory explanation of its import: why it should remove the problem of the guarantee was unclear.

An alternative response to the problem was offered by Daniel Defoe and Francis Grant. They suggested that the Treaty of Union itself would have the status of a 'fundamental', such that any subsequent breach of its terms by the united parliament would 'dissolve the constitution and very being of the parliament, and overthrow the Union' [Defoe, *Essay at Removing National Prejudices*, 26]. The most important point thus secured was the Protestant religion and Presbyterian church government, which were made 'fundamental to the new constitution, and therefore not changeable' [Grant, *The Patriot Resolved*, 18]. Quite how the treaty and the accompanying acts relating to the churches were to work in this way neither Defoe nor Grant could specify. There was no suggestion that the treaty would form part of a system of public law, as the Treaty of Westphalia did within the law of the empire in Germany, and no provision for a higher court to adjudicate on any alleged breach of its terms. Much sport however could be made with the pretended sovereignty of the estates and the freeholders, a full and credible answer to the question of the guarantee remained difficult to provide.

VI

Simply retracing the sequence of claims and counter-claims over Scotland's sovereignty is likely, however, to yield only a partial understanding of the debate. Above all, such an approach is liable to encourage undue emphasis on the Scottishness of the participants' concerns. But if we now recall the transformations in the concept of sovereignty which I identified earlier in the work of Hobbes, we can recognise certain additional features of the debate, which will complicate and enhance our sense of its significance. In highlighting these, I am not claiming that they reflect the direct influence of Hobbes; what I do suggest is that the issues he had raised had entered the mainstream of Scottish political thinking.

One feature of the debate which is brought into focus is the marked reluctance to appeal to the sovereignty of the people, among opponents of the Union just as much as its supporters. Historians now make much of popular opposition to the treaty in the winter of 1707-7, pointing to the incidence of petitioning and mob activity; the implication is presumably that the Union lacked democratic legitimacy. But it is striking that no contemporary thinker offered to justify the actions of 'the people'. For all the talk of the consent of the freeholders, the debate threw up no Scottish Locke. James Steuart, one-time author of the *Ius Populi Vindicatum* (1669), had since risen to be lord advocate; but having done the clergy's bidding, and executed Aikenhead, he retired to his tent and said no more. The Hobbesian insistence that the individuals who formed a commonwealth had no part in its sovereignty went unchallenged.

A second post-Hobbesian feature of the debate was the widespread acceptance that Scotland's sovereignty could no longer be defended against an English conquest. While the government's reluctance to divert troops away from the war effort on the continent gave the Scots some room for manoeuvre, conquest was clearly the ultimate sanction. Godolphin more than once threatened privately to impose the Hanoverian succession by force; and the example of Cromwell left no doubt as to the threat's credibility. Well aware of this, Ridpath, Hodges and Fletcher all made it clear that war would be a disaster, and must be avoided: union by conquest was the worst possible outcome of the crisis. It was for this reason that all three argued for a confederal union, rather than separation. But the prospect of war was no more palatable to the Union's supporters, who avoided any reference to arguments from conquest (although Grant, at least, had used them to justify William's accession in 1689). Hence, perhaps, the liking for the Grotian formula of a communication of rights - even if to use it the unionists had to ignore Fletcher's earlier sharp observation that the examples of 'communication' offered by Grotius had only taken place following the conquest of one party by the other [*Account of a Conversation*, in *Political Works*, 196].

But perhaps the most interesting Hobbesian feature of the debate was the prevalence within it of erastianism (the doctrine that churches are rightly subordinate to the civil power). As enacted by the two parliaments, the Union established both the Presbyterian and the Anglican churches on terms clearly incompatible with the *jure divino* pretensions of many of their clergy. The danger was spotted by the more rigorous Presbyterians, such as Robert Wylie, James Webster and the author of the engagingly-titled *Smoaking Flax Unquenchable* (1706). But the Presbyterian laymen - Ridpath, Hodges, Defoe and Grant - were unconcerned: what divided them was not the erastianism of the treaty, but the question of whether its provisions were guaranteed. The episcopalians Seton and Cromarty were even more pronounced in their erastianism, Seton having earlier advocated the unification of the two churches along with the parliaments [*The Interest of Scotland in Three Essays*, Part I]. Knowing that they would only inflame Presbyterian opinion, the episcopalians were more discreet during the last phase of the debate, in 1706-7. But as long as presbytry was established on a 'civil' basis, the prospects for their toleration would be much improved. So it turned out: the Union legislation represented the triumph of an erastian consensus among the Scottish lay elite at the expense of the clergy.

It is true that the collusion between episcopalian and Presbyterian was short-lived. In 1712 the Tory administration in London re-opened the questions of lay patronage and toleration. In support, Cromarty not only justified greater toleration for episcopalians, but suggested that Presbyterians who continued to put allegiance to the covenants before that owed to the state should be treated in the same way as the Jacobites and papists, and barred from office [*The Scottish Toleration Truly Stated*, 16-17]. There was an anguished response from William Carstares, the former confidant of William III, who had guided the Union settlement through the general assembly. But Carstares' complaint was not against an infringement of Presbyterian right: what vexed him was the loss of 'concurrence' between the church and the civil power [*Case of the Church of Scotland*, 3-4]. Those who had feared that the treaty could not be guaranteed were right; but what was insecure was the erastian basis of presbyterianism.

While the Hobbesian transformations of the concept of sovereignty can thus be found in the arguments of both supporters and opponents of the Union, it seems clear that they worked more to the advantage of the former. But this did not make the unionists into simple-minded apologists for the sovereignty of Westminster. For they had also taken Hobbes's point that sovereignty was justified by its utility. What mattered, they argued, was not sovereignty itself, but the 'advantages' which union and a common parliament could be expected to bring. Among Scotland's *Great Advantages by an Union with England*, the title of his pamphlet in 1706, Seton numbered the improvement of trade, industry and agriculture, and the opportunity for Scots to share the rights of liberty and property long enjoyed by the English. In these ways, he thought, the Union would assert 'our sovereignty and independency' more than any other measure [*Scotland's Great Advantages*, 11]. Cromarty was equally explicit. 'The notion of a kingdom per se' was but an abstraction when set against 'the riches, honour and safety of all, and every individual' [*Trialogus*, 5-6.]. And when Francis Grant reviewed the advantages, religious as well as secular, which the Union would bring, he reckoned that very little had been sacrificed to obtain them. 'What was our nominal sovereignty? The phantome of a body ... without a head' [*Patriot Resolved*, 21].

The Union debate, I suggest, had enabled the Scots to get the question of sovereignty into perspective. They had learned from the difficulties encountered by Fletcher and Ridpath how elusive the supposedly ancient sovereignty of their crown and parliament had become. But they were also made aware by the Union's opponents that a united parliament could not guarantee that particularly Scottish interests would always be respected. With no obvious solution to this dilemma, the leaders of the Scottish debate drew on what I have called the Hobbesian transformations of sovereignty to step back from the brink. Giving no credence to theories of popular sovereignty, they made it clear that the governing elite must take responsibility for finding a solution. They recognised that for a country in the position of Scotland to insist on taking its sovereignty to the length of absolute independence would simply advertise its vulnerability to conquest by its larger neighbour. But they also recognised and welcomed the opportunity afforded by the Union crisis to assert the sovereign power of the civil magistrate over the *jure divino* pretensions of the clergy. In short, they recognised that discussion of sovereignty was always a matter of weighing risks against benefits. They had learned the most important Hobbesian lesson of all, that sovereignty was a means, not an end, to be judged by the advantages it brought. In the words of article 18 of the treaty, its measure was the 'evident utility of the subjects within Scotland'. The idea of sovereignty has its uses, but it is always simple-minded to regard it as sacrosanct, wherever it may be located.

References:
[John Hamilton, Lord Belhaven, attrib. to], *A Defence of the Scots Settlement at Darien, with An Answer to the Spanish Memorial against it* (1699); [William Carstares], *The Case of the Church of Scotland with relation to the Bill for a Toleration to the Episcopal Dissenters* [1712]; [George Mackenzie, earl of Cromarty], *A Friendly Return to a Letters Concerning Sir George Mackenzie's and Sir John Nisbet's Observation and Responce on the matter of the Union* (1706); [George Mackenzie, earl of Cromarty], *Trialogus* (1706); [Daniel Defoe], *An Essay at Removing National Prejudices against a Union with England*, Part III (1706); Andrew Fletcher, *Speeches by a Member of the Parliament* (1703), repr. in Andrew Fletcher, *Political Works*, ed. John Robertson (Cambridge, 1997), 129-173; Andrew Fletcher, *An Account of a Conversation Concerning a Right Regulation of Governments for the common Good of Mankind* (Edinburgh, 1704), also repr. in *Political Works*, ed. Robertson, 175-215; [Francis Grant], *The Patriot Resolved, in a Letter to an Addresser, from his friend, of the same sentiments with himself, concerning the Union* (1707); Sir George Mackenzie, *Observations on the Acts of Parliament* (Edinburgh, 1687); George Ridpath, *Scotland's Sovereignty Asserted* (Edinburgh, 1695); [George Ridpath], *Scotland's Grievances Relating to Darien* (1700); [George Ridpath], *An Historical Account of the Ancient Rights and Power of the Parliament of Scotland* (1703); [George Ridpath], *Considerations upon the Union of the Two Kingdoms* (1706); [William Seton of Pitmedden], *The Interest of Scotland in Three Essays* (1700, 2nd edn., London 1702); [William Seton], *Scotland's Great Advantages by an Union with England* (1706); William Seton, 'Speeches, on the ... Union, ...1706', in Daniel Defoe, *The History of the Union between England and Scotland* (London, 1786).

Further Reading:
William Ferguson, 'Imperial Crowns: a neglected facet of the background to the Treaty of Union of 1707', *Scottish Historical Review*, 53 (1974), 22-44; William Ferguson, *Scotland's Relations with England: a Survey to 1707* (Edinburgh, 1977); *A Union for Empire. Political Thought and the British Union of 1707*, ed. John Robertson (Cambridge, 1995); Christopher A. Whatley, *'Bought and Sold for English Gold': Explaining the Union of 1707* (Glasgow, 1994).

5

Scottish Sovereignty in the Eighteenth Century

ALEX MURDOCH

The title of this essay is intended to draw attention to the point that continuation of a distinctive system of Scottish government within a union state after 1707 arguably represented the continuation of Scottish sovereignty within the British union, although the fragile nature of that sovereignty in the later part of the seventeenth century was apparent to many contemporary observers and was reflected in the Scottish debate over the union negotiations with England. Despite the work which has been published in the last quarter century, sceptics still point to the lack of Scottish legislation passed by the Westminster parliament and the lack of Scottish impact on British central government as an indicator of subordinate provincial or client status for Scotland that at times, particularly in the first half of the century, verged on colonial subjugation. I would like to interrogate the arguments of the sceptics by considering Scottish politics and government after 1707 in several distinct periods as discussed below. The case presented here is that sovereignty reserved to Scotland under the terms of the Treaty of Union survived throughout the eighteenth century and that it grew and developed in a dynamic manner rather than becoming a static and increasingly irrelevant feature of modern Scottish society.

I

1707-1725: From Union to Subordinate Kingdom
  The Scottish Court party, led by the duke of Queensberry and the duke of Argyll, certainly planned that the Scottish union with England would feature a significant element of 'executive devolution' in Scotland. The Scottish privy council would continue to act as an executive in Edinburgh, the lord chancellor of Scotland would continue to lead the legal system in Scotland preserved by the Treaty of Union and in London there would be a secretary of state for Scotland serving in the ministry. Instead, pro-Union but anti-court Scottish politicians managed to persuade the Westminster parliament to abolish the Scottish privy council in its first session as a 'British' parliament. The existence of a secretary of state with responsibility for Scotland persisted throughout various vicissitudes until 1725, but on an increasingly detached basis from the rest of London government. The lord chancellor of Scotland ceased to hold office in a fit of absence of mind as part of the abolition of the privy council. A new warrant for the office had been issued to the earl of Seafield after the union, but doubts were raised over the validity of his commission, and although Seafield was still being referred to as lord chancellor as late as March 1708, this ceased to be the case shortly thereafter. Seafield, however, became one of the Scottish representative peers in the House of Lords. Yet while the title of lord chancellor vanished in Scotland, the great seal of Scotland entrusted to the chancellor continued to be held there and the now keeper of the great seal of Scotland became the highest paid officer on the still separate Scottish civil list. The office has been assumed to have been a sinecure, but in fact the keeper of the great seal of Scotland was always one of the most important of the Scottish representative peers in London,

who took the lead in speaking on Scottish issues in the House of Lords throughout the century. Indeed, in 1713 the title of lord chancellor of Scotland was revived for the former earl of Seafield, who by then had inherited the more senior title of earl of Findlater, and it was as lord chancellor of Scotland that he moved for the repeal of the Treaty of Union in the House of Lords in 1713.

There is widespread awareness of the Jacobite rebellion of 1715 in Scotland and the indication it gave of the instability of the union settlement. Fewer are aware of Patrick Riley's work on the impact of the English Tory ministry of 1710 on the union settlement, taking office as a government without any identification with the desirability of union with Scotland, and determined that the union would be implemented on English terms. This in effect meant that the sovereignty reserved to Scotland under the terms of the Treaty of Union came under attack, and although this was most noticeable in church affairs, where an unsympathetic Anglican English Tory party saw no reason to defend the privileges of a Presbyterian Church of Scotland, it also affected Scotland through the medium of a series of calculated political snubs directed at the Scottish politicians at Westminster, designed to emphasise their subordinate status. In effect the Church of Scotland lost legal authority in Scotland after its attempts to prevent public episcopalian worship in Scotland were overturned on appeal from the court of session to the House of Lords in the Greenshields case. Legislation then followed that required all church of Scotland ministers to swear an oath of allegiance to the government, episcopalians in Scotland be allowed to worship freely provided they took an oath of allegiance to the government and renounced Jacobitism, and the reintroduction as a property right of the entitlement of landowners and the crown to nominate ministers to Church of Scotland parishes under the law of patronage. Yet there were also attacks on Scotland which did not involve the church. The Hamilton case of 1711 denied the duke of Hamilton admission to the House of Lords on the strength of his British peerage as duke of Brandon. This was extended to include Scottish peers who had previously held British peerages, such as the duke of Queensberry as duke of Dover. With the end of war with France finally in sight by 1712, the Tory ministry also proposed to introduce the malt tax in Scotland, from which Scotland had been exempted specifically under the terms of the Treaty of Union for the duration of the war.

When the earl of Findlater moved for the repeal of the Act of Union in the House of Lords, he noted four grievances in particular in his speech, none of which related to presbyterianism or the Church of Scotland. These were first, the abolition of the Scottish privy council; second, the refusal to admit British peers to the House of Lords; third, the attempt to impose a malt tax and an increased level of taxation generally; and fourth, 'the ruin of our trade and manufactures', which meant trade in general with France and Holland, and woollen manufactures in particular, sacrificed on the altar of the economic interests of Yorkshire. Later, during the Jacobite rebellion of 1715, similar grievances against the union were published by the Jacobites in Perth: English discrimination against Scots woollens and linens, increases in taxation, failure to pay money due as part of the equivalent agreed in the Treaty of Union, the interference of the House of Lords as a court of appeal in Scots law, the abolition of the Scots privy council, refusal to admit Scots peers with British peerages to the House of Lords, and the use of court influence over the Scots parliament in 1705-7 to obtain its approval for the union. After the rebellion, two threads of continuity can be recognised in the litany of complaints in Scotland about misgovernment under the union until 1725; English pressure to intervene in the Scottish taxation system increased in relation to the tobacco trade and the malt tax was viewed as oppressive by the Scots; and post rebellion policy in the Highlands after 1715 represented resentment at English interference in what many unionists regarded as an internal Scottish problem best left to Scots to solve. This all blew up with the crisis over the introduction by the Walpole ministry of the malt tax into

Scotland in 1725, albeit on a reduced level in relation to England and Wales, which led to a different stage of Scottish government and a different attitude to Scottish sovereignty.

II

1725-1742: The Campbells as 'Undertakers'
The events of 1725 led the Walpole ministry to retreat from any intention to implement political union on a meaningful basis in Scotland, and instead to introduce a policy of marginalising Scotland in relation to Westminster politics. The attempt to extend the malt tax to Scotland in 1725 led to such widespread resistance that Walpole abandoned the idea of governing Scotland through favour to all unionists and instead adopted a variant of the system of 'undertakers' he used in the management of Ireland. There was no Scottish parliament, but 1725 demonstrated the continued sovereignty of the Scottish legal system and of the church, and in addition it led to the foundations of the distinctive Scottish banking system which became such a feature of Scottish economic growth during the eighteenth century. The younger brother of the second duke of Argyll, the earl of Islay, was sent to Scotland in his capacity as an extraordinary lord of the court of session and lord justice general of the court of justiciary, both offices which gave him the right to sit as a judge in each of the highest Scottish courts. The secretary of state for Scotland, the duke of Roxburgh, was sacked for resistance to government policy, and his office of keeper of the privy seal of Scotland given to Islay, who was not given the vacant secretary's post. This instead was allowed to lapse and was not revived until the fall of the Walpole ministry in 1742. Islay's offices, however, allowed him to put government pressure on the courts, liaise with the military under General Wade and the new lord advocate, Duncan Forbes, and to call the tax collectors of the customs and excise networks in Scotland to account by threatening the corrupt and inefficient with dismissal. In effect, he became lord chancellor of Scotland in everything but name, and *de facto* he reintroduced a crypto-privy council into Scottish affairs. He also developed a policy for Scotland which he implemented under Walpole until 1742, involving both carrot and stick.

The element of force and intervention manifested itself in at least five ways. First, there was closer intervention on a continuous basis in the Scottish legal system with Islay based in London and active in the House of Lords, corresponding with the two most talented Scots lawyers of their generation, Duncan Forbes and Andrew Fletcher, Lord Milton (nephew and heir of the great patriot). It was no mistake that one was a highlander and that the other was from Lothian, nor was it a mistake that neither of them was from the west of Scotland. Second, tax collection became subject to more bureaucratic controls, although these increased controls did not lead to significant increases in tax revenue collected in Scotland. Third, the government under Islay and his legal aides began systematically to intervene in the general assembly of the Church of Scotland and in the church generally to demonstrate the superiority of law and the state over the church. Fourth, military control was extended over the Highlands in particular and the whole country in general under the command of General Wade, an Irish Protestant familiar with the penal security system in Ireland. Fifth, university reforms were undertaken that were designed to convert Scots colleges from seminaries to train ministers into secular centres of learning that taught a liberal science and humanities curriculum aimed at the sons of the gentry more than the ministry. This included bringing Francis Hutcheson from Dublin to the chair of moral philosophy at the University of Glasgow. The carrot was economic investment by the government in Scotland. The Campbells founded the Royal Bank of Scotland as part of this, using Equivalent debentures issued in 1707 to capitalise their bank and given a monopoly of banking such tax revenues as were raised in Scotland by the government. The commissioners and trustees for the improvement of the fisheries and manufactures of Scotland were also appointed to administer funds promised under the Treaty of Union, with a brief to invest them in economic expansion in linen textile manufacture in particular. This was linked to government subsidies to encourage the export of linen cloth and yarn and the re-export of tobacco from America via Scottish ports to the European continent. While Forbes as lord advocate became associated with the stick, Fletcher of Saltoun's nephew Lord Milton became associated with economic policy, serving both as a trustee for the commission for the improvement of fisheries and manufactures and as a key member of the board of the Royal Bank of Scotland.

This system, often discussed in terms of Scottish management, could be said to have reduced Scotland to colonial or at least provincial status (my argument is that there is a significant difference and that the latter is not necessarily negative), or it could be said that Scotland became a client state within the broader grubbiness of the Walpolean regime. The standard accounts refer to this system either ending in 1746 with the Jacobite rebellion (put forward by Enlightenment historians) or persisting to the 1760s until it just ran into the sand of wider political change that made it redundant (the more sceptical political and social perspective). In fact, as pointed out above, the system ended with the downfall of the Walpole ministry in 1742.

III

1742-1765: Semi-independence Part I, The Campbell Protectorate
Walpole's fall from power brought a new ministry into power which wanted to return to the policy of favouring all unionists in Scotland equally. As part of this policy, the office of secretary of state for Scotland was revived and given to the hapless East Lothian peer the marquess of Tweeddale. His administration, if one can use that term to describe the activities of those who attempted to supplant the Argathelian interest in Scotland, failed to prevent the Jacobite rebellion of 1745 from becoming more than a minor incident in the Highlands. The failure of the Tweeddale regime, however, did not result in the restoration of Walpole's system of management, although the former Islay (from 1743 third duke of Argyll in succession to his brother) resumed a significant role in Scottish government and in the task of reconstruction following the rebellion. The office of secretary of state for Scotland lapsed again in 1746 with Tweeddale's resignation, but the third duke of Argyll did not just have a different name, he had a vastly different role from that he assumed in 1725 as earl of Islay. He no longer, as an elder statesman in his sixties, acted as director of policy in Scotland for an English prime minister determined to keep Scotland from playing a disruptive role in British politics. Instead, he acted as a defender of Scottish sovereignty within the union in the aftermath of the Jacobite rebellion, parrying government interventionism and preserving the independence of the Scottish legal system, continuing to act as an extraordinary lord of the court of session, lord justice general (head of the court of justiciary), having also exchanged in 1733 the office of keeper of the Scottish privy seal for the more prestigious post of keeper of the great seal of Scotland, the most important on the Scottish civil list. Whereas in the 1730s Islay had ruthlessly kept loyalty to the regime in mind as an essential requirement for promotion to the Scottish bench, by the 1750s Argyll sought to sponsor those with obvious talent, promoting men such as Henry Home, who became Lord Kames, or James Boswell's father, Alexander, as Lord Auchinleck.

He did not do this on his own, of course, but through the political interest he had developed in his earlier career and with the help of protégés like Lord Milton who had with him become expert on the operation of Scottish government. In some ways, Argyll's actions protecting the sovereignty of Scotland after the end of the Forty-Five mirrored the programme he pursued when he directed Walpole's intervention on the part of the British state in 1725, except that the stick involved really did come from London and was motivated by mistrust of Argyll, who like his elder brother after the 1715 rebellion was viewed as too pro-Scottish and too soft on Jacobitism. Lord Chancellor Hardwicke and the duke of Newcastle as one of the secretaries of state pushed for a post rebellion settlement that would exclude the Campbell interest. This led to legislation such as the infamous Disarming Acts, often denounced as cultural genocide, and legislation directed at the Scottish episcopalian church, blamed by the duke of Cumberland for much of the support for the rebellion.

The act relating to Scotland, however, passed by the Westminster parliament after the Forty-Five which has received most attention was the act abolishing heritable jurisdictions in Scotland, written by the lord chancellor of England to attack what he perceived as the primitive feudalism of Scots law. Argyll spoke in support of the bill in the House of Lords, although his exposition relating to the historical conditions which had made devolved legal jurisdictions necessary in a Scotland dominated by the absolutist monarchy of the Stewarts was received in complete incomprehension by the majority of his listeners. 'The Duke of Argyll made the most exotic speech I ever heard,' an ambitious and hostile newly elected Scottish M.P. wrote to Duncan Forbes, 'had I not been informed before that he was to speak for the bill I should have thought from his facts and reasonings that he was intended to vote against it' [*More Culloden Papers*, v, 182]. Part of Argyll's agenda was to fight off plans to expropriate the native population in the Highlands and introduce plantations on the model of Ireland. In 1752 a much delayed act provided for the annexation of Jacobite estates by the government in what was the first attempt at land nationalisation in Britain. Both acts were implemented in Scotland by the Argyll interest and implemented in such a way that their punitive intentions when passed at Westminster were transformed into the kind of economic development package the earl of Islay had introduced twenty-five years earlier in 1725. The court of session eventually settled claims in compensation for the loss of heritable jurisdictions which brought £164,000 into the hands of Scottish landowners, including Argyll, who could be said to have financed the construction of his new Gothic castle at Inveraray out of the proceeds. Payments by the British treasury of debts due on the Perth and Lovat estates annexed in 1752 led to expenditure of a further £142,000 after adjudication by the court of session and the passage of parliamentary legislation in 1759 and 1770. By 1757 Argyll was acting as British broker in Scotland to raise troops on a substantial scale for the war effort against France, particularly in North America. It was this legacy of directing Scottish affairs that he left to his nephew the first earl of Bute when he died in 1761, described by his followers as 'the father of his country'.

In many ways the earl of Bute did not understand the sovereignty of Scotland passed on to him by his uncle, and once Argyll's chief lieutenant, Andrew Fletcher, Lord Milton, succumbed to senility in 1765 the old Campbell interest ceased to function in any meaningful way. Many at the time believed that this was only natural, that Argyll and Milton represented the generation of Scottish politicians that had negotiated the union and literally fought to keep it in place against both Presbyterians and Jacobites. The new generation, represented by figures such as the third earl of Bute, James Boswell, or Lord Kames, believed that the time had arrived to complete the union and dispense with Scottish sovereignty within it, just as their ideological successors like Francis Jeffrey would attempt to do in 1832.

IV

1765-1784: Semi-independence Part II, The Enlightenment
We know now how sadly mistaken were those who expected to complete the union in the early years of the reign of George III. From the time Bute gave up any pretence

to direct Scottish public affairs until the election of 1784 Scottish government received no direction from the people above, as Adam Ferguson described them, but it is no mistake that this period coincided with the great years of achievement of the Scottish enlightenment, with its public concern with the problems of national improvement in the economy, culture and society of Scotland. The politics of this period in Scotland became very complex, partly because anything connected with Scotland was viewed with intense suspicion at Westminster, which left Scotland to the Scots. In terms of Scottish sovereignty, however, this was a period in which the general assembly of the Church of Scotland, the faculty of advocates, the court of session itself, and even the convention of royal burghs began to emerge as civic institutions that sought to address political and economic issues in Scotland. The Scottish banking system emerged as a key Scottish institution in this period, developing as a result of the union rather than preserved as a condition of it. The French tobacco monopoly was paying £100,000 cash a year into the Scottish banking system from 1748 to 1775 to finance purchases of tobacco imported by Glasgow merchants from Virginia. It was during this most open period of Scottish sovereignty during the eighteenth century that the country became known for cultural achievements associated with its universities, as well as economic success associated with its landowners and merchants. Someone like William Robertson, devoid of secular political ambition, could emerge between 1760 and 1780 as a leader of both the Church of Scotland and the University of Edinburgh, serving as a spokesperson for an ideology of universal and inclusive improvement that would transcend the old political divisions between Presbyterian and Jacobite. Yet Robertson and his allies insisted on continuing to operate within Scottish institutions representing Scottish sovereignty within the union, and this example directly influenced Benjamin Franklin and John Witherspoon and some of the others who introduced the federal principle into the government of the United States from 1776 to 1789. The growing cultural confidence of the enlightenment became reflected in economic activity as the town council of Edinburgh embarked on the construction of a new town to embody the modernisation of the country, the construction of a Forth-Clyde canal was financed by public subscription to help provide the transportation network to underpin the development of the growing economy of the Scottish central belt, and the inward investment from England in enterprises like the Carron ironworks near Falkirk demonstrated how the political stability achieved after the last Jacobite rebellion could lead to further economic growth. Adam Smith published the *Wealth of Nations* in 1776, and then spent the remainder of his career in Edinburgh advising the government on the administration of customs taxation on Scottish trade.

V

1784-1805: The Dundas Despotism

From 1784 Henry Dundas came to prominence at Westminster when he gave up his Scottish offices in 1784 (but not the lucrative sinecure of keeper of the signet seal of Scotland formerly held by Lord Milton) to take up British responsibilities at the admiralty and the board of trade. This allowed him to return to the Campbell system in league with the grand nephew of the Campbells, the third duke of Buccleuch, but with the roles reversed. Instead of the great Scottish peer sitting with the cabinet in London and sending down instructions to his lawyer assistant in Scotland, it was the lawyer Dundas who was part of the ministry in London and corresponded with his principal supporter in Scotland, one of its largest landowners, the duke of Buccleuch. This analogy can be pushed too far. It is clear that Buccleuch never did the detailed managerial administration that Milton had done for Islay/Argyll. Dundas's nephew the lord advocate, Robert Dundas, acted more in that capacity. But Buccleuch did lend his considerable authority and wealth to Dundas's career, allowing him to overcome the social obstacles facing a commoner attempting to influence politics by reviving a political system based on aristocratic privilege.

There was another distinction. Dundas and Buccleuch were children of the Scottish enlightenment. They had been taught by Robertson and Smith. They were aware of the legacy of Hume. Whereas Argyll and Milton in their old age had made the careers of Robertson, Smith and Hume possible through their patronage, Dundas and Buccleuch inherited the intellectual legacy left by these men. It has to be said that while in the short term Dundas and Buccleuch succeeded in uniting the landed class and most of the professional and mercantile class behind a programme of political stability and commercial revolution, they failed to anticipate the social impact of the economic development they encouraged, and came to doubt the wisdom of their early idealism. In 1797 Dundas wrote to Buccleuch arguing that war time militia regiments would be necessary in a post-war period to maintain order in the emerging manufacturing regions of Scotland, given that they were increasingly cut off from the stabilising and conservative authority of landowner and church. By 1809 the duke was reported by one of his factors as of the opinion that manufactures in general had been pushed too far in Britain, and that development of textile manufactures on his estates had not raised the value of his land, but rather rendered his residence on them disagreeable, 'if not disgusting'.

Times, of course, had changed. Scottish sovereignty based on the political identity and institutions of the landed class appeared far more questionable to far more people in Scotland in the age of the American and French revolutions than they had before. The culmination of Dundas's career as head of the unionist regime in Scotland was not his impeachment and resignation in 1805, which marked the end of his political career, but the achievement of union with Ireland in 1801. Dundas's advocacy of union with Ireland in 1801 on the precedence of Scotland applied an eighteenth-century solution to a nineteenth-century problem, although he would not live to see just how problematic his neat solution to the consolidation of imperial authority would become. The Dundas despotism, however, was not just about integration into an expanding British state and empire and the denial of democracy in Scotland. After all, democracy was denied in all of Britain, in the American republic, and in France as well as Scotland after 1784, as bourgeois elites moved to monopolise the sovereignty represented in the constitutions concerned. The Dundas despotism was also about further adapting the feudal legacy of Scottish sovereignty as it had survived the union and been modified by the enlightenment to meet new challenges involving rapid economic and social change. By the post-war period following the deaths of Dundas and Buccleuch, it appeared that in this respect they had failed, and that this legacy was abandoned after 1815, but Graeme Morton's work indicates that the stateless unionist nationalism of nineteenth-century Scotland was a dynamic adoption of the sovereignty of Scotland in the eighteenth century that built on Scottish institutions and law, while reducing the domination of the landed elite that had led the country throughout the eighteenth century.

As part of this process, Scottish sovereignty in the eighteenth century came to be seen by reformers and radicals in Scotland as part of the feudal legacy of 'Old Corruption' that had to be swept away along with the landed class that personified it. That was a normal aspect of the endless process of reinvention undergone by any nation. What we should not forget, however, is that in terms of eighteenth-century Britain, Scotland was not a client state and the society which produced the Scottish enlightenment was not static in terms of institutions and the sovereignty they represented. For better or worse, the institutions guaranteed under the terms of the Treaty of Union survived to form the basis of the civic society of nineteenth-century Scotland. The terms of the Treaty of Union guaranteeing state support for Scottish economic development were fulfilled due to determined political pressure from Scotland that transcended traditional divisions in Scottish politics during the eighteenth century. New institutions like the Scottish banking system were created to meet the challenges of changing times. Old institutions, like the Church of Scotland, came to play a secular and dynamic role in modernisation. At the end of the century, demands by ever greater numbers of Scots for access to political recognition in Scotland were deflected during the war which more than any other created the British state, just as similar demands were deflected in England, Wales, Ireland and beyond. When political reform was achieved finally in Scotland, Scottish sovereignty did not end with it, although it was eclipsed by the growing Scottish role in a British Whig and later Liberal party. In other words, Scottish sovereignty was not feudal and static; it became modern and continued to be dynamic, but it was not associated with a parliament. In the eighteenth century this was viewed as a blessing by those, like Lord Kames, who argued that until the Treaty of Union in Scotland the country had been divided solely into those who were 'tyrants' and those who were 'slaves'. There were those at the end of the eighteenth century who wondered if anything had changed, and who demanded that the sovereignty reserved to Scotland under the Treaty of Union be made more accessible to the majority of the population rather than remain the property of its landed elite.

Further Reading:
John D. Brims, 'The Scottish "Jacobins", Scottish Nationalism and the British Union', in *Scotland and England 1286-1815*, ed. R.A. Mason (Edinburgh, 1987); John D. Brims, 'The Scottish Association of the Friends of the People', in *Conflict and Stability in Scottish Society 1700-1850*, ed. T.M. Devine (Edinburgh, 1990); T.M. Devine, *The Tobacco Lords* (Edinburgh, 1975); Michael Fry, *The Dundas Despotism* (Edinburgh, 1992); Bruce Lenman, *The Jacobite Risings in Britain, 1689-1746* (London, 1980); Elaine W. McFarland, *Ireland and Scotland in the Age of Revolution* (Edinburgh, 1994); Allan Macinnes, *Clanship, Commerce and the House of Stuart, 1603-1788* (Edinburgh, 1996); Alexander Murdoch, *The People Above: Politics and Administration in Mid-Eighteenth-Century Scottish Politics* (Edinburgh, 1980); P.W.J. Riley, *The English Ministers and Scotland, 1707-1727* (London, 1964); John Robertson, *The Scottish Enlightenment and the Militia Issue* (Edinburgh, 1985); John Stuart Shaw, *The Management of Scottish Society* (Edinburgh, 1983); John Stuart Shaw, *The Political History of Eighteenth-Century Scotland* (Basingstoke, 1999); Richard Sher, *Church and University in the Scottish Enlightenment* (Edinburgh, 1985); *Scotland and America in the Age of Enlightenment*, ed. Richard Sher and Jeffrey Smitten(1990); Ronald Sunter, *Patronage and Politics in Scotland 1707-1832* (Edinburgh, 1986); *More Culloden Papers*, ed. Duncan Warrand, vol. v (Edinburgh, 1930).

6

Sovereignty in the American Revolution

H. T. DICKINSON

There were a great many causes of the American Revolution, but the really fundamental issue was the constitutional dispute between British imperialists and American patriots. These protagonists disagreed sharply and profoundly about the nature and location of sovereignty in particular. Each side believed that its interpretation of constitutional issues was the legitimate one and the only one that could secure life, liberty and property. It was the seriousness of this dispute that led each side to take up arms.

At the end of the seventeenth century many men on both sides of the Atlantic saw the past as a struggle to limit the absolute power of the monarch, to safeguard the privileges of parliament and to protect the liberty of the subject. Afraid of the arbitrary authority of the monarch, they had sought protection from the common law, customary rights, traditional practices and fundamental law. They had come to believe in an ancient constitution that limited the monarch, established the rule of law and government by consent, and preserved a wide range of civil liberties.

The decades after the Glorious Revolution witnessed the steady growth in the power of the legislature in both Britain and the American colonies, but this development led to different attitudes towards the constitution. In Britain, the growing power of parliament, combined with the traditional fears of an arbitrary monarch, encouraged the belief that the legislature - composed of the king, the House of Lords and the House of Commons - was the sovereign authority in the state. As such it was absolute, arbitrary and irresistible. But, because this power could be exercised only with the agreement of crown and parliament, it was not seen as a threat to liberty. By locating sovereignty in king, Lords and Commons, the propertied elite in Britain believed that they had managed to create a constitution that achieved stability while retaining government by consent.

At the same time, the legislative assemblies in the American colonies were also growing in political importance and constitutional significance. Seeking to model their practices on the House of Commons and seeking every opportunity to enhance their influence, they achieved a similar control over the purse strings that made them indispensable to the executive. The colonial elite soon learned to restrict the powers of their own governors, but they were less able to curb the authority of the executive and parliament in Britain. In their view therefore the sovereign parliament in Britain posed as much of a threat to their lives, liberty and property as had any Stuart monarch. Thus, while seeking to augment the authority of their own colonial legislatures, they desired to restrict the authority of parliament. In responding to the constitutional threat from parliament they adhered as strongly as ever to their seventeenth-century interpretation of the constitution with its emphasis on common law, long-established customs, prescriptive rights and fundamental law. The colonists began to use against parliament many of the arguments that parliament had previously used against the crown.

The constitutional disputes which arose between Britain and the American colonies in the 1760s and 1770s included a wide range of issues, but at the heart of these constitutional struggles was profound disagreement over the nature and location of sovereignty. It was this dispute that persuaded both sides to resort to an armed struggle. In exploring why sovereignty is central to an understanding of the American Revolution, this essay will examine why Britain sought to exercise sovereignty over the American colonies and why the American patriots resisted these efforts. It will demonstrate next how each side sought to justify its constitutional claims. It will then show why it proved impossible to find any satisfactory compromise to these conflicting constitutional claims. Finally, it will briefly investigate how the new American nation endeavoured to re-define and re-locate sovereignty in ways very different to those adopted in Britain.

I

The exercise of sovereignty
Although successive British ministries were not engaged in a determined conspiracy to destroy the liberties of the American colonists, they did seek to exercise the sovereign authority of parliament to tax and legislate for the colonies. Faced with the heavy expenses of empire, parliament required the colonies to bear a higher proportion of these defence costs. Since the colonies were also increasingly important to Britain, in commercial and strategic terms, parliament wished to increase metropolitan control over these colonies so that Britain could continue to reap financial and commercial benefits. In seeking to ensure colonial compliance with these policies ministers did not request the agreement of the colonial assemblies, but relied on parliament's sovereign authority throughout the empire.

The Stamp Act of 1765 was the first revenue act passed by parliament with the deliberate aim of imposing an internal tax on the American colonies. When coordinated colonial resistance to this measure persuaded parliament to repeal this act in 1766, British imperialists insisted that there could be no surrender of parliament's sovereign authority. The Declaratory Act of the same year insisted that parliament possessed the constitutional authority to make laws and statutes for the colonies 'in all cases whatsoever'. The Townshend duties of 1767 were a return to the policy of raising revenue by external duties, but the money raised was designed to meet the expenses of the colonial executive and judiciary in order to free these from the financial control of the colonial assemblies. This was an exercise of parliamentary sovereignty designed to increase Britain's control over the colonies. When colonial protests led to the repeal of most of these duties in 1770, Lord North deliberately retained the duty on tea as evidence of parliament's sovereign authority. The Tea Act of 1773 was designed in part to inveigle the colonists into paying the tea duty and hence into implicitly acknowledging the sovereignty of parliament. When this act was violently resisted in the colonies, parliament passed the Coercive Acts of 1774 as proof of its constitutional right to impose its authority on the colonies. The colonists opposed these acts by renewed cooperation and preparations for armed resistance. The issue between British and the American colonies had quite clearly gone far beyond a dispute over taxation. The question now was whether the British parliament possessed sovereign authority over the colonies or whether the colonies were in effect independent of the British legislature.

For their part, the American colonists made a clear distinction between the British constitution, the constitution of the British empire, and the constitutions of the American colonies. They acknowledged that parliament possessed sovereign authority over the affairs of Britain. They were also ready to recognise parliament's superior, though not unlimited, authority over matters of trade and defence that concerned the British empire as a whole. What they did not accept was that parliament had unlimited constitutional authority over the internal affairs of the colonies. In accepting the supreme superintending authority of parliament over the

British empire, the colonists allowed that Britain could pass laws concerning the regulation of the Atlantic trade in order to advance the welfare of all the British territories and, incidentally, to promote the wealth of Britain herself. While they sometimes complained about the economic consequences for themselves of such parliamentary regulation, the colonists did not challenge parliament's constitutional right to pass such legislation. They were even prepared to concede that the colonies gave their implied consent to such measures because they were for the greater good of the whole empire. The colonists did not agree however that parliament possessed the right to interfere, with taxes or legislation, in the purely internal affairs of the colonies. The colonies possessed their own constitutions and internal taxation and legislation were both seen as the preserve of the colonial assemblies. The colonial grievances against Britain stemmed therefore from a firm conviction that the constitution of the colonies placed internal sovereignty in their own legislative assemblies.

The colonies were determined to defend the constitutional rights of their legislative assemblies and to resist the encroachments of parliament. Each colony increasingly regarded itself as a distinct state so far as the government of its internal affairs was concerned and within each state the legislature was regarded as the sovereign authority. Sovereignty within the British empire did not rest with parliament alone, but was distributed among the various states and was exercised by the various legislatures for different purposes. Parliament might be the greatest of these legislatures, but its authority was limited outside Britain and particularly with respect to the internal affairs of the American colonies. The constitution of the British empire was in essence federal rather than unitary.

When their constitutional rights were seriously infringed by parliament, the colonists united in effective action to preserve what they clearly regarded as their constitutional rights. They first combined against the Stamp Act of 1765 because they regarded it as a constitutional innovation which levied an internal tax when levying such taxes was seen as the preserve of their own assemblies. They renewed their coordinated resistance against the Townshend duties in 1767 because Britain intended to use the revenue to render royal officials independent of the assemblies. When Lord North retained the tea duty in 1770 and passed the Tea Act in 1773, the colonies were fully aware that he was acting to preserve the constitution claim to parliamentary sovereignty. When the Coercive Acts of 1774 seriously threatened to undermine their constitutional rights, the American patriots finally realised that they might have to defend these rights by force of arms. It was parliament's claim to sovereign authority over the internal affairs of the colonies that led directly to the American War of Independence.

II

Justifying rival constitutional claims
The American colonists initially encapsulated their constitutional claims in the slogan 'no taxation without representation', but they went on to develop a whole host of arguments justifying their claim that they were not subordinate to parliament. These protests in turn provoked British imperialists into explaining precisely why parliament was sovereign. The result was an intense and profound ideological war that led to an irreconcilable breach between the protagonists.

The American colonists put forward a host of historical arguments, claiming that they had inherited the liberties of freeborn Englishmen, long before they laid claim to the natural rights of all men. They claimed, for example, that they had the right to enjoy the liberties of Englishmen because the first colonists had migrated as free men, they had carried the prescriptive rights of Englishmen with them, and their descendants had inherited them. Some colonists insisted that they had migrated to escape religious persecution and had risked all in an effort to increase their liberty. Others argued that they had migrated to improve their condition and they would not have taken such enormous risks to settle in the wilderness if they were to end up in a worse position. No one would have migrated in order to lose their freedom. Moreover, they had spent their lives and their labour, their blood and their money, in founding the colonies and in creating trade which greatly enriched the mother country. Hence they had more than recompensed Britain for any expenses incurred in defending them and they had bought their liberty at a high cost.

British imperialists challenged these migration arguments. Some claimed that the colonists had abandoned their rights on leaving England, while others maintained the migrants had voluntarily sacrificed their constitutional rights in England in return for religious and economic benefits in America. It was also claimed that the colonists had sought and secured legal permission to migrate and they therefore remained subject to the authority that had allowed them to leave. There was no evidence to prove that the migrants believed that they were giving up their obligations as English subjects when they left for the new world or that the constitutional authorities in England had released them from their duties as subjects. If the colonists were still within the realm, they had to meet the same obligation as subjects at home. If the colonists were without the realm, then they had no claim to the same rights as those left at home. The colonists could not choose to claim all the benefits, while refusing all the obligations, of those subjects remaining in the mother country.

The colonists maintained that the constitution they took with them to America enshrined limited monarchy, government by consent, the rule of law, no taxation without representation, and a range of civil liberties including trial by jury, freedom of expression and the right to resist arbitrary power. They based their notion of this ancient constitution on the authority of common law, immemorial custom, fundamental law, the contract between ruler and ruled, and their own colonial charters. Only much later did they appeal to the universal and inalienable natural rights of man. These various appeals were rarely seen as competing alternatives, but were regarded as mutually reinforcing. The colonists did not claim a natural right that could not also be grounded in an appeal to English constitutional theory. They regularly stressed that their rights were inherited and were secured by long uninterrupted possession. They maintained that they had all the same rights as subjects in Britain and that they had always possessed them to an equal degree. Thus, they were defending old rights, not claiming new ones.

The colonists made much of the contracts made with the king on first migrating. They referred in part to their actual charters, but also to the various prior discussions, the conditions of migration, and the subsequent customs and practices in the colonies. In their view, there was both an actual contract with the crown and an implied contract with the English people. They appealed to their charters not as original contracts clearly setting out their constitutional rights and privileges, but as evidence of a public compact and covenant that implied a contractual relationship between crown and colonists. Although they recognised that the terms of their charters were often vague, especially on political issues, they regarded them as important constitutional symbols clearly indicating that the colonists had rights and that government was limited. The practices of the early colonists also demonstrated that they had enjoyed a considerable measure of self-government from the outset and had been able to establish law courts and legislative assemblies, provided they did not pass laws contrary to those in operation in the mother country. This encouraged the colonists to believe they were living by the common and constitutional laws of England.

In reply, British imperialists insisted that the colonial charters did not confer extensive or specific constitutional rights. These charters were mainly concerned with trade and property rights. While they had created corporations capable of making by-laws, they had not established independent legislatures exempt from parliament's sovereign authority. No charter allowed colonial assemblies to make laws contrary to the laws and statutes of England. The charter of Pennsylvania allowed the colonists there to tax themselves, but it also stated that subsequent acts of parliament could levy taxes on the colony. The 1633 charter of Maryland explicitly exempted that colony from royal but not from parliamentary taxation. Moreover, since all charters had been granted by higher authority, the colonists were still subordinate to that authority and, as had occurred in the past, colonial charters could be amended or revoked by that superior authority. The British imperialists mis-read their seventeenth-century constitutional history as much as their colonial opponents. They claimed that the first colonists had migrated under the sovereign authority of the king in parliament, not under the authority of the monarch alone. They went on to assert that even if their charters were from the crown the colonists remained subordinate to the sovereign parliament.

The American colonists claimed - and were allowed - many of the constitutional rights of Englishmen, including the rights to a jury trial, free assembly, petition, freedom of conscience, a free press, and the security of their life and property under the rule of law. They were also allowed the right to establish law courts and representative legislative assemblies. What they found particularly hard to sustain was their claim that their assemblies should enjoy full legislative autonomy with respect to the internal affairs of the colonies. Their British opponents repeatedly claimed that parliament had regularly passed laws and taxes that applied to the colonies. To meet this challenge, the colonists insisted that almost every single measure could be classed as a means of regulating the Atlantic trade or of securing commercial benefits for Britain. Only the Post Office Act of 1711 looked like a precedent for parliament's right to impose an internal tax on the colonies, but even this measure could be described as being a means of promoting commercial relations between the colonies and the colonists had given their implied consent to this particular act. In contrast, the Stamp Act was an innovation which was bitterly resented and almost unanimously opposed by the colonies.

British imperialists never really understood the constitutional distinctions which American patriots drew between internal and external taxes levied by parliament or between parliamentary taxes designed to regulate imperial trade and those taxes designed to raise revenue. In their eyes all earlier acts passed by parliament and accepted by the colonies were clear constitutional precedents for parliamentary sovereignty. There were numerous precedents demonstrating parliament's right to legislate for or to tax the colonies and repeated examples of laws passed by the colonial assemblies only becoming lawful when approved by the king and his advisers in England. Colonial assemblies were therefore subordinate legislatures, while parliament was fully sovereign. In defending their claim to government by consent the American colonists used the slogan 'no taxation without representation'. This had long been an English constitutional claim and the House of Commons was particularly conscious of its right to initiate taxes and loans because it was the representative chamber in parliament. The American patriots referred to their own long tradition of levying internal taxes in the colonies and noted that parliament did not claim to be able to impose taxes on the Irish people - only the Dublin parliament could do that. Parliament also refrained from taxing the Channel Islands and the Isle of Man. Wales, moreover, had not been taxed until it had secured representation in parliament, while both Chester and Durham had eventually been granted representation at Westminster because it seemed a constitutional grievance that they had previously been taxed when not represented in parliament.

Several members of parliament were impressed by the American claim to 'no taxation without representation'. When drafting the Stamp Act, George Grenville himself had recognised that the issue of colonial representation had to be faced. He put forward the doctrine of virtual representation which maintained that parliament virtually represented the whole nation and not just the minority of men who possessed the right to vote. Parliament represented all the important interests in the nation and was elected by a wide range of propertied men. Once elected, each MP represented the whole nation. By the same token, every individual person was represented not be a particular MP, but by the whole House of Commons. All MPs were expected to act in the interests of the whole nation. Every individual and place was not directly represented, but a large body of men was enfranchised and a wide range of interests were represented.

British imperialists clung to the notion of virtual representation because it was the only way to justify parliament's right to bind all the unenfranchised people in Britain. The American patriots firmly rejected this doctrine because it entirely failed to serve their interests and to defend their liberties. They argued forcibly that there must be a community of interest between the people and their representatives in the legislature. They were adamant that MPs at Westminster could not properly represent the particular interests of the colonies. Representatives needed to have some knowledge and interest in the people and the property within their constituencies, and they ought to be responsible and accountable to their constituents. This was not possible if the members of a particular legislature could pass laws which they did not have to obey or, worse still, raised taxes which they did not have to pay. The doctrine of virtual representation betrayed these expectations and allowed parliament to act unconstitutionally.

III

The failure to find a constitutional compromise
The dispute over parliamentary sovereignty struck so hard at the vital interests of both Britain and the American colonies that neither side showed much interest in reaching a compromise and, by the early 1770s there seemed on be no middle ground between the subordination or the independence of the colonies. When the colonies first raised the cry of 'no taxation without representation', there was some discussion on both sides of the Atlantic over whether the colonies could be represented in parliament. It soon became very apparent to all however that American representation in parliament was quite impractical. The colonists in particular were adamant that their colonial assemblies should remain sovereign over internal colonial affairs and they soon dropped any proposal that they should send representatives to Westminster. They feared that limited representation would leave them in a permanent minority in parliament, while conferring legitimacy on parliament's claim to sovereign authority over their own internal affairs. Both American patriots and British imperialists also soon recognised the insuperable practical obstacles imposed by great distances and slow means of communication. In addition, the British were unwilling to see large numbers of colonists creating a perpetual and disruptive faction in parliament. Some even feared that the seat of empire might cross the Atlantic to Philadelphia, if American demographic and economic growth rates continued to exceed those of Britain.

None the less, alarm at the widening breach between Britain and the American colonies encouraged many British commentators to propose a variety of solutions to the crisis. Josiah Tucker and Adam Smith actually suggested that it was better to concede independence to the colonists than risk full-scale war, but many more commentators advocated some kind of compromise. Thomas Pownall urged a new imperial relationship in which parliament would abandon any claim to levy internal taxes on the colonies, but would still have authority to raise external taxes and impose trade regulations. By 1774 he was arguing in favour of a return to the pre-1763 situation, but he still urged the colonies to levy a regular revenue to meet the general costs of the empire. William Pitt insisted parliament could not tax the colonies, but he remained adamant that parliament must retain full control over trade regulations and imperial defence. As late as 1775 he hoped that the colonies could be persuaded to grant the king a perpetual revenue which would be put at the disposal of parliament. Edmund Burke was also ready to abandon British efforts to tax the colonies in return for colonial requisitions to meet some of the costs of empire and he still expected parliament to regulate the Atlantic trade. He did not see that upholding the doctrine of parliamentary sovereignty, even while not deploying it, offered no guarantee to the colonists that their lives, liberty and property could be safeguarded.

Critics of the British government outside parliament proposed more generous conciliatory schemes. James Burgh suggested that the colonists should be allowed to send temporary representatives to parliament or to hold an inter-colonial convention in order to negotiate their contribution to imperial defence. John Cartwright proposed that all the North American colonies from Quebec to Florida should become separate states, each owing allegiance to the crown and loosely linked to Britain in a 'Great British League and Confederacy'. Each state would raise and pay for its own militia, but the British navy would defend the Atlantic trade routes, and Britain would control foreign policy and arbitrate in any dispute between the other states. Cartwright also wrote in favour of a system of judicial review which would establish a court which could declare whether acts of parliament were constitutional or not. This proposal found little favour, though Jeremy Bentham gave it some thought before rejecting it because it gave too much power to the judges. Richard Price favoured some kind of federal union based on a strong sense of common interest, common loyalty to the crown, and a common council to discussion issues affecting all parts of the empire.

Such radical proposals found little support in parliament. Lord North was alarmed at the outbreak of armed hostilities and he greatly feared the loss of the American colonies, but he was not prepared to offer any concession which involved the abandonment of parliamentary sovereignty. In his proposals of 1775 and 1778 he made it clear that Britain had abandoned for ever all efforts to impose parliamentary taxes on the colonies and he was even prepared to repeal all the offending legislation passed by parliament since 1763. These were major concessions, but the prime minister still expected the colonies to acknowledge the sovereign authority of parliament and to agree to vote supplies to meet part of the costs of imperial defence. This money would be controlled by the treasury of the respective colony and spent in that colony, but parliament would decide when to request money, how much should be raised in total, and what amount each colony would contribute. Moreover, parliament would still be able to pass legislation to regulate imperial trade. From a purely constitutional point of view, Lord North was seeking to elicit from the Americans a tacit recognition that the sovereign authority in the empire lay with parliament, though he was ready to promise that this authority would not be used. After a decade of debating parliamentary sovereignty however the Americans were well aware that the very nature of parliamentary sovereignty meant that they could never be given an absolute guarantee that a future parliament would hold to any bargain that the colonies might strike with Lord North. No parliament could bind the decisions of a future parliament or even the acts of a subsequent session of the same parliament. Once they had conceded the constitutional point about parliamentary sovereignty, the Americans could have no future security for their lives, liberty and property because parliament could retract every concession and it would still be acting constitutionally in doing so.

Despite British accusations that they were regularly changing the grounds of their dispute with the mother country, American patriots were in fact remarkably consistent in their constitutional hostility to parliamentary sovereignty. This made it difficult for them to propose any compromise acceptable to parliament. In 1774 Joseph Galloway put forward the most famous compromise proposal when he laid his Plan of Union before the Continental Congress. Galloway suggested that the colonies should retain their own assemblies to control purely internal legislation and taxation, but he advocated that every three years these assemblies should elect representatives to a grand council. This would meet in America at least once a year to discuss and legislate for all matters affecting the affairs of the colonies in which Britain and any of the colonies was concerned. This grand council would be a distinct but inferior branch of the British legislature, united and incorporated with it, and having the same rights and privileges as the House of Commons. Imperial legislation could originate in any branch of the British legislature and it would need the approval of both parliament and the grand council. Galloway's plan initially found some support in congress, but delegates later expunged it from the minutes, probably because it might appear to weaken the assemblies and concede the doctrine of parliamentary sovereignty.

The only solution to the imperial crisis that the American patriots would accept by the early 1770s was a repeal of all parliamentary legislation since 1763, an unequivocal British renunciation of the constitutional doctrine of parliamentary sovereignty, and a clear agreement between parliament and the colonies that the latter's own assemblies were the sovereign authority over the internal affairs of the colonies. From the late 1760s the colonists had begun to emphasise their dependence on the crown alone and by the early 1770s they were declaring that they were in essence self-governing states owing allegiance to the same monarch as Britain. Moreover, in their view, the monarch's power over them was as limited as it was over Britain. They were prepared to offer the king requisitions to help pay the costs of their defence, but such an offer only served to alarm parliament because it threatened to render the king financially independent of parliament or at least increase his patronage which he could deploy to influence parliament. Fortunately for the preservation of parliamentary sovereignty in Britain, George III had no intention of agreeing to American suggestions that the colonies only connection with Britain was through the crown. In defending the sovereignty of parliament, however, George III lost his American colonies.

IV

Sovereignty after the Declaration of Independence
The dispute over sovereignty rent the British Atlantic empire asunder. Both British imperialists and American patriots agreed that either the American colonies must be subordinate to a sovereign parliament or they must be independent. There was no middle ground on which to reach a viable compromise. Both sides in this dispute believed they were upholding English constitutional values and were defending life, liberty and property. But the dynamics of constitutional developments on both sides of the Atlantic had produced a constitutional dilemma which was to prove insoluble. British liberty required a sovereign legislative able to impose firm limits on the power of the crown. American liberty required freedom from an omnipotent parliament. The War of American Independence was in fact a conflict between these constitutional visions, both of which owed their origins to the determination to resist the exercise of absolute, arbitrary power.

Despite its military defeat, Britain continued to uphold the doctrine of parliamentary sovereignty because it served its own interests so well. This constitutional doctrine was credited with saving the country from the evils of absolutism and catholicism, with establishing the rule of law and government by consent, and with combining economic success, social stability and personal liberty. The British constitution possessed these inestimable virtues because it was both a mixed government and a balanced constitution. Britain's mixed form of government secured all the benefits of monarchy, aristocracy and democracy, while avoiding the dangers inherent in each in its pure form. The balance of king, Lords and Commons ensured harmonious relations between all three elements in the sovereign legislature, while representing all the important interests in the state. Over the next half century political changes actually strengthened British support for the doctrine of parliamentary sovereignty. Economical reform seriously reduced crown patronage and made the legislature more independent of the crown and more dependent on the electorate. The growing power of public opinion and the beginnings of electoral reform made parliament more responsible and more accountable to the people at large. The nineteenth century saw the doctrine of parliamentary sovereignty more firmly entrenched than ever.

In the new United States of America it took more than a dozen years to replace the rejected doctrine of parliamentary sovereignty with a firmly established alternative view of constitutional sovereignty. While the Declaration of Independence rejected the sovereignty of parliament, it did not create a new constitution or establish where ultimate sovereignty lay. The Continental Congress recommended that all thirteen former colonies should each adopt a new state constitution. It did not recommend a particular form of constitution, but it did suggest that these should rest on the authority of the people and should include a full and free representation. Very quickly in some states, but more slowly in others, new written constitutions were drafted to establish the form of government, clarify the system of representation and delineate the liberties of the subject. These new constitutions created a fundamental law superior to the normal laws subsequently passed by the legislature. Some states simply confirmed their existing political systems, several drafted bills of rights, while Massachusetts made some effort to have its new constitution ratified by the whole adult male population. While no new constitution was fully democratic, either in how it was drafted or in its system of representation, considerable effort was made to endorse the notion of popular sovereignty. Several states asserted that the people were the sole source of legitimate power and all of them insisted on the accountability of elected representatives. They all ensured that the executive was elected for limited periods and could be controlled by the legislature and that the legislature was elected on a broad franchise at frequent intervals.

This wave of constitution making created governments for thirteen separate states. Although the Continental Congress gave some unity to these states, there was no formal national government in America for several years. The new state legislatures, jealous of their rights and fearful of the corrupting tendencies of power, were very reluctant to cede power to a new central government. Few Americans believed that an extended republic was feasible in any case. There was also as yet little sense of an American national consciousness and loyalty to one's particular state was a much stronger impulse. It was the needs of war and the fear of internal disorder that helped promote a measure of national union. A working division of power was attempted by the Articles of Confederation which were adopted in 1778, but not approved by the individual states until 1781. These Articles explicitly allowed each state to retain its 'sovereignty, freedom and independence', though an implicit division of sovereignty was established because congress did have some, though limited, powers expected of a national government. The state legislatures elected delegates to the Continental Congress, but this body could not levy taxes on its own initiative and had to rely on voluntary contributions from the states to finance the war effort. Congress did sometimes speak in the name of the American people, but the states remained the source of its authority. In certain respects, particularly during the war, congress did act like a national government in regulating coinage, borrowing money, establishing a post office, raising armed forces, coordinating the war effort, negotiating foreign alliances, and making peace. Congress could not wage war effectively or sign alliances or trade agreements however without the support of at least nine states. Many of its decisions were no more than recommendations which the individual states were left to enforce. In the early 1780s it was clear that congress under the articles could not reconcile major divergent interests between the states over such issues as slavery, the balance of representation between large and small states, and claims to western lands.

The weakness of the national government was apparent in war and peace. Concern over this grew as the more conservative propertied elite came to fear civil war, popular insurrections and the abuse of power by state legislatures dominated by sectional interests. Advocates of constitutional reform pressed the need for change, but it took several years to reach an agreement on a new constitution. Only after very considerable public debate did a constitutional convention chosen by the state legislatures meet in Philadelphia to draft a new Federal Constitution in 1787. At the heart of these debates was the question of the nature and location of sovereignty. The problem facing all protagonists was how to divide sovereignty - normally regarded as indivisible and irresistible - between the national and the state governments in such a manner that national, local and individual interests would all be safeguarded. While some thought such a division could not be achieved, some of the most influential Founding Fathers found a remarkable and a radical solution to this question.

The framers of the new Federal Constitution tried to achieve energy, stability and liberty by a new distribution of authority. They recognised the impossibility of creating a unitary state with a single sovereign government. To persuade the states to accept a stronger national government it was decided that the most acceptable yet radical solution was to place ultimate sovereign authority in the hands of the people. From the premise of a sovereign people it was possible to argue that both the national and the state governments possessed only limited powers delegated to them by the sovereign people. No government could claim to be sovereign; all were the servants of the people performing specific functions allowed to them by the people. The people were credited with the authority to elect and approve of the special convention set up to draft the constitution. The new constitution began with the words 'We, the People' instead of 'We, the states'. It was drafted in the name of the people and it was acknowledged as having created the new fundamental laws of the state. It was also subsequently accepted that this new constitution needed to be ratified by the people in special conventions held in each state. This constitution therefore was not a treaty between thirteen sovereign states, but a new form of government drafted in the name of the people and submitted for ratification by the people not by the state legislatures. To satisfy some of the critics of this constitution other measures reinforced the rights and authority of the people. An extensive Bill of Rights, protecting the individual from executive and legislative power, was attached as the first ten amendments to the constitution even before it was submitted for ratification. It was also agreed that the constitution could be amended in future.

The new Federal Constitution was designed to provide a whole raft of checks and balances to prevent the growth of arbitrary power, while curbing the reckless exercise of popular sovereignty. The personnel of the executive, legislative and judicial branches were kept separate at both federal and state levels. The legislature at both levels was divided into two chambers. At the federal level the Senate was elected on a geographical basis by the state legislatures, while the House of Representatives was elected from large constituencies directly by the people. The federal and the state legislatures were granted full powers over different spheres and for different purposes. The federal government was delegated power over external matters such as war, peace, diplomacy, currency and foreign commerce, while the states were left to look after internal order and the prosperity and improvement of their inhabitants. Representatives and office holders were elected for different terms to make it difficult to construct a long-term majority in control of both the executive and the legislature.

The new constitution recognised the people as the sovereign authority. It was repeatedly stressed that the people delegated their sovereign power to different individuals and bodies of men for short periods and for certain limited ends. A wide franchise and repeated elections rendered those at all levels of government ultimately responsible and accountable to the people. The Federal Constitution thus divided and distributed sovereignty not unlike the manner long advocated for the British empire by American patriots in their disputes with parliament. The basic power of government was divided without dividing sovereignty itself - that lay with the people. Only the people at large created government at all levels, decided how powerful any particular government institution should be, and held them accountable by frequent elections on a broad franchise. Furthermore, the people retained the right to bear arms and to resist arbitrary power. In the last resort, they even retained the right of revolution.

The new constitution had established a fundamental law which could limit the power of the legislature and the executive. No one contended that even the powers of the federal or state governments were absolute or arbitrary. Judges faced with a conflict between the fundamental law of the constitution and any legislative or executive act had to decide in favour of the former. This concept of judicial review was not written into the constitution, though it was implied in it and it was strongly advocated by many of the framers of the constitution. Over the next decade or two the judges of the Federal Supreme Court ensured that it became enshrined in constitutional practice. This system of judicial review was not meant to make the judiciary supreme, but to allow the judges to defend the sovereign people and the fundamental law of the constitution.

Further Reading:
H.T. Dickinson, *Liberty and Property: Political Ideology in Eighteenth-Century Britain* (London, 1977); H.T. Dickinson, 'The Eighteenth Century Debate on the Sovereignty of Parliament', *Transactions of the Royal Historical Society*, 5th series, 26 (1976), 189-210; H.T. Dickinson, 'Britain's Imperial Sovereignty: The Ideological Case against the American Colonies', in *Britain and the American Revolution*, ed. H.T. Dickinson (London, 1998), 64-96; H.T. Dickinson, '"The Friends of America": British Sympathy with the American Revolution', in *Radicalism and Revolution in Britain, 1775-1848*, ed. Michael T. Davis (London, 2000), 1-29; Jeffrey Goldsworthy, *The Sovereignty of Parliament: History and Philosophy* (Oxford, 1999); Willi Paul Adams, *The First American Constitutions* (Chapel Hill, NC, 1980); Jack P. Greene, *Peripheries and Center: Constitutional Developments in the Extended Politics of the British Empire and the United States, 1667-1788* (Athens, GA, 1986); Jack P. Greene, 'Competing Authorities: The Debate over Parliamentary Imperial Jurisdiction, 1763-1776', *Parliamentary History*, 14 (1995), 47-63; Richard R. Johnson, '"Parliamentary Egotisms": The Clash of Legislatures in the Making of the American Revolution', *Journal of American History*, 74 (1987), 338-62; Donald S. Lutz, *The Origins of American Constitutionalism* (Baton Rouge, 1988); Edmund S. Morgan, *Inventing the People: The Rise of Popular Sovereignty in England and America* (New York, 1988); John Phillip Reid, *Constitutional History of the American Revolution* (4 vols., Madison, WI, 1986-93); Gordon S. Wood, *The Creation of the American Republic 1776-1787* (New York, 1993).

7

Ireland: From Legislative Independence to Legislative Union, 1782-1800

THOMAS BARTLETT

The years 1782 to 1789 have generally been portrayed as a sort of golden age of the Irish parliament: but the subsequent decade, culminating in bloody rebellion and in the extinction of that institution, has been viewed much less favourably. By and large, historians have found few grounds to revise the verdict of Sir Jonah Barrington, who dubbed these twenty years *The Rise and Fall of the Irish Nation*. And yet, it may be suggested that the contrast in these decades is more apparent than real. With hindsight, it is clear that the 1780s, for all the self-congratulation and the oratorical fireworks attendant on the achievement of Irish legislative independence, was a period of missed opportunities. If not exactly the locust years, this decade had in fact offered a period of leisure that ought to have been taken advantage of in order to resolve those problems that would prove so intractable in the tumultuous 1790s. From an early date, the numerous flaws in the new constitutional dispensation between Britain and Ireland that came into existence in 1782 were apparent but, in the event, nothing was done. William Pitt was not far wrong when he later criticised the parcel of measures that made up the 'Constitution of 1782' as entirely backward-looking, as being nothing more than the mere destruction of another system. That interim arrangement of 1782 had, by 1789, taken on the character of a (profoundly unsatisfactory) final settlement. By that date, the hopes engendered by the winning of legislative independence in 1782 had gone, and the stage was set for the confrontations of the 1790s which were to end in rebellion and the end of the Irish parliament.

I

The euphoria over the 'Constitution of 1782' proved shortlived, for it quickly became evident, to British ministers no less than to Irish patriot politicians, that it was by no means a final adjustment. The first sour note was struck by Henry Flood, the one-time opposition leader-turned-officeholder, who now, in an effort to regain his credibility among the patriots, pronounced the 'simple' repeal of the Declaratory Act - a cornerstone of the 'Constitution of 1782' - to be entirely inadequate and demanded that the British government formally renounce its declared right to legislate for Ireland. Reaction to Flood's initiative was unfavourable: Henry Grattan - widely regarded as the father of Irish legislative independence - quickly declared himself satisfied with 'simple repeal'; British ministers were outraged at the overt impugning of their good faith; and the Dublin wits were quick to point out that, logically, Flood's position was untenable (a renunciation could, after all, itself be renounced). Overall, Flood's campaign smacked too much of mischief-making with a view to self-promotion. None the less, it took hold, particularly among the Volunteers.

The support of the Volunteers, the paramilitary defence force which had played such a vital role in achieving legislative independence was crucial for Flood's campaign. The Volunteers had been without a defined mandate since the constitutional victories of April 1782, and the approaching end of the American war promised to make them entirely redundant. Flood's doubts about 'simple repeal' offered them a new role as guardians of the constitution, and they were quick to embrace it. Pressure mounted for the British government to enact an immediate 'Renunciation' Act, and in January 1783 this was conceded.

In the eyes of some the 'Constitution of 1782' was now complete; but in fact, all that the struggle for 'Renunciation' had achieved was to highlight the deep residual distrust with which British policy and British politicians were viewed in Ireland and to demonstrate the unsatisfactory nature of the 'Constitution'. 'Renunciation' did nothing to render Irish parliamentary independence any more secure; it may in fact have weakened it, not merely because it turned Flood against Grattan but because it increased British anxiety at what had been already given away to Ireland. With the radical surgery on Poynings' Law and the repeal of the Declaratory Act, British politicians professed themselves puzzled as to what was now the link between Britain and Ireland. A shared king was all very well, but it was hardly sufficient on a day-to-day basis. Again, despite the repeal of the Declaratory Act and the passing of the Renunciation Act, British parliamentary sovereignty remained secure, but the exercise of it was unthinkable; and the veto retained by the king could not be used except *in extremis*. On the British side, therefore, clarification was sought, and pressure grew for a treaty that would unequivocally re-affirm Ireland's connection to Britain and her position within the empire. In Ireland, however, the mood was rather different. British capitulation over 'Renunciation' had fuelled patriot hopes that their next venture might meet with equal success. Having at last adjusted the constitutional connection between England and Ireland to their satisfaction, the patriots and their Volunteer allies (some said masters) would now seek to alter the political relationship between the Irish parliament and the Irish people.

II

Perhaps surprisingly, the question of parliamentary reform had hitherto attracted little attention in the Irish parliament: the focus of patriot endeavour had been fixed on the Anglo-Irish nexus rather than on the equally flawed relationship between the Irish parliament and the 'Irish people'. With the winning of the 'Constitution of 1782', however, the question of parliamentary reform was raised, both with a view to safeguard the legislative gains and also to ensure that there would be no backsliding by Irish members of parliament. It was, however, only when the struggle over 'Renunciation' was satisfactorily concluded, that the issue of reform was brought forward in a sustained manner. Articles appeared in the *Dublin Evening Post*, the *Freeman's Journal* and the *Hibernian Journal* in January 1783, pointing out the numerous anomalies in the Irish representation and stressing how vulnerable such absurdities rendered the constitutional gains of 1778-83. The Volunteers, as ever, eager to pick up the ball and run with it, were soon calling for a more equal representation of the people in parliament; and in September 1783 at Dungannon, county Tyrone, a reform convention attended by 500 Volunteer delegates from 278 corps throughout Ulster came together. Some fifteen MPs were there, and a leading role was taken by the delegate of the Derry Volunteers, Frederick Augustus Hervey, earl bishop of Derry. The main business was to plan a national convention on reform to be held later in Dublin, but the delegates took the opportunity to draft a series of resolutions which would be considered in Dublin. These resolutions called for annual parliaments, a secret ballot, an end to decayed boroughs, more MPs for large towns and counties, the vote for all Protestant males of modest property, compensation for borough owners who in consequence of reform lost their 'property', and the expulsion of most pensioners from the Irish parliament.

Prudently, the delegates decided to defer all discussion of the question of Catholic eligibility for the franchise until the national convention would meet in Dublin.
Reaction to these developments in ministerial circles in London was deeply hostile. The duke of Portland claimed that it was 'high treason' even to suggest parliamentary reform in Ireland; Lord North, more restrained, spoke of 'insurmountable difficulties'; Charles James Fox wailed that if reform were conceded 'Ireland is irretrievably lost forever' and he forecast 'either a total separation or a civil war between us' [Bartlett, 106]. In Dublin, the lord lieutenant, Northington, was, however, reassuring: he was well aware of a certain nervousness, even among reformers, at the spectacle of the Volunteers, a paramilitary body, seeking to perpetuate their importance by dictating to the elected representatives of the Irish nation in the matter of parliamentary reform. Moreover, he could see that there were serious divisions between Flood and Grattan, and between Charlemont and the earl bishop of Derry on such matters as the content of the reform proposals, and the strategy to be pursued in order to achieve them. Equally, he well realised the capacity of the question of political rights for Irish Catholics to generate dissension. On all these counts, Northington was quietly confident that the Irish campaign for parliamentary reform would fall apart. So it proved. The national convention was soon in disarray over the catholic question; a plan for parliamentary reform concocted by Flood was refused a reading by the Irish House of Commons and a later one in March 1784 was also barred. Thereafter, enthusiasm for reform ebbed. Dublin Castle's determination to play the 'Catholic card' in order to remind all right-thinking Protestants of the reality of the Catholic menace began to take effect. Rumours of popish plots and French intrigues were played up, and circulated: by August 1784, the chief secretary, Thomas Orde, was claiming that the alarm of the Catholic design has had a wonderful operation and he expressed his confidence that the jarring interests of religion and property would immeasurably benefit Dublin castle.
By this stage, it was clear that the only hope for reform in Ireland lay in its success in England, where William Pitt, the prime minister since late 1783, was on record as being a supporter. Constitutionally, Ireland may have been a sister kingdom with an equal legislature; but practical politics dictated that the greater country should lead and the lesser follow. Ireland's formal constitutional subordination may have gone in 1782, but where weighty issues were concerned, a certain prudent inferiority still remained. Hence, when Pitt's bill went down to defeat in the British House of Commons in April 1785, it killed any chance reform may have had in Ireland.
The Irish reform movement failed, first, because the vested interests in the Irish parliament were too well entrenched. The great Irish parliamentary families of Shannon, Ponsonby, Ely, Leinster and Devonshire (and a host of lesser fry) had backed legislative independence in 1782 for that had cost nothing, would render them 'popular', and might even enhance the price of their boroughs: but parliamentary reform threatened both their 'interests' and their pockets, and was therefore to be resisted. In addition, the British government, and British politicians of all parties, were unalterably opposed to reform in Ireland, foreseeing enormous problems if the Irish parliament were freed from aristocratic control and made more accountable. British political control in Ireland, already diminished by the 'Constitution of 1782', would be further attenuated by a widening of the boundaries of the Irish political nation. Parliamentary management, despite the adjustment of 1782 still the prime duty of the lord lieutenant and his chief secretary, would be rendered more problematic than ever if there were reform, as both current and earlier holders of these offices constantly proclaimed. These reasons - internal opposition from powerful interests and external resistance to reform in Ireland - go some way towards explaining that movement's failure. In the end, however, it was the failure

to include Catholics in reform plans that was decisive: the Catholic question, declared William Drennan, a leading Belfast reformer, was our ruin.

The initial exclusion of Catholics from the reform proposals, the resolute refusal to contemplate enlisting their support in the campaign, all combined to render the movement for parliamentary reform a minority interest. The Catholic Relief Acts of 1778 and 1782 had brought the Catholics into the political scale: though still voteless as well as seatless, none the less, Catholics could no longer be ignored, and it was an act of folly for the reformers to do so. Without Catholic support, the agitation for reform could always be dismissed as sectional if not sectarian, partial, interested and the product of envy, frustration and resentment. With Catholic support, it could scarcely have been seen as anything other than national. This conclusion was the central one drawn by reformers when, some years later and under the inspiration of the French revolution, they set out once again to campaign for parliamentary reform.

Ironically, those who had argued that parliamentary reform was not necessary were to a large extent vindicated by the stout defence which the Irish parliament now offered in its opposition to Pitt's wide-ranging proposals for a commercial and defensive treaty. Just as the Irish parliament had refused to be intimidated by the Volunteers, so too it refused to be swayed by the blandishments of William Pitt. Perhaps the legislative independence of the Irish parliament was going to mean something after all?

III

At the time of the concessions that constituted the 'Constitution of 1782' there had been a good deal of discussion among British politicians (and some Irish) concerning the need to conclude some sort of treaty between the two countries in order to clarify their new relationship. None doubted that some such arrangement - the term 'a final adjustment' was much canvassed - was necessary for the preservation of the remaining connection between Ireland and Britain: but it was not until 1784 that an opportunity offered to achieve this.

John Beresford and John Foster, respectively chief commissioner of the Irish revenue board and chancellor of the Irish exchequer, were anxious to expand Ireland's trade by winning fresh concessions (and confirming old ones) from Britain in the area of Anglo-Irish commerce. In the event, Pitt too had been impressed with the desirability of putting the Anglo-Irish relationship on a new, firmer footing. His plans, though never wholly formulated, were clearly much wider in scope than those of Foster and Beresford. There were three distinct elements to Pitt's proposals: parliamentary reform in Ireland on a Protestant basis; the substitution of an Irish Protestant militia for the (by now) religiously promiscuous Volunteers; and finally and centrally, an imperial treaty which would both re-affirm Britain's sovereignty and fix (Foster preferred 'rivet') Ireland's position within the empire. What Pitt appears to have been aiming at was a junction of the Protestant interest in Ireland with that in Britain. This united Protestant front would then set its face resolutely against the demands of Irish Catholics (and possibly Irish Presbyterians) while bidding defiance to those Catholic powers (France and Spain) that had tilted the balance against Britain in the American war.

Before any of this could be accomplished, however, Pitt was clear that a commercial arrangement with Ireland, loosely based on that proposed by Foster should be undertaken. Unlike the latter's scheme that of Pitt was much wider in scope, embracing commerce certainly, but also bringing in both constitutional and defence points not included in the original proposal. Specifically, Pitt maintained that the constitutional connection between Ireland and Britain would be strengthened immeasurably by Ireland agreeing to pay a defined annual contribution towards imperial naval charges. To this end, Foster's original scheme, against his wishes, was expanded during discussions in London with Pitt and his advisers, and ten propositions were submitted to the Irish parliament in February 1785 for its consideration. Here an opposition conducted by Grattan was mounted, the ten propositions were increased to eleven, and two important amendments were made, again contrary to Foster's wishes. These gave Ireland, first, a greater say in the disposal of her contribution towards naval charges, and second, they provided that Ireland need make no contribution at all in time of peace unless her budget balanced.

These resolutions on arrival in London immediately came under fire. Commercial interests, ably orchestrated by members of the parliamentary opposition to Pitt, protested against the generosity of the provisions and forecast ruin for themselves if they passed into law. Pitt himself was aghast at the provision that no contribution would be made unless the Irish budget balanced, and he moved to have that struck out. Similarly, he insisted on widening the scope of the provisions in order to bring in general imperial matters. As a result of commercial clamour and ministerial misgivings, the eleven propositions had by now expanded to twenty. What had begun life as a modest Anglo-Irish trade arrangement had now taken on the character of an elaborate imperial treaty complete with defence and constitutional provisions.

The twenty British resolutions, as Foster had warned, evoked much protest on their arrival in Ireland, and they were denounced in a series of addresses as being destructive of the constitution no less than the trade of Ireland. In the Irish parliament, too, where the proposals had been cast in the form of a bill in August 1785, opposition soon centred on the implications for Ireland's legislative independence if the proposals passed. In particular, the fourth proposition quickly gained notoriety for it demanded that the Irish parliament should agree to enact in the future such trade laws as were enacted in the parliament of Great Britain.

Much of the criticism directed at the bill or indeed at the twenty resolutions on which it was loosely based was ill-conceived: Grattan in particular made a fool of himself by revealing his lack of understanding of commercial matters; and other hostile speakers were scarcely better informed. None the less, argument was overcome by rhetoric, the solid commercial advantages of the plan were ignored, and the threat to Irish legislative independence was highlighted. In the vote, the result was so close that Dublin castle chose to consider it a defeat, and the bill was withdrawn.

The failure of the commercial propositions was significant for the working of the 'Constitution of 1782'. It marked, in the first instance, a humiliating rebuff for Pitt, exposing him as a poor manager of men. He felt this rejection deeply, and thereafter had scant regard for Irish politicians or their vaunted legislative independence. Moreover, Pitt was confirmed in his view that the Anglo-Irish constitutional connection was dangerously flawed and that the mutual faith and understanding that Foster had claimed to be the new basis of the Anglo-Irish relationship would soon prove to be worthless. In addition, the collapse of the commercial propositions inevitably put an end to those more grandiose schemes involving a possible parliamentary reform and the formation of a Protestant militia which Pitt had at one time contemplated for Ireland. Parliamentary reform - on a Protestant basis only - had perhaps never been likely, if only because Dublin castle had set its face against it, but the proposed Protestant militia to absorb the Volunteers had been regarded by Dublin castle as highly desirable. In the aftermath of the 'defeat' on the commercial propositions, however, there would be no imperial treaty, and therefore, there could be no Irish Protestant militia and no parliamentary reform. Pitt's rebuff over the commercial propositions meant that the anomalous, ambiguous and dangerously vague relationship between Britain and Ireland would remain unreformed and that hence the much sought-after final adjustment would continue to prove elusive.

Lastly, it was noticeable that in the various debates on the commercial propositions the idea of a union was aired for the first time in public. Lord North protested in the

British House of Commons that the commercial privileges to be offered to Ireland were so extravagant that they should have accompanied a union between the two countries. Grattan, too, took up this point, but he denounced Pitt's plans as 'an incipient and a creeping union: a virtual union' and he concluded by saying that, in opposing the bill, 'I consider myself as opposing an Union *in limine*' [Kelly, *Prelude*, 190]. It would be quite wrong to say that from this point on, Pitt worked for a union between Britain and Ireland, but equally it is clear that union was somewhere on the political agenda of both countries, that it had its spokesmen, and that its merits were openly canvassed.

In the event, the next controversy to upset Anglo-Irish relations, the so-called Regency crisis of 1788, further prompted a discussion of the merits or otherwise of union. The details of this crisis need not detain us. George III was pronounced deranged in October 1788 and a regent was to be appointed during what was hoped would be a brief incapacity. Matters were initially complicated by the fact that the obvious candidate for regent, George's son, the Prince of Wales, was a firm friend of Charles James Fox, Pitt's leading rival. Pitt therefore prudently proposed that the prince be appointed regent with restricted powers; Fox agreed with the appointment but, understandably, was opposed to the condition of restricted powers. Matters were further complicated when the Irish parliament sought to intervene in the wrangle over the regent's powers. A new prime minister in England, a likely consequence of the Prince of Wales succeeding his father with full powers, was bound to result in a new lord lieutenant in Ireland; and those Irish politicians who were close to Fox - such as Grattan and the Ponsonbys - were expected to profit from this change. In addition, George III was king of Ireland, and the appointment of a regent could be held to fall within the Irish parliament's powers: hence, intervening in this matter would assert Irish legislative independence in the most unmistakable manner. Irish politicians surged towards what they thought would be the winning side and, casting caution to the wind, passed an address calling on the prince to take up his responsibilities with unrestricted powers. A small delegation was deputed to bring this request to the prince in person, but soon after the delegates' arrival in London, George III recovered his wits and the crisis was over. The whole affair, commented W.W. Grenville had been 'the most absurd and ridiculous farce' [Bartlett, 119].

But farce or not, a degree of significance attaches to the episode, for it once again demonstrated to Pitt the flawed nature of the 'Constitution of 1782' and it confirmed his worst fears about the unpredictability of the 'giddy' Irish parliament. John Fitzgibbon, soon to be appointed lord chancellor of Ireland had been one of the few to stand their ground when others - dubbed the 'Regency rats' by the lord lieutenant, Buckingham - had rushed to jump on the prince's bandwagon, and he had endorsed Pitt's reading of the situation. Fitzgibbon was convinced that the Irish parliament's intervention into the regency debate had actually undermined the common monarchy which had provided an hitherto unchallengeable bond between the two countries. What would have happened, mused Fitzgibbon, if the Irish parliament had chosen someone other than the candidate of the British parliament - a member of the Stuart family, say - for the position of regent? To everyone's surprise, an element of dynastic insecurity - similar to that which had provided the essential context for the Anglo-Scottish union of 1707 - had now entered Irish politics; because of Irish assertiveness (or giddiness) during the regency crisis, the independent Irish parliament, and the 'Constitution of 1782', could now be seen as a threat to the link offered by sharing the same monarch. By 1789, the ties of love and mutual affection and the security offered by a common king had been shown to be quite insufficient to keep the Anglo-Irish relationship on a secure footing. Moreover by that date, time for leisured reflection and remedial action was running out.

IV

Within a matter of weeks of the opening of the states-general in Paris in May 1789, the term 'the French Revolution' had begun to make an appearance in Irish newspapers: and throughout the country, but especially in Belfast and Dublin, those groups who had previously been in favour of political reform drew inspiration and encouragement from the unfolding of the stirring events in France. In July 1790, the Volunteers, since 1785 largely moribund, marched to celebrate not the battle of the Boyne but the fall of the Bastille, and in Belfast there was much talk of new clubs and new alliances. By October 1790, the lord lieutenant, Westmorland, had come into possession of a document entitled 'The Belfast Constitutional Compact' which consisted of a series of resolutions calling on Presbyterians and Catholics to make common cause against 'extorting tithe-mongers and ecclesiastical plunders' and pledging support for the Catholics' 'just claim to the enjoyment of the rights and privileges of freeborn citizens' [Bartlett, 125]. This preliminary intelligence of a potential alliance between Catholics and Dissenters appeared to be confirmed during the summer of 1791. In July of that year, the lord lieutenant drew attention to a pamphlet circulating in Belfast and Dublin concerning 'the establishment of a Brotherhood', and he pronounced it be 'a very dangerous paper' [Bartlett, 126]. This discussion document was the work of William Drennan and it prepared the way for a club to be set up in Belfast in October 1791 (and in Dublin a few weeks later) entitled The Society of United Irishmen.

Drennan had drawn the lesson from the debacle of the mid-1780s that parliamentary reform would prove elusive until the Catholics were brought to lend their weight and numbers to the campaign. As it happened, Theobald Wolfe Tone, a young Dublin barrister, was thinking along similar lines, and in a remarkable pamphlet, *An Argument on behalf of the Catholics of Ireland*, published in August 1791, he maintained that 'Irishmen of all denominations' had to band together 'against the boobies and blockheads' that governed them in order to achieve parliamentary reform. Tone's *Argument* had a great impact. It quickly ran through a number of editions and was disseminated widely - even Westmorland read it, and he commended it to the foreign secretary, Lord Grenville, as 'a pretty specimen of the sentiments of Irish reformers' [Bartlett, 126]. Its publication led to Tone being invited to Belfast to attend at the inaugural meeting of the new society for which Drennan had called. Here, he took charge, suggesting the name of the new society - the United Irishmen - and composing its key resolutions calling for the destruction of English influence in the Irish government by means of a union of all the people, maintaining that this could only be accomplished through a thoroughgoing parliamentary reform, and claiming that no such reform could be 'practicable, efficacious or just' which did not include Catholics.

Tone's pamphlet was relentlessly realistic both in its reasons for the failure of the previous reform movement and in its signposting the way forward. Undoubtedly it and other similar productions contained many home truths: for example, that the 'Constitution of 1782' had merely resulted in increased 'corruption' in the Irish parliament; but Tone's pamphlet went further by directly addressing the question of the Catholics' capacity for liberty and by concluding on the basis of events in France that Catholics could in fact be trusted. French Catholics had captured the Bastille, separated church from state, and had proved ardent in the cause of liberty: if French Catholics in the most catholic country in the world could do all this, why not Irish Catholics?

Tone's arguments may have made sense to Irish Presbyterians, but for Catholics it was all rather different, and there can be no doubt that an alliance along the lines he proposed could hardly be other than extremely problematic. Presbyterians had ever been the most implacable enemies of Catholics and catholicism: much history would have to be repressed before a genuine alliance could take place. More than this, however, Catholics were well aware of how shabbily they had been treated in the recent past by the Presbyterian reformers of the early 1780s. At the various reform conventions, the largely Presbyterian delegates had decided that neither the proposed reform on the franchise nor on seats in parliament was to be extended to Catholics. In short, the reformers - Presbyterians foremost among them - had let the Catholics down in the 1780s, why should Catholics trust them now?

In addition, there was the British government to be considered. For a generation, London had been the object of Irish Catholics' prayers and petitions. Indeed the credit for previous catholic relief measures had been claimed by the British government for it had urged a reluctant Dublin castle to undertake them, and had pushed them through a lethargic, if not hostile, Irish parliament in 1778 and 1782. Why should Irish Catholics run the risk of sacrificing the goodwill of the British government by entering into an alliance with those whose capacity to deliver on their promises was questionable, indeed whose very *bona fides* on this issue were suspect? At the same time, it was obvious that certain tactical advantages could be won by the Catholics if they or their leaders could impress upon the British government that only through the granting of significant concessions could the threat posed to English government in Ireland by the proposed catholic-dissenter alliance be averted. There can be no doubt that this was the argument used most forcefully and frequently by the new and energetic secretary of the Catholic Committee, Richard Burke (Edmund's son) during the years 1791-2, and undoubtedly this point had an effect on the British government. Time after time, members of the British government sought to impress upon the Dublin castle administration the danger posed by such an alliance: 'I may be a false prophet', wrote Grenville, the foreign secretary, to Westmorland on 20 October 1791, 'but there is no evil that I should not prophesy if that union takes place at the present moment and on the principles on which it is endeavoured to bring it about' [*Fortescue MSS*, ii, 214].

In Grenville's view, there was nothing for it but for substantial and immediate concessions to be made to Irish Catholics. Westmorland tried to resist Grenville's logic but in so doing he contradicted his own earlier alarmist statements by now playing down the threat posed by a dissenter-catholic alliance. His protests against bringing forward the Catholics were brushed aside. The outbreak of war on the continent in 1792 and the near certainty that Britain would be drawn in (duly confirmed in February 1793) lent an added urgency to concession and a growing impatience with the panics and apprehensions of Dublin castle, and Irish politicians. In 1792 a minor Catholic Relief Act was put through the Irish parliament and in 1793 a much more substantial one was enacted which gave the vote to Irish Catholics in the county constituencies on the same terms as Irish Protestants. This latter concession was forced through a deeply reluctant Irish parliament by the British government, and this is instructive. No peerages, pensions or promises were required to make the Irish parliament perform a u-turn (a similar proposal had been rejected months earlier). Rather, plain speaking (or brutal threats), and a fear of being outrun by the British government in the race for the Catholic vote did the trick. The conclusion was clear: when the British government unequivocally expressed its wishes on a particular matter, the Irish parliament could not resist it. The weakness of the 'Constitution of 1782' was thereby starkly revealed, and a lesson was learned by certain Irish politicians. The Irish parliament, hitherto a bulwark of the Ascendancy was now seen as a Trojan horse: Irish unionism was born.

The major concessions to the Catholics in the years 1792-3 had, it was believed, successfully detached that body from any active support or involvement with the radical reformers. Moreover, the outbreak of war with revolutionary France in early 1793 gave Dublin castle its opportunity to move against a radical group which was both pro-French and anti-war and which appeared to be isolated. Measures were soon taken to harass its members. A Convention Act was passed which, by outlawing assemblies purporting to have a representative character, closed off to the United Irishmen the tried and tested method of putting pressure on the government. Similarly, the disbandment of the Volunteers and the setting up of a militia under the firm control of the government removed the danger that the United Irishmen might engage the older body in the reform campaign. That potent configuration of popular, parliamentary and paramilitary forces that had won the 'Constitution of 1782' would not be permitted to recur. Moreover, in a further show of the castle's determination, leading United Irishmen were arrested on charges of seditious libel for criticising government policy; a secret committee of the Irish House of Lords was set up in order to substantiate allegations that the United Irishmen were involved in treasonable activities with the French; and in Belfast a military riot served to overawe the city. Finally, following revelations at the trial in mid-1794 of a French emissary, the Rev. William Jackson, the Society of United Irishmen was suppressed by government decree. It re-emerged a short time later; but now it was a secret, oathbound conspiracy dedicated to seeking military support from revolutionary France in order to achieve an Irish republic.

The later history of the revolutionary conspiracy of the 1790s lies beyond the scope of this paper: but already by 1795 the shape of the threat to the government, and the nature of the response - both official and unofficial - that would be made to that threat was clear. The recall of the well-meaning viceroy, Earl Fitzwilliam in that year, and his replacement by Lord Camden, was a clear sign that conciliation was not a policy option. In addition, Fitzwilliam's dismissal revealed that what was now known as 'catholic emancipation' - the right of catholic candidates, if elected, to take their seats in the Irish Commons - was not to be conceded lightly. Instead, the very real danger of an insurrection in Ireland in association with a French invasion force would be met by new, draconian, laws, and new forces would be established or imported. A new ideology of 'Protestant Ascendancy' would be fostered, in order to combat the pleas of the United Irishmen to sink denominational rivalries into a common Irishness. Moreover, extensive use would be made of spies and informers, and ultimately the armed forces of the crown would be encouraged to act beyond the law. By 1798 the spiral of violence and counter-terror provoked by popular insurgency and official counter-insurgency had reached a point where Dublin castle welcomed an insurrection, reasoning that an open rebellion could be more easily crushed than a secret conspiracy.

William Pitt, too, was not displeased at news of rebellion in Ireland for it offered him the opportunity to propose that legislative union between Britain and Ireland that he had long desired; and he moved swiftly to seize it. At the very least, a union would give the perfect riposte to those who had in the rebellion sought separation; and to that extent union could be urged as a key instrument of counter-insurgency, a vital strategic imperative drawing Britain and Ireland closer and closer so as to frustrate those Irish Jacobins and their French allies who had sought to prise them apart. Indeed, in his main speech advocating the union proposals in the British House of Commons, Pitt made much of this imperial point. But Pitt also saw union as the final solution to those problems that had been bedevilling Anglo-Irish relations since 1782. In particular, he spoke of the profoundly unsatisfactory nature of the 'Constitution of 1782' - that 'mere destruction of another system' - and of the continuing failure to reform it. He pointed to the ever-present danger of a clash between the two 'independent' parliaments of Britain and Ireland - a clash, he claimed, only narrowly averted at the time of the regency crisis. Moreover, it was only in an united parliament, he maintained, that the catholic question could be solved with benefit to Irish Catholics and without danger to Irish Protestants. And not only the Catholic question: the new imperial parliament would function as an impartial legislature, far removed from the clamour and prejudice of local factions, calmly and dispassionately adjudicating in the interests of all on the various problems that might arise within the entire empire, an assembly where contentious matters such as tithes or the provision of salaries for Catholic priests could be coolly deliberated on.

Central to Pitt's understanding of Ireland was his belief that the 'Constitution of 1782' had failed, that Irish politicians had failed and that there could now be no alternative but union. Irish political failure in Pitt's eyes was compounded by Irish financial failure, for he was all too well aware that Irish finances by the late 1790s were a total mess and that only British subventions kept Dublin castle from bankruptcy. Pitt's unflattering verdict on the Irish political structure, his firm conviction that there was no option other than union, and his resolute, and publicly avowed, determination not to rest until that was accomplished were guaranteed to ensure ultimate victory. As in 1793, so in 1800: when a British government unequivocally declared its intentions towards Ireland, it could not be denied. The sham of the 'Constitution of 1782' was exposed. At midnight on 31 December 1800, the experiment of Irish legislative independence came to an end, the union between Great Britain and Ireland came into effect, and over five hundred years of Irish parliamentary history came to a close.

References and Further Reading:
Thomas Bartlett, *The Fall and Rise of the Irish Nation: The Catholic Question, 1690-1830* (Dublin, 1992); G.C. Bolton, *The Passing of the Irish Act of Union* (Oxford, 1966); Historical Manuscripts Commission, *The Manuscripts of J.B. Fortescue*, ii (London, 1894); Patrick Geoghegan, *The Irish Act of Union* (Dublin, 1999); Jacqueline Hill, *From Patriots to Unionists: Dublin Civic Politics and Irish Protestant Patriotism 1660-1840* (Oxford, 1997); Edith M. Johnston, *Great Britain and Ireland 1760-1800* (Edinburgh, 1963); Ann C. Kavanaugh, *John Fitzgibbon, Earl of Clare* (Dublin, 1997); James Kelly, *Prelude to Union: Anglo-Irish Politics in the 1780s* (Cork, 1992); James Kelly, *Henry Grattan* (Dublin, 1993); James Kelly, *Henry Flood: Patriots and Politics in Eighteenth-Century Ireland* (Dublin, 1998); R.B. McDowell, *Irish Public Opinion 1750-1800* (London, 1944); R.B. McDowell, *Ireland in the Age of Imperialism and Revolution 1760-1801* (Oxford, 1979); A.P.W. Malcomson, *John Foster: the politics of the Anglo-Irish Ascendancy* (Oxford, 1979); *A New History of Ireland, IV: Eighteenth-Century Ireland 1691-1800*, ed. T.W. Moody and W.E. Vaughan (Oxford, 1986); Gerard O'Brien, *Anglo-Irish Politics in the Age of Grattan and Pitt* (Dublin, 1987); Neil Longley York, *Neither Kingdom nor Nation: The Irish Quest for Constitutional Rights, 1698-1800* (Washington DC, 1994).

8

Church-State Relations in Scotland after the Union

STEWART J. BROWN

When England and Scotland entered into legislative union in 1707, there was no provision for the creation of a single religious establishment. On the contrary, the Union settlement established two fundamentally different religious systems – the Anglican and the Presbyterian – within the same state. This was remarkable. Most of Europe at this time viewed religious uniformity, and a close alliance of church and state, to be essential for state building. The Peace of Westphalia of 1648 had confirmed the principle of 'cuius regio eius religio' in central Europe, with only limited toleration for religious minorities. Imperial Russia, for example, was ruthless in its efforts to suppress the Old Believers after 1667. In 1685 the French state of Louis XIV had revoked the Edict of Nantes, as part of a policy aimed at the elimination of protestantism, while the French state also used political force to suppress the Jansenists after 1713. In 1731 the Austrian empire expelled the Protestants of Salzburg, driving some 20,000 into exile.

And yet in 1707, a unified British state was created, with a single parliament, and two distinct religious establishments, each recognised as the true church within its respective portion of the state. It was not simply a matter of the state granting toleration to a minority tradition, but of the state recognising two churches as the true body of Christ. They were, moreover, churches that did not recognise one another as true churches and did not share a common communion. They were also churches with a history of deep mutual antagonism. For probably most Anglicans in 1707, presbyterianism was associated with the revolution of the 1640s, the desecration of churches and cathedrals, the Solemn League and Covenant of 1643 and the killing of Charles I, the martyr king. For most Presbyterians, Anglicanism was responsible for the persecution of the Covenanters, especially during the killing times of the 1680s, when people had been hunted down for worshipping without warrant from a bishop. In recognising these conflicting religious systems as established churches within the same state, the Union of 1707 created what was in many respects a religiously schizophrenic state, a political system that seemed certain to be unstable. And yet the religious settlement of the Union of 1707 survived.

What was the relationship between a Scottish national religion on the one hand, and a British state in which that Scottish national church was a minority tradition? This chapter will explore this question, giving attention to three periods in Scottish history, when questions surrounding church-state relations were particularly acute. The first was the period following the Act of Union, up to and including the Toleration and Patronage Acts of 1712. The second is the period of the 'Ten Years' Conflict' between church and state in the years 1833-1843, a conflict over both the use of state funds for church extension in an increasingly pluralist society and the power of the church to regulate patronage. The third was the decade of 1920s and the major Presbyterian effort of those years to revive the influence and authority of the established Church of Scotland, an effort that included both the Presbyterian church reunion of 1929 and the campaign to suppress and marginalise the Roman Catholic community in Scotland.

I

In 1689 the estates of Scotland had re-established presbyterianism within the national Church of Scotland, and abolished bishoprics, cathedrals and diocesan jurisdictions. Its decision to end episcopacy was not based on religious principle; rather, episcopacy was deemed 'contrary to the inclinations of the generality of the people'. This was questionable. The Church of Scotland had been episcopal in organisation since 1662, and the resistance of the Presbyterian Covenanters had been largely broken by the mid-1680s. In truth, the numbers of committed episcopalians and Presbyterians within the church in 1689 were probably evenly balanced, while the large majority of the Scottish people was prepared to accept whatever system of ecclesiastical government the state agreed to recognise. Initially, William III had hoped to frame a comprehensive settlement in Scotland, one that would have combined both Presbyterian and episcopal elements. In the event, the king agreed to re-establish presbyterianism – in part because he was influenced by the Scottish Presbyterian minister, William Carstares, who had served as a chaplain to William in Holland, but probably more because of the continued loyalty of the majority of the Scottish episcopal hierarchy to the exiled Stewart family. At the same time, William felt little commitment to the Scottish Presbyterian settlement, and there was considerable anger in London over the treatment of the Lowland Scottish episcopal clergy, many of whom were 'rabbled', or violently ejected from their churches and homes by well-organised Presbyterian mobs.

The Presbyterian settlement remained fragile in 1705-6, as, driven by economic and diplomatic pressures, Scotland entered into the negotiations for parliamentary union with England. There was still a substantial episcopalian presence in the Scottish establishment. As late as 1703, according to figures compiled by Carstares, there were 649 Presbyterian ministers, and 164 episcopal ministers in the Church of Scotland, with another 124 parishes vacant. Within the Church of England, many were unhappy with the treatment of the Scottish episcopal clergy, who, despite their Jacobite loyalties, remained for most Anglicans the only ordained clergy in Scotland. For many, the Union negotiations offered an opportunity for a new religious settlement, one that might end the persecution of the Scottish episcopalian and lead to greater uniformity among the established churches of England and Scotland.

The Presbyterian clergy were thus not surprisingly apprehensive over the Union negotiations. To diminish Presbyterian opposition to the Union, the Scottish parliament passed in 1706 the Act of Security, confirming the Presbyterian settlement. Despite some opposition from Church of England bishops in the House of Lords, the Scottish Act of Security was inserted into the Act of Union of 1707, along with a similar guarantee for the preservation of the Anglican settlement in the English establishment. For Scottish Presbyterians, the Act of Security meant that the church courts would have the power to suppress the remnants of episcopalianism, and organise the whole of Scotland's population under Presbyterian pastoral care and discipline.

But the Act of Security and the Presbyterian hopes of religious uniformity were soon challenged. In 1709, two years after the passing of the Union, James Greenshields, an episcopalian minister who had been ordained in 1690 and had held curacies for some years in Ulster, returned to his native Scotland and began officiating in Edinburgh, using the Anglican *Book of Common Prayer* in his services. He was summoned before the presbytery of Edinburgh which ordered him to desist, but he refused to recognise its authority. The presbytery then turned to the city magistrates, who had him arrested and imprisoned. Greenshields appealed to the court of session, the supreme civil court in Scotland, arguing, among other things, that the same liberty of worship granted to Presbyterian ministers in Ireland should be allowed to episcopal clergy in Scotland. The court of session refused his petition, though Greenshields was released from prison after several months of confinement. He appealed to the British House of Lords, which agreed to hear the appeal and which in March 1711 reversed the court of session decision. Greenshields was now permitted to conduct worship with the *Book of Common Prayer*, while the magistrates had to pay damages and costs. This successful appeal to the House of Lords in an ecclesiastical case established the House of Lords as the supreme court in Scottish ecclesiastical as well as civil matters. It was also probably a breach of the Treaty of Union, and aroused considerable resentment among the Scottish Presbyterians.

Following the Greenshields decision, the Union parliament passed two acts affecting the Presbyterian settlement in Scotland, which taken together seemed to point towards the restoration of episcopacy in the Scottish church. Both these acts were passed with no attempt to consult representatives of the Church of Scotland, and against strenuous opposition from within the church. First, in 1712, parliament passed a Toleration Act for Scotland, granting legal protection for episcopalian worship, when conducted according to the *Book of Common Prayer* by clergy ordained by English or Irish bishops. Scottish Presbyterians were angered at being obliged by parliament to permit episcopalian worship, which in effect licensed schism and thwarted the efforts of the national church to secure religious uniformity in the country. They were still more angered over a provision in the act which required Presbyterian and episcopal clergy to subscribe the same oath of allegiance, abjure the Pretender and pray for the queen. In the eyes of the Union parliament, it seemed, there was little difference between the Presbyterian and episcopal clergy in Scotland.

The Toleration Act was soon followed by the Patronage Act of 1712, which restored lay patronage for the selection of ministers in nearly all the parishes of the Church of Scotland. Patronage had long been regarded as a grievance in the Scottish Presbyterian tradition, being associated with the medieval Latin church and ideas of ecclesiastical hierarchy. Since the Reformation, patronage had tended to be revived during periods of episcopal government within the church and abolished during periods of Presbyterian ascendancy. Thus, it had been revived with the restoration of episcopacy in 1660, and abolished with the re-establishment of presbyterianism in 1690. The Patronage Act of 1712 was passed against strenuous protests from the Presbyterians in the Church of Scotland, who viewed it as yet another blow to presbyterianism. There were reasons for Presbyterian fears. Many of the patrons were episcopalian landowners. Further, when the bill was sent from the Commons to the Lords, there was not even a provision that the clergyman presented to a living in the Church of Scotland had to be a Presbyterian, and it was only through the last-minute efforts of the duke of Argyll that such a clause was added. For Presbyterians, the two acts were clear breaches of the religious provisions of the Treaty of Union. Carstares feared they may have been intended to provoke Presbyterian unrest, giving parliament an excuse for further legislation against the Presbyterian settlement. 'These are heavy blows', he wrote of the Toleration and Patronage bills in March 1712. 'I hope we shall not be so unwise as to gratify the expectation and desire of our enemies in being the beginners of disorders' [Story, 336].

In May 1714 the general assembly of the Church of Scotland sent an address to Queen Anne on the religious state of the country, in which it complained of the growing confidence of the episcopal clergy, who were not content to worship according to the *Book of Common Prayer* in their own meeting houses, but were now beginning to do so in parish churches. In Aberdeen, the episcopalians had taken over the Old Church for the conduct of worship, while in some districts the episcopal clergy were maintaining their own ecclesiastical discipline in defiance of that of the Presbyterian establishment. For the general assembly, the two acts of 1712 were rapidly undermining the influence and authority of the Presbyterian establishment.

The moves to change the religious settlement in Scotland were brought to an end with the Jacobite rising of 1715. In that year, while William Carstares, the architect of the Presbyterian settlement, lay dying, the widespread support of the Scottish episcopalians for the Stewart cause ensured the survival of the Presbyterian establishment. An Anglican-dominated parliament found that whatever the attractions of religious uniformity, the Union and the Hanoverian succession would best be secured by maintaining the Presbyterian establishment in Scotland.

After 1715, parliament ceased its interventions in the Scottish religious settlement and allowed the Scottish Presbyterian establishment to consolidate its hold over the country. In the following decades, the Scottish church developed and expanded its parochial institutions for the religious instruction and pastoral care of the Scottish people, building on institutions defined in the sixteenth and seventeenth centuries, but now enjoying the relative peace in which to secure those institutions. The episcopalians declined to a remnant, surviving mainly in the more remote Highlands and islands. The years after 1715 brought the consolidation through the Lowlands of what Tom Devine has termed 'the parish state', with an effective system of regular public worship, pastoral visiting, catechising of the young, kirk-session discipline, parochial education and parish poor relief, which served to define communities. Presbyteries regularly visited the parishes within their jurisdictions, to supervise the parish ministers, review the religious condition of the parishioners and ensure the proper maintenance of church and school buildings. Increasingly, parish populations grew familiar with the Shorter Catechism and the Westminster Directory of Public Worship. These years witnessed the formation of Presbyterian Scotland; they were, in the view of such later Presbyterian divines as Thomas Chalmers, the golden age of the Church of Scotland. With a Scottish parliament no longer sitting in Edinburgh, the Presbyterian church courts, especially the annual meetings of the general assembly, became forums for public discourse.

Following the defeat of the Jacobite rising of 1745, the Presbyterian hold over the country was further strengthened, and there was a steady expansion of Presbyterian worship and discipline in the Highlands and islands. There were, to be sure, problems, largely relating to popular opposition to lay patronage in the church, with sporadic rioting against the settlement of patrons' candidates after about 1730, and some Presbyterian secessions from the established church after 1733. But the Presbyterian seceders did not challenge the existence of the Presbyterian establishment in Scotland. Nor was patronage without its benefits. The relations between the landed classes and the church grew closer, as landowners, ministers and kirk-sessions shared a common aim in preserving social and political order. Under the leadership of William Robertson and the Moderate party from the mid-1760s, the Presbyterian church became one of the major supports of the Union in Scotland. It distanced itself from its covenanting past, emphasising instead a social order based on the subordination of ranks and obedience to the powers that be. Against the general movement among European states toward religious uniformity, the Presbyterian establishment had survived within the predominantly Anglican British state. But that establishment had not received all the support it had looked for from the state. For all the autonomy granted to the Presbyterian establishment, the Toleration Act was not repealed, while the Patronage Act mitigated against the appointment of a clergy zealous for the revival of the covenants.

II

In the early 1830s the relations of church and state in Scotland again came under severe strain, with the beginning of what became known as the 'Ten Years' Conflict' between the established Church of Scotland and the British state. The origins of the 'Ten Years' Conflict' were to be found in the massive social changes of the late eighteenth and early nineteenth centuries. These included a considerable growth in population and an increase of commerce and manufactures. This expanding population, particularly in the manufacturing towns and cities, placed considerable pressure on the parochial structures of the established church. In Glasgow or Edinburgh, parish populations swelled to 10,000 or more, far beyond the capacity of a parish clergyman to provide pastoral care, the parish church to accommodate for public worship, or the systems for parish discipline, education or poor relief to work effectively. As a result, the parish state was breaking down in much of Scotland.

Along with these social changes, there was change in the nature and extent of religious dissent. In 1790 about 10 per cent of the Scottish population attended churches outside the religious establishment. Between 1790 and 1830, however, there was a massive growth in dissent, until probably more than a third of the Scottish population adhered to one of the dissenting denominations. In part, this growth resulted from a new conversionist zeal among the dissenting churches, inspired by the evangelical awakening of the later eighteenth century. While the established church remained largely defined by its historic parochial system, evangelical dissenters were more flexible in their mission to the Scottish people, employing itinerant preachers, holding open-air services, forming congregations in the new population centres growing up at distances from the parish churches. The growth of dissent was also influenced by the reformist and democratic ideas associated with the American and French revolutions, which placed emphasis on individual choice in religious matters. A large and growing portion of the Scottish population chose to step outside of the parish state, with all its communal associations, and instead follow their individual conscience, finding their own voice within a dissenting church. A considerable number of the new evangelical dissenters, moreover, were not Presbyterians, but were Congregationalists or Baptists, with no residual loyalty to the old Presbyterian establishment. A new, religiously pluralist Scotland was emerging. Further, from the late 1790s, many of the older Presbyterian seceders experienced 'new light' on the issue of religious establishments, giving up the teachings of the Westminster Confession of Faith on the alliance of church and state. Instead, they embraced the voluntary principle, holding for the separation of church and state, along the lines of the new North American republic.

The response in the Church of Scotland was to seek to revive the institutions of the parish state in industrialising and urbanising Scotland. From about 1810, several leaders of the established church developed practical programmes for improving the provision of pastoral care, parish education and parish poor relief, especially in over-large urban parishes. They included Stevenson Macgill of Glasgow, Andrew Thomson of Edinburgh, Robert Burns of Paisley, and above all Thomas Chalmers, parish minister in Fife and Glasgow, and from 1828, professor of divinity at the University of Edinburgh. These men embraced the piety and missionary zeal of the evangelical awakening and were passionate in their commitment to reach the lapsed and irreligious masses. Along with the new programmes for the urban parish ministry, they also began pressing for church extension, or the creation of additional established churches. In this, they drew encouragement from the church building grants which parliament had granted to the Church of England in 1815 and 1824. Their aim was to revive the social influence of the established church, as a means to restore the cohesion of a society in the midst of rapid change. While professing a spirit of toleration towards the dissenting population of Scotland, they also hoped that a programme of church reform and extension would draw dissenters back into the establishment. Theirs was the old aim of religious uniformity.

In 1834 the evangelical wing, led by Thomas Chalmers, gained the support of the general assembly of the Church of Scotland and brought the assembly to take two major initiatives, aimed at restoring the parish state of the Presbyterian establishment. First, the assembly acted to limit the unpopular Patronage Act of 1712, by granting the male heads of family in a parish the power to veto a patron's presentation to the ministry of that parish. The assembly hoped this would put the long-standing patronage dispute to rest, and now create a popular national church. Some began embracing again the language of the covenants, calling for a godly commonwealth. Second, the assembly began a national church extension campaign, aimed at erecting hundreds of new parish churches and schools. The building of new parish churches, combined with the return of the seceder churches to the established fold, would greatly multiply the number of parishes, until the whole population of Scotland was organised into small, close-knit parish communities. The established church would revive its control of education, poor relief and the social order. Presbyterian leaders envisaged the church extension campaign as a co-operative venture between church and state, with members of the church raising money to build new churches and schools, and the state providing permanent endowments, to help pay the salaries of the clergy and schoolmasters. It was the responsibility of the British state, they argued, to ensure that the size of the established church in Scotland was commensurate with the size of the Scottish population. The British state, they believed, should assist in achieving the Presbyterian commonwealth. During the next five years, the church extensionists built, through private contributions, nearly 200 new parish churches, many in impoverished urban districts. These years also witnessed a revival within the established church, with giving for home and overseas mission activity increasing fourteen-fold. One of the Presbyterian secession denominations, the Original Burgher Synod, reunited with the established church in 1839, raising hopes that other dissenting bodies would also return.

But in its larger aims, the Church of Scotland was disappointed. The negotiations with the government for a parliamentary grant for endowments for the new churches proved unsuccessful. The majority of dissenters in Scotland, led by the Congregationalists, organised widespread resistance to any state endowment grant, insisting that the godly commonwealth envisaged by the church extensionists would threaten their civil rights. The more representative, post-1832 parliament could not ignore such arguments, especially coming from a large and well-organised part of the Scottish nation. In 1838 the government of Lord Melbourne announced that it would not provide additional grants of public money to endow new churches. For leaders in the established church, the state's refusal to provide grants for church extension was a great betrayal of the Scottish people, a thwarting of the effort to revive the ideal of a covenanted nation, under the guidance of a popular church. For leaders of the state, on the other hand, church extension ultimately represented a threat to the civil rights of dissenters, an attack on the emerging culture of religious pluralism, and a challenge to liberal society.

The distrust engendered by the controversy over church extension, meanwhile, had contributed to a further conflict, this one concerning patronage and the church's Veto Act. In a series of legal judgements beginning in 1838, the civil courts found the church's Veto Act to be an illegal encroachment on the civil rights of patrons and their candidates in appointments to church vacancies. The church courts, however, refused to recognise the authority of the civil courts in matters of ecclesiastical appointments. Scottish church leaders now turned to parliament for a legislative solution. But neither the Whig nor Tory parties in parliament was prepared to support legislation that would give the Church of Scotland the freedom from civil control in church appointments that it asked. Politicians suspected that Scottish church leaders were ambitious for power, and believed that their aspirations for the godly commonwealth and religious uniformity had to be curbed in the interest of preserving civil liberties and social harmony. The national church would need to be brought under civil control in the new, more religiously pluralist society. In 1843 the conflict between state and church culminated in the Disruption of the Church of Scotland, as over a third of the more zealous Presbyterian clergy and nearly half the lay membership left the establishment to form the Free Church of Scotland. With the Disruption, the Church of Scotland became a minority establishment. Its parish structures gradually ceased to be the main providers of social services, and its ecclesiastical courts ceased to be forums for debates on national issues. The parish state was gradually dismantled. For some, the Disruption was the result of the insensitivity of a predominantly Anglican British State to Scotland's Presbyterian religious settlement, and the unwillingness on the part of parliament to recognise any institutions outside its control. It must be observed, however, that the people of Scotland were divided over the church extension and patronage questions, and a more pluralist, urbanised society was breaking down the structures of the established church and parish state well before the Disruption gave those structures such a shake. It is significant that there was no call within the new Free Church for a repeal of the Act of Union.

III

In the aftermath of the Great War of 1914-1918, there was a further effort to restore the authority of the Presbyterian establishment in Scotland. The war had, for many, demonstrated the value of national unity, and had raised hopes that national unity would be preserved in the post-war era, providing the basis for social reconstruction. Leaders of the Scottish Presbyterian leaders naturally wished to participate in the work of reconstruction. Some went further, and hoped that the national church might take the lead. They drew encouragement from the movement for Presbyterian church union, which promised to restore the unity and social influence of the national Church of Scotland after decades of fragmentation and denominational strife.

The Presbyterian church union movement in Scotland had begun in the 1890s. The Presbyterian churches had grown weary of the denominational strife and ecclesiastical controversy that had characterised so much of the nineteenth century, and especially the decades after the Disruption. There was a new commitment in all the Presbyterian churches, established and non-established, to contributing to social improvement. Under the influence of the trans-Atlantic 'social gospel' movement, Presbyterian leaders in all the Scottish denominations worked to reconcile the social classes, improve housing conditions, and ensure more generous social welfare provision. There was a growing feeling that the Presbyterian churches would have a far greater social influence if they could end their divisions and work closely with the civil authorities. In 1900 the two largest non-established Presbyterian churches, the Free Church and the United Presbyterians, joined to form the United Free Church. In 1908 the United Free Church began formal union discussions with the established Church of Scotland. During the Great War, the United Free Church and the Church of Scotland co-operated in holding conferences and issuing reports on social issues, with the aim of working closely with the British state in the work of post-war reconstruction. The nation should 'covenant together' as of old, proclaimed Professor W.P. Paterson, moderator of the general assembly of the Church of Scotland, in his closing address at the assembly of May 1919. That same assembly gave a hero's welcome to Field Marshal Sir Douglas Haig, an elder in the Church of Scotland and the architect of victory on the western front. Here was a potent symbol of a new triumphalist alliance of Scotland's national church and British state.

In the 1920s a west of Scotland Presbyterian minister, John White of the Barony Church, Glasgow, emerged as the leading figure in the Church of Scotland. A proponent of the 'social gospel' in his pre-war ministry, White had also served with courage for over a year at the western front as a chaplain with the Cameronians, and had seen action at the Somme. After the war, his thought moved in a conservative direction. He hoped to see a united Church of Scotland, now in close alliance with the British state, working to restore a Christian commonwealth in Scotland, in which the church would once again become the centre of civic as well as religious life, influencing social policy at the national level, and defining the social ethic at the parish level. Under White's leadership, the church union movement gained the support of the Unionist government at Westminster, which proved vital in getting legislation through parliament that smoothed the way to Scottish Presbyterian reunion. The leaders of the United Free Church insisted that parliament must recognise the spiritual independence of the established Church of Scotland as a condition for church union. Representatives of the United Free Church and Church of Scotland together drafted a set of nine Articles Declaratory, as a new constitution for the united church. The key article was the fourth, which proclaimed that the church was 'subject to no civil authority ... in all matters of doctrine, worship, government and discipline'. Parliament had refused to accept such a claim in 1843, but, in 1921, parliament gave the articles statutory approval. Four years later, in 1925, parliament passed an act commuting the teinds into a capital sum and also giving the church the freedom to create new parish churches without the approval of parliament.

In October 1929 the Church of Scotland and the United Free Church came together in an incorporating union. The overwhelming majority of Presbyterians were now united in a single national church. John White became the first moderator of the general assembly of the united Church of Scotland, and he was the man of the hour. As soon as the union was completed, White led the church in a campaign to reassert its social influence and authority. In 1930 the church initiated the Forward Movement. It appointed twelve commissions of experts to investigate different aspects of social policy, publishing their reports in early 1931 under the title of *The Call to the Church*. There was a major conference in Glasgow in October 1931, bringing together some 2,500 delegates, and this was followed by twelve 'Missions to the Kingdom' conducted throughout Scotland, aimed at reclaiming the nation for the established church. In 1933, White announced the beginning of a new church extension campaign, aimed at reviving the parish system for the pastoral supervision of the nation. The church called for the building of scores of new churches, and also church halls, which were to become centres of community life. The slogan for the campaign was 'the church in the midst'. There would be an effort to restore the idea of a Presbyterian commonwealth, with a close alliance of church and state. Special attention was given to the new housing areas being developed on the peripheries of the older cities. White meant to revive the church extension campaign of the 1830s, and he was compared to Thomas Chalmers. Where Chalmers's church extension campaign had foundered in large part because of the opposition of dissenters and the lack of co-operation of the state, however, White now faced little opposition from Protestant dissent and he had the support of the state.

The main obstacle to the campaign to revive the Presbyterian commonwealth in post-war Scotland was the country's large Roman Catholic population. Where in the early eighteenth century, it was the episcopal church, and in the early nineteenth century, Protestant dissent, now it was Catholicism that stood in the way of the aspirations of the established church. Catholicism had been growing steadily from the early nineteenth century, largely as a result of Irish migrants attracted by employment prospects in industrialising Scotland. The migration had largely ceased by the 1920s, as a result of the collapse of traditional Scottish heavy industry. But there was now a large Catholic population, some 600,000, located largely in the west of Scotland, and this population had no desire to be part of a revived Presbyterian commonwealth organised around the parochial structures of the reunited national Church of Scotland.

In 1922, with the Presbyterian church union moving towards completion, the general assembly of the Church of Scotland, in response to petitions from church courts in the west of Scotland, appointed a special committee to investigate the issue of Irish immigration. That committee's report to the general assembly of 1923 was vitriolic in its denunciations of Roman Catholics of Irish parentage living in the west of Scotland, and it called for immediate state action to deal with this 'menace'. During the next six years, under John White's leadership, the Church and Nation Committee organised and led a national Presbyterian campaign, calling for the state to legislate for the restriction of immigration from the newly formed Irish Free State and for the deportation of much of the Irish-born population residing in Scotland. The Presbyterian churches proclaimed the campaign to be primarily one of preserving the purity of the Scottish race from pollution by an 'inferior race' of Catholics of Irish ethnic background. The rhetoric was bitter. The Catholics were non-Protestant and therefore non-national; they took jobs from native Scots and they seduced Scottish women into Catholic marriages; they were outside the covenant, and must be either marginalised or expelled. White hoped to be able to announce at the first general assembly of the united Church of Scotland in 1929 that the government would be responding to the church's demands and introducing legislation to reduce the size of the Catholic population. In this, however, he and his supporters were disappointed. Despite numerous Presbyterian deputations, petitions and reports on the subject, the Unionist government declined to take legislative action. The united Church of Scotland continued its campaign after 1929, seeking to make Catholics economic scapegoats in a nation suffering the effects of world depression. But without encouragement from the state, the campaign waned from the mid-1930s, and in 1938, it was brought to a close. The British state had declined to co-operate with a revived Presbyterian church in joint action directed against the Catholic population in Scotland. That population remained, its civil rights protected. By the later 1930s the movement to revive the Presbyterian commonwealth was waning. The Forward Movement and the church extension campaign had failed to mobilise the nation behind the idea of a revived parochial establishment. There was no revival of an authoritative national church or of a national religion in Scotland, though by the later 1930s, there were signs of a revival of the Church of Scotland as a Christian church, witnessing for spiritual and moral values against the rise of totalitarian systems on the continent.

IV

At the Union of 1707, the British state had done something unusual. It had agreed to the establishment of the Anglican church in one part of the state, and the establishment of the Presbyterian church in another. It was a decision rooted in considerations of political expediency. The predominantly Anglican British parliament, to be sure, initially granted only a grudging acceptance of the Presbyterian Church of Scotland, and it may well have moved after 1712 toward restoring episcopacy – had not the episcopalians forfeited such support by their continued loyalty to the Stewarts. But after 1715, the parliamentary state co-operated with the Presbyterian church for the maintenance of a Christian social order in Scotland, and encouraged the Church of Scotland in its positive work of providing pastoral care, religious observances and religious and moral instruction to the Scottish people.

The British parliamentary state, however, also acted at certain periods to curb the church's aspirations to achieve religious uniformity in Scotland, in the interest of protecting certain religious minorities. In this, its policies in Scotland mirrored its policies in England and Ireland, where there was also a steady movement towards toleration of religious minorities. The Toleration Act, forced on Scotland in 1712 by the predominantly Anglican parliament, was probably viewed by many of its Anglican supporters as preparing the way for the establishment of episcopacy in the Church of Scotland. But the broad policy of toleration for Protestants continued even after the Jacobite rising of 1715 brought an effective end to the prospect of an episcopal establishment in Scotland. This toleration was later expanded to include other Dissenting communities as they emerged and found their political voice. In the 1830s parliament declined to support a church extension campaign that Protestant Dissenters viewed as a threat to their basic civil liberties. In the 1930s parliament declined to support legislation called for by the church against the Catholic community in Scotland.

In these three episodes, the British state acted as an independent, reasonably objective force, restraining the national church's drive for religious uniformity and a comprehensive authority. There was a continued tension between the Scottish national church and the British state, and a rough balance was struck. In all of this, it must be said, the Church of Scotland was acting according to its mission as a national church. It is the role of a national church to strive to expand its pastoral care and religious instruction to the whole population, to seek the conversion of all. The church would not be true to its mission if it did less. It believed it was the true church within the realm of Scotland and that it had a responsibility under God to seek to draw the whole of Scotland's population into its communion. But the British state had a responsibility to preserve the civil rights of all its subjects, including religious minorities, and from the early eighteenth century, it increasingly came to fulfil this responsibility, curbing the drive of the national Church of Scotland for religious uniformity. Significantly, the church broadly accepted this situation. Although thwarted in its ambitions by the state, the church never pressed for the repeal of the Union. It benefited too much in its mission from the Union and the empire. The great figures in the history of the Church of Scotland – William Carstares, Thomas Chalmers and John White – were all staunch supporters of the Union, and while frustrated in their larger ecclesiastical aims, they never questioned the continuance of the Union.

Further Reading:
C. G. Brown, *Religion and Society in Scotland since 1707* (Edinburgh, 1997); S. J. Brown, *Thomas Chalmers and the Godly Commonwealth in Scotland* (Oxford, 1982); S. J. Brown, '"Outside the Covenant": The Scottish Presbyterian Churches and Irish Immigration, 1922-1938', *Innes Review*, 42 (1991), 19-45; S. J. Brown, 'The Campaign for the Christian Commonwealth in Scotland, 1919-1939', in *Crown and Mitre*, ed. W. M. Jacob and N. Yates (Woodbridge, 1993), 203-22; T. M. Devine, *The Scottish Nation 1700-2000* (London, 1999); A. Muir, *John White* (London, 1958); R. H. Story, *William Carstares: A Character and Career of the Revolutionary Epoch (1649-1715)* (London, 1874).

9

Cultural Independence and Political Devolution in Wales

KEITH ROBBINS

No discussion of 'Sovereignty, Devolution and Independence' within 'the Isles' would be complete without a consideration of Wales. Yet it is not an easy task to do so. Arguably, it is only in the last half of the twentieth century that Wales appears to occupy a significant place in this matter. Indeed, from one perspective, what is remarkable is that it should have a place in this discussion at all. Other contributors to this volume, whether speaking of Scotland, Ireland, the North American Colonies or the 'British Dominions' all have complex constitutional pasts, with their separate parliamentary pedigrees to examine at different points in time. It is in such a context that Wales appears almost anonymous. The assembly (not parliament) which has now been set up in Cardiff cannot be meaningfully said to have had a predecessor. The fact, too, that its establishment was only carried by a very small majority in a referendum - in which approximately half of the electorate did not trouble to vote - is a further illustration of ambiguity. The absence of a Welsh parliament naturally reflects the history of Wales and a lengthy time-frame - though it can only be sketchily treated - is required in order to shed light on the paradox suggested by the title of this paper. It is that emphasis, rather than an analysis of events in the 1990s, which characterises this contribution.

I

There was an aspiration to create a parliament, however we interpret the term, to be held at Machynlleth in mid-Wales, at the time of Owain Glyndwr's revolt at the beginning of the fifteenth century. In itself that would have been a novelty. Although individual Welsh princes in previous centuries had aspired to a degree of overlordship, they had not been able to achieve it completely or permanently. The Anglo-Norman invasions had produced a patchwork of jurisdictions and further complicated the 'Welsh question'. From an English perspective Wales was remote and inhospitable. The Statute of Rhuddlan (1284) set the seal on Edward I's comprehensive conquest and destroyed the infrastructure of a Welsh polity. The magnificent castles signified subjection. Divided between 'Wallia Pura' and the March, Wales lacked the military strength and internal coherence to achieve lasting independence. The idea of a parliament died with the failure of the rebellion. Glyndwr himself, however, was never captured and retained a mythic appeal in Wales over subsequent centuries. Penal laws reinforced English control. Some hopes lingered that the Welsh (the 'true Britons') would somehow regain either independence or even contrive to assert their supremacy in 'Britain'. The reality was that neither the Welsh nor the Scots could penetrate far beyond their frontiers, making England, in the eyes of Norman Davies, one of the safest locations in the world.

    The advent of Henry Tudor (some of whose ancestors had fought with Glyndwr) to the English throne brought an unexpected but prophetically satisfying twist to the story. Here was an English monarch who had the prudence to call his eldest son Arthur. It was, however, his second son, Henry who succeeded and who in a series of acts (1536-43) effectively brought about the union of England and Wales. If what Thomas Cromwell achieved was a sovereign state in a new sense, Wales joined that state more or less contemporaneously with its inception. The Marcher lordships were dissolved and four new counties were created to add to the six already in existence. Each was represented in the House of Commons. English law and administration was established and the English language became officially paramount, though the subsequent translation of the Bible into Welsh, an aid to the consolidation of the Reformation in Wales, was a major factor in maintaining the Welsh language. The supremacy of England in this relationship was incontestable, though penal laws against the Welsh, which had often in any event ceased to be used, were revoked. This process of incorporation - which paradoxically entailed formalising the English-Welsh border - occurred before Wales had achieved what we might call the scaffolding of statehood.

All that is boldly put. For present purposes the essential point is that sufficient Welsh gentry were to hand to make the system work. There was no rebellion in Tudor Wales. Outnumbered by English MPs though they inevitably were, Welsh MPs played their part in the evolving aspirations and conventions of the English parliament. The Welsh ancestry of the Tudors suggested that now the Welsh and the English should be equal in all things. An emphasis on a Welsh/British consciousness could still be combined with unqualified loyalty to the regime and the unitary state. One of that state's key men, Robert Cecil, investigated his Welsh pedigree and took an interest in Welsh antiquities. In London, the 'Welsh Wizard', John Dee, urged Elizabeth I to claim the overseas 'British Empire' which King Arthur and Prince Madoc had obligingly bequeathed her. In Snowdonia, however, heroic ancestral fights against the English were still revered. No sixteenth-century Welsh writer, it seems, contributed to the literature on the political union of Britain. When it appeared imminent, the prospect of a Scottish succession to the throne of England did not initially excite Welsh observers, the view being taken that the people of the Dominion of Wales were 'more able to mainteyne a regal estate than be the Scottes'. Eventually, however, it was found that the accession of James VI and I was also a fulfilment of Merlin's prophecy. A Welsh translation of James's *Basilikon Doron* laid stress on the Stuart descent from Owen Tudor.

In the seventeenth-century War of Three Kingdoms a mere principality could not be other than a junior player. Charles I was substantially able to transfer to himself that affection for the crown which had spilled over in Wales from the Tudors to the Stuarts. Welsh gentry neither at Westminster nor at home wished to give way to 'base men'. At this juncture, only a small minority of Welshmen were committed to radical Puritanism and parliamentary liberty. Such Welsh parliamentarians who did oppose the king had no wish to abolish monarchy but only to curtail its abuse of authority. In the wars themselves Wales remained largely royalist, though individuals showed a marked ability to detect the way the wind was blowing. It was a civil war in Wales which replicated, to varying degree, the balance of forces beyond its borders. It was not a separate affair which could have had a separate Welsh outcome. There would be winners and losers in Wales, but the struggle would be resolved elsewhere. The MP for the Cardigan Boroughs was one of those who signed the king's death warrant. It is reasonable to suppose however that the great majority of Welshmen were horrified by his death. The *Eikon Basilike* was swiftly translated into Welsh. The Rump Parliament did not gain the support of the county community in Wales. During the protectorate years, under the new constitution, each Welsh county, except Merioneth, was given two seats, and the boroughs of Cardiff and Haverfordwest one each. Fearful of insurrection, Cromwell relied on a key group of men, some of whom had risen from obscurity, to keep control but he was not able to establish a generally acceptable form of government. The restoration seems to have been generally welcomed. Displaced gentry resumed what they regarded as their rightful places - at Westminster no less than in their localities.

II

Taking a broad sweep, we may suggest that after 1660 a pattern of Welsh parliamentary participation was re-established and endured without substantial amendment for some two centuries. Some kind of loose 'Welsh interest' can be identified under the early Stuarts but it did not reappear after 1660. When MPs from Scotland came to Westminster they did not find an organised 'Welsh party' but rather individuals who voted as they saw fit. Welsh MPs did not invariably find the House of Commons the most attractive of venues when they came up to London, and some did not come with any great regularity. Some individuals, particularly lawyers, rose to great heights, though, if Judge Jeffreys is accounted a Welshman, they were not invariably liked. Some showed themselves particularly susceptible to venality, though that was not a distinctively Welsh characteristic. There were few active supporters of James II in 1688. Old court favourites made way for new ones under William and Anne. The circle of country gentlemen from whom Welsh MPs were drawn seems to have narrowed even further at this time. Particular families dominated their 'neighbourhoods', a term they interpreted generously. They formed an elite which had come to regard itself, through patterns of education, intermarriage with English families and commercial partnerships as thoroughly 'Anglo-Welsh' in orientation. Local feuds and office-holding rivalries formed the stuff of Welsh politics and party labels can be only loosely attached. Some historians see Welsh politics at this time as being largely untroubled by the ideological principles displayed in England. At the same time, for those interested, news began to travel more quickly and make it possible to hear about parliamentary matters even in remote Welsh places. On the whole, if party labels are accepted, Wales was predominantly a Tory country, though divisions between Jacobites and Hanoverian supporters allowed some well-financed Whigs to make headway. It was not until 1727 that there were more Whigs than Tories returned for Wales. Under the Hanoverians official assistance at elections and the bestowal of patronage from outside steadily ensured a Whig ascendancy, though of course that was not a specifically Welsh phenomenon.

The electoral manoeuvres of eighteenth-century Wales cannot be pursued in more detail here. Peter Thomas concludes that the system had fallen into the hands of an ever smaller group of powerful landowners. Electoral alignments frequently bore little relation to national politics at Westminster - though, again, this need not be thought an exclusively Welsh phenomenon. Such distinctive character as Welsh politics possessed, he suggests, comes from the social structure of Wales rather than from any sense of a cohesive national identity. It also appears to be the case that such impetus as there was towards parliamentary reform in the 1780s came from outside Wales and it was only in Caernarfonshire and Denbighshire that reform committees were established. Indeed, throughout the eighteenth century it might be said that at the parliamentary level the Anglo-Welsh border had little or no significance. Sir Watkin Williams-Wynne, with his seat at Wynnstay, sometimes naughtily referred to as 'the Prince of Wales', was one of the leading British Tories under the first two Georges, though he may perhaps be more accurately regarded as an archetypal politician who sat in 'the country interest'. He was indubitably Welsh. His grandfather, Sir William Williams, the founder of the north-east Wales dynasty, had become Speaker of the House of Commons in 1681. Sir Watkin could play a major role, it was said, in the politics of ten counties - on both sides of an Anglo-

Robbins

Welsh border that had little political significance for him. It was in Staffordshire that his judiciously named horse 'Old England' came in first in his presence at a race meeting organised by the Staffordshire Tories. Sir John Phillips, a Pembrokeshire baronet and notable figure, was another Welsh politician whose career and interests spanned the border with ease.

It is only if the analysis is confined to this level, however, that appearance could be mistaken for reality. Eighteenth-century Wales was not just 'old England'. No visitor could be unaware of the still continuing vitality of the language and the culture which it nourished. The contentious assumption that only English could be the language of the future had not yet taken hold. It was true that some old traditions were dying but other opportunities, made possible by printing, were opening up. Edward Lhuyd, the distinguished Welsh keeper of the Ashmolean museum in Oxford had stimulated a growing interest in the diversity of Britain. It was also the case, by later in the eighteenth century that economic and industrial changes - the exploitation of minerals - were already evident. Wales was indeed different, whether one relished or despised it, but the notion that it might constitute some kind of independent political entity with a parliament of its own scarcely surfaced. Scotland, after all, had forfeited its parliament in an Anglo-Scottish Union which appeared to consolidate Great Britain at last. Any Welsh parliamentary proponent would first have had to decide its location - and no city presented itself. Such boroughs and towns as Wales possessed were small indeed. North and Mid-Wales were substantially serviced from Liverpool, Chester and Shrewsbury, while small towns in the south and west like Carmarthen or Cardiff might be regarded as little more than satellites of Bristol. The afore-mentioned Sir John Philipps was significantly an MP for Carmarthen and an MP for Bristol. There was no university in Wales. It was Jesus College, Oxford (attended by Sir Watkin) and the London inns of court which gave Welshmen, clergymen included, their higher learning. In short, at this level, well-established roles and networks looked secure. One would look in vain to detect any significant impact on Welsh representation in parliament and in expectations of and attitudes towards Westminster arising from the economically-determined changes that were taking place in Welsh society. The 1832 Reform Act brought only a modest increase in the size of the small Welsh electorate. Elections, in any event, remained something to be avoided if possible. Particular families - Cawdor, Dynevor, Vaughan, Mostyn, Bulkeley and others - remained strongly in evidence, though some 'new' candidates began to come from industrial or commercial families in such constituencies as Merthyr and Swansea. Their interests did not invariably coincide with those of large landowners. Three Sir Watkin Williams-Wynnes, to give examples of survival, represented Denbighshire between 1796 and 1885.

III

It is the general election of 1868 which is normally regarded as marking the end of 'old politics' in Wales. The preceding decades had seen some turmoil. The population of Wales passed the million mark for the first time in the 1841 census - a 78 per cent increase since 1801. Merthyr Tydfil, with 46,000 people in 1851, suddenly became the largest community in Wales, more than double its nearest rival, Swansea. Merthyr had seen an insurrection in 1831 and Newport had its Chartist rising in 1839. From a London perspective, though not only from a London perspective, this new urban Wales was a raw and volatile place. Not that the countryside was quiet. The appearance of the lady 'Rebecca' and the riots that followed in South-West Wales after 1839 revealed a disturbed and disturbing world which was equally puzzling to Queen Victoria and Sir Robert Peel. Railway-building (which focused on routes across Wales to England and Ireland rather than within Wales itself) made Wales seem both closer to Westminster but at the same time more distant in its modes and mentalities. Its industrial development produced new perspectives at both ends of the Great Western Railway. Parts of Wales, perhaps even the whole of Wales, could no longer be thought of as a perpetually peripheral principality. It remained to be seen what political significance this might have. The world needed Welsh coal and slates - as was evident in the growth of the south-eastern and even north-western ports in Wales.

Such changes, of course, were not confined to Wales and in turn generated demands for 'Reform'. However, it does not appear that Wales provided the spark or took the lead in the multifarious reforming movements in Britain in the first half of the nineteenth century. Both the Birmingham Political Union and the London Working Mens' Association established 'offshoots' in industrial Wales. Likewise, later, Chartist emissaries came to Wales to spread the cause. It took some time for the Anti-Corn Law League to make an impact in Wales. The Peace Society was disappointed by the lack of interest in Wales and its missions were initially disappointing. It has been noted that Wales was even slower to embrace the Scottish-inspired temperance movement than England. The first two temperance societies for Welshmen were not in Wales at all but in Liverpool and Manchester. It is ironic, therefore, that reforming enthusiasms which, later in the century, and long afterwards, came to be thought 'typically' Welsh, were substantially 'imports'

IV

Perhaps part of the reason lies in what still made Wales substantially different within the United Kingdom of Great Britain and Ireland to which it anonymously belonged: language. It was, for example, only when a Welsh-speaking Welshman from Manchester took the anti-corn law crusade to North Wales that considerable support for the cause was forthcoming. Again, the peace cause was thought to suffer because the Quakers of Neath, where the only auxiliary of the London Peace Society existed, were (damningly) thought 'essentially English in outlook'. Chartists in England had to be told that the eloquence of their emissaries was to little avail since their audiences in Wales could not understand them. They needed a Welsh 'minder' on hand. In time, through translations and digests in the burgeoning Welsh-language periodical literature, the language-gap was bridged, but it was a reality. But how to deal with language raised the most emotional and difficult of issues and gave Welsh political culture its distinctive flavour. There were, literally, two languages of reform and they complicated every question. Insofar as Wales was, initially, on the receiving end of English-based reforming movements it was not because it had no grievances and was supine. It was rather because all the urges to improvement touched a raw linguistic nerve. The 1847 report of the commissioners examining education in Wales was the classic instance. No reader of the report could possibly suppose that Wales was England, but would that Wales, in future, have to express itself through English? Religion, with which language was also intimately bound up, gave Wales another and different emotional focus. With the exception on the calvinistic Methodists, largely with Welsh-speaking congregations, all other Welsh religious bodies had their counterparts in England. The issue of disestablishment was an issue across Britain. Nonconformity was a minority in England. It was a majority in Wales. In England and Wales a campaign might succeed. In England on its own, a campaign by English nonconformists would fail. In Wales a campaign on its own might succeed. So, during decades of struggle, Welsh nonconformists decided to go it alone. It would be necessary to extract a major symbolic success from the Westminster parliament.

And that is why the 1868 outcome was so significant. The ambition was expressed in the election address of Henry Richard, a Liberal victor at Merthyr, who claimed that the landed proprietors, in alliance with the church, assailed again and again in the House of Commons though they had been had never stood up to defend his calumniated countrymen. 'We are the Welsh people,' he declared 'not you' [Morgan (1970), v]. Wales was 'ours' and its feelings, principles and sentiments would at last have a place in the House of Commons. This was language which echoed across the counties and met a powerful response. The Liberal triumph woke the spirit of mountains and shattered the political power of landlordism. In detail, Lloyd George's 1910 rhetorical flourish needs modification, but the substance is correct. It is also correct that the Welsh result was not out of line but in one sense simply another illustration of a general British outcome. Nevertheless, it ushered in an era of Liberal dominance in Welsh parliamentary representation (and in local government) that substantially lasted until the First World War.

Even so, it was an ambivalent dominance, or perhaps one should say that it was a further expression of that ambivalence which history, geography and language had bequeathed inescapably to Wales. It was still a country without a capital city though the civic grandeur expressed by early twentieth-century Cardiff laid a claim that other parts of Wales were reluctant to endorse, suspecting that this monstrous urban newcomer was not really Welsh at all. Wales now had a national institution - the University of Wales - formed of the federation of the three university colleges established in the 1870s and 1880s. A national library and a national museum were in the offing. These were all the national symbols of Liberal Wales - but the uncertainty surrounding their implications reflected the ambiguity of their origins. They were, to greater or lesser degree, a product of London-Wales. Gwynn Williams has noted that, since the eighteenth century, successive groups of London Welshmen took the lead in Wales itself. Certainly, Anglesey-born Sir Hugh Owen, a poor law commissioner at Somerset House, falls into this category. A man of demonic energy, what really engaged his enthusiasm was the idea of a university for Wales. The college which began in Aberystwyth in 1872 owed a great deal to him. His circle shared the conviction, however, that anything which might separate the inhabitants of the principality from the great English community would prove a great evil. The role of men like Owen as 'go-betweens' was critical. Even Henry Richard, 'spokesman for Wales' falls into this 'go-between' category. Born near Lampeter, in a county in which at that time only a small proportion of the population spoke English (three-quarters of Cardiganshire's population was still monoglot Welsh at the time of the first language census of 1891) he had made his career both as a nonconformist minister and then secretary of the Peace Society in London. He proclaimed the Welsh nation in Merthyr but when he attended the House of Commons he did so in a London which had become his home city. The expansion of the press in Wales brought a closer acquaintance with the politics of Westminster at a popular level than had probably ever been the case before. The historian of the nineteenth-century press in Wales stresses that the newspaper market was not confined to titles edited, printed and published within Wales. By 1852, the London *Times* could reach Carmarthen on the evening of the day of publication. Liverpool and Manchester newspapers employed Welsh correspondents. The *Liverpool Mercury* had become the most widely read daily newspaper on the Lleyn peninsula by 1870. Ministerial editors of Welsh-language denominational journals also made a point of reading both the secular and religious press published in England so as not to be ignorant of the affairs of the world.

V

As far as the affairs of Wales in parliament were concerned the Welsh Liberals succeeded in establishing, in a way that was novel, that Wales was different and that in certain respects it required separate legislative provision. The long-drawn-out campaign in Wales for the disestablishment of the Church of England achieved success in parliament in 1914. Although it had taken a long time, this achievement demonstrated that an outcome could be delivered which satisfied the Welsh majority. The church issue, however, was only one of a number of matters where distinctive Welsh needs were pressed - concerning land tenure, secondary education and other matters - and were substantially satisfied. Such legislation had not been easily accomplished because Welsh Liberals found that their influence was greatest within the British Liberal party when that party was least effective and able to deliver the legislation they desired but in the end it existed. This peaceful and constitutional change showed what could be done by a 'Welsh parliamentary party' that gave a coherence of objective to 'Wales at Westminster' that had not existed before. It also showed that there were non-Welshmen at Westminster who had a sympathetic understanding of what was going on in Wales. Of no one was this more true than of Gladstone himself, though Welsh Liberals experienced his equivocations to the full. His marriage had taken him across the border into Wales for tree-felling and other purposes. And there were lesser figures than Gladstone whose cross-border activity was of great importance. One such was the English Anglican, Etonian and Oxonian, Stuart Rendel, MP for Montgomeryshire from 1880 until 1894, sometimes referred to as the 'Member for Wales'.

It cannot be said, however, that the monarchy made much contribution to this process of mutual understanding. Before she came to the throne, Victoria had indeed spent eleven weeks on the island of Anglesey and she cruised round the Welsh coast with Prince Albert in 1847. During her entire 64-year reign however she spent only seven nights in Wales (compared with seven years in Scotland and seven weeks in Ireland). On her death in 1901, the journal *Y Genedl Gymreig* (*The Welsh Nation*) believed that there had been no greater grief anywhere in the empire than had been expressed in Wales.

The very success of Welsh Liberals at Westminster, however, posed fresh problems for some of them. They had demonstrated that Welsh MPs need not be marginal and their self-confidence grew. So, was serving the needs of Wales to be the limit of their aspiration? The holding of significant office within British government in the nineteenth century had been an Anglo-Scottish duopoly. Why should not Welshmen break into this exclusive preserve? Here was a dilemma which confronted Tom Ellis, 'the forerunner', MP for Merioneth (a constituency where 93.7 per cent spoke Welsh in 1901) from 1886 until his youthful death in 1899. He became Liberal chief whip in 1894 and might confidently have expected major office if the Liberals returned to power in the new century. But was this a betrayal of Wales? A decade or so earlier this attractive product of Aberystwyth and Oxford had been thought of as the potential 'Parnell of Wales'. The Manchester-born David Lloyd George, MP for the Caernarfon Boroughs, experienced the same dilemma, though he seems to have resolved it without undue difficulty. Welsh-speaking and nonconformist (though nonconforming in his nonconformity), and to a later Keynesian eye the epitome of a disagreeable Welshness, he yet felt suffocated by his beloved homeland and yearned, successfully as it turned out, for a role in British and world politics beyond his 'stunted principality'. He became the first, and so far only, prime minister of the United Kingdom whose mother tongue has not been English.

VI

Wales faced England, and parliament was in England, but Wales also faced Ireland. When rural Wales was disturbed, it sometimes seemed to British governments in London that Wales was perhaps another Ireland. Were not both countries 'Celtic'? At the time of 'Rebecca' there were suspicions that the organisers were in contact with agitators elsewhere. In Scotland, the church was being rent in twain, in Ireland there was clamour for repeal of the union and even in secluded Wales there was insurrection. In her letters Rebecca did sometimes refer to oppression suffered at the hands of Saxons and reporters sent to the area claimed to have found bitter distrust or hatred of Englishmen. Its historian however insists that the politics of Rebeccaism did not include nationalism, though the government's reaction to the riots perhaps stimulated it. Nevertheless, there were sufficient similarities to make some suppose that Wales would follow Ireland in demanding 'home rule' and/or the repeal of the union with England. The 1881 Irish Land Act produced demands for the same kind of legislation in Wales. An appeal to 'Celtic solidarity' however had limited appeal outside scholarly realms. In the nineteenth century an Irish presence made itself felt in Wales. Even before the famine, Irish immigrants had settled in the iron-and coal-producing villages of south Wales and elsewhere. Afterwards, their numbers increased substantially. The Irish-born and their descendants came to form a significant proportion of the population in urban centres. Their identification as Catholics (though it was with less than complete success that the church kept this a reality) emphasised their apparently anomalous presence in Protestant Wales. And it has been pointed out that the Catholic church abandoned its 'Welsh district' as a territorial unit by consigning the six counties of north Wales to an English diocese at the very time that nonconformity was fashioning a Wales in its own image. Irishmen were supposed to tend towards drunken violence. Following the Burke and Cavendish murders in Dublin in 1882 there were riots directed against Irishmen in Tredegar. The tensions inherent in these circumstances did not suggest a common Welsh/Irish strategy. While probably most Welsh Liberals could reconcile themselves to Irish home rule they were not its enthusiastic advocates and expressed deep concern for the freedom of conscience of Irish Protestants if it did come about.

Nevertheless, home rule did come onto the Welsh political agenda but, in the event only fitfully, erratically and unsuccessfully. The establishment of county councils, and the consequential transfer of power at a local level, in Kenneth Morgan's judgement, eventually blunted the appeal of the wider objective of Welsh home rule. The unanimity shown by Welsh Liberals on other matters was absent when it came to this subject. In an 1888 debate on a bill to establish a standing committee to consider all bills relating to Wales only eleven Welshmen troubled to vote for it and the proposal failed. Some English MPs, particularly from just over the border, believed that the committee would have nothing to talk about. It was only the language, spoken in their view by an insignificant and illiterate minority (in fact 54.4 per cent in 1891) which made Wales any different from Shropshire. It was not the view of the Englishman who was the MP for Arfon, but the motion failed. In 1907 a Welsh standing committee was established. More fundamentally, when the idea of home rule was pressed it - as it was by the enthusiasts of Cymru Fydd (Young Wales) in the middle 1890s it revealed the fissures in Welsh society. Not only was the Liberal party organisationally divided between northern and southern federations, there were also significant differences of attitude, differences which reflected the economic and social changes which had occurred and were continuing to occur.

Cardiff's MP, representing a great commercial and cosmopolitan town which boasted the largest Liberal association in Wales, spoke against anything which would sever his constituents from their economic relations with the industrial areas of England. In the years just before 1914 the home rule idea revived (in a context, of course, where 'home-rule-all-round' was being floated in some quarters as a way of resolving the Irish impasse). The most active advocate of Welsh home rule was E.T. John, who had made his money as a Middlesbrough iron manufacturer but who had returned to Wales and won East Denbighshire in 1910. He introduced the first ever Welsh Home Rule bill into the Commons in March 1914 but it did not progress beyond the formal first reading. Lloyd George lent it no assistance. It is difficult not to agree with Kenneth Morgan that at this juncture Wales was much more divided by sectional, regional, or class antagonisms than unified by the appeal of autonomy. Then came the Great War in which it was a Welshman who led Britain to victory. That victory was followed by a war in Ireland in which that same Welshman made his final contribution to Celtic solidarity by partitioning Ireland.

VII

The decision to create the national assembly for Wales comes eighty years after the end of the First World War. One might be tempted to believe that it came about because those antagonisms to which Morgan referred have been overcome and that the path not taken for a century after 1868 has at last been followed. In 1966 Gwynfor Evans won the Carmarthen by-election for Plaid Cymru - though in the general election of that year Labour won 32 out of the 36 Welsh seats at Westminster - and took the party's first seat at Westminster. Certainly, it was in the 1960s that there was substantial movement both in internal Welsh politics and in the place of Wales in the British constitutional and administrative structure took place. Until that point the era of Labour dominance in Welsh politics and its brief periods in British government had not resulted in any substantial change in the position of Wales. A devolutionary strand had never been absent from Welsh Labour politics but in the climate of social and economic dislocation in the inter-war period it had been sectional or class solidarity on an all-British basis which had predominated. The struggles over church disestablishment came to seem to belong to a different world. The periodic censuses continued to record the erosion of the Welsh-language community but, for some, personal well-being (even if that meant exile to the motor industries of Birmingham or Oxford) was more important than the survival of the language. In circumstances in which the English resolutely refused sufficiently to see the advantages of socialism, frustration and resentment sometimes boiled over at the minority place which Welsh-majority Labour inevitably occupied within the Westminster parliament.

Plaid Genedlaethol Cymru, founded in 1925, seemed predominantly to be a cultural defence movement only masquerading as a political party. It attracted some intellectuals and literary figures but was under suspicion in some quarters for alleged fascism. Welsh Labour MPs, particularly from mining constituencies, though never homogeneous, gained a reputation for being on the left of the party. Although giving temporary hospitality to Ramsay MacDonald, Welsh MPs were very largely Welsh. The sectional emphasis of Labour as a whole, however, was reinforced by the large number of Welshmen who entered Westminster as MPs for English constituencies. Cardiff-born Mont Follick (Loughborough) was, however, the only one among them to have also been the secretary in Madrid to the exiled sultan of Morocco. It was not until 1947 that a modest regional council of Labour was formed. The following year came a council for Wales, an advisory body. The most prominent Welsh member of the post-war Labour government, Aneurin Bevan, a Welsh MP, had once famously declared that Welsh sheep did not differ from English sheep. Later, he could detect a few differences but not sufficient to warrant diversion from the task of building British socialism. After 1951 creeping territoriality is discernible. The Conservatives gave a hard-pressed minister the additional dignity of being minister of Welsh affairs.

In the background was a 'parliament for Wales' campaign of fitful vitality. The analogy with Scotland began to be pressed more strongly. The first secretary of state for Wales was appointed in 1964 - the first two holders of the post being Welsh speakers. The Conservatives retained the post in 1970 and appointed a Welshman who sat for an English constituency. The Welsh Office based in Cardiff began to give Wales a bureaucratic identity. Labour was in trouble in Wales from which an invigorated Plaid was the beneficiary. There was protest both about its economic policies which were not thought sufficiently attuned to the needs of Wales and, in local government, certain scandals pointed up the perils which could stem from long periods of single-party dominance. Following the Crowther-Kilbrandon royal commission, which reported in 1973, came the proposals embodied in the Scotland and Wales Bill which envisaged devolution for Wales based on an 80-member assembly and the 1979 referendum. In a 59 per cent turnout, only a fifth of voters supported the proposal. The campaign had seen the re-emergence of all of the old fears and antagonisms. The vigorous language campaigning of Cymdeithas yr Iaith (Welsh Language Society) seen in some quarters as a necessary assertion of identity, was found in others to represent unacceptable cultural aggression. It appeared to be the 1890s all over again. The result, even in the north-west where Plaid Cymru had established a firm parliamentary base at Westminster was negative. Whatever else the outcome showed, it revealed that Wales remained a community of communities, each to some extent apprehensive of the other, a picture disguised by an electoral system which had created an illusion, at different times, that Wales was solidly Liberal or solidly Labour. It is the reality of that diversity, made politically effective by a different electoral system, which is now evident, a diversity which the history recounted in this paper might lead one to expect.

Further Reading:
British Consciousness and Identity: The Making of Britain 1533-1707, ed. Brendan Bradshaw and Peter Roberts (Cambridge, 1998); D. Hywel Davies, *The Welsh Nationalist Party 1925-1945: A Call to Nationhood* (Cardiff, 1983); Norman Davies, *The Isles: A History* (Basingstoke, 1999); R.R. Davies, *The Revolt of Owain Glyndwr* (Oxford, 1995); *Politics and Society in Wales 1840-1922: Essays in Honour of Ieuan Gwynedd Jones,* ed. Geraint H. Jenkins and J.B. Smith (Cardiff, 1998); Geraint H. Jenkins, *The Foundations of Modern Wales 1642-1780* (Oxford, 1993); Philip Jenkins, *A History of Modern Wales 1536-1990* (London, 1992); Aled Jones, *Press, Politics and Society: A History of Journalism in Wales* (Cardiff, 1993); David J.V. Jones, *Rebecca's Children: A Study of Rural Society, Crime and Protest* (Oxford, 1989); I.G. Jones, *Mid-Victorian Wales: The Observers and the Observed* (Cardiff, 1992); K.O. Morgan, *Wales in British Politics 1868-1922* (Cardiff, 1970); K.O. Morgan, *Modern Wales: Politics, Places and People* (Cardiff, 1995); *The National Question Again: Welsh Political Identity in the 1980s,* ed. John Osmond (Llandysul, 1985); Keith Robbins, *Nineteenth-Century Britain: Integration and Diversity* (Oxford, 1998); Peter D.G. Thomas, *Politics in Eighteenth-Century Wales* (Oxford, 1998); Rayland Wallace, *Organise! Organise! Organise! A Study of Reform Agitations in Wales 1840-1886* (Cardiff, 1991); J.G. Williams, *The University Movement in Wales* (Cardiff, 1993).

10

Sovereignty and Independence in the Dominions

GED MARTIN

'There shall be a Scottish Parliament' [Himsworth and Munro, 120]. The confident language of the Scotland Act implies that Westminster has engaged in this exercise many times before, and that a tested blueprint from the overseas empire can be applied north of the border. Does this mean that in Scotland, too, the creation of a subordinate legislature will be but a step to complete independence?

Expatriate Scots played a major role in Dominion politics. John A. Macdonald from Glasgow largely designed Canadian Confederation, while the author of the first effective draft of Australia's federal constitution, Andrew Inglis Clark, was the son of a migrant from Kinghorn in Fife. Yet there was a surprising absence of reference to the Scottish example in the formation of overseas constitutions. Until recent times, Scotland seemed satisfied with its status within the United Kingdom, and so offered no model for colonial devolution. Macdonald sought to reassure the people of Quebec when he defended the confederation scheme in 1865, likening the partnership of French- and English-Canadians to the relationship between England and Scotland. It was an 'obligatory' principle of the Act of Union 'that the Scottish law cannot be altered, except for the manifest advantage of the people of Scotland' and only then with 'the sanction of the majority of the Scottish members in Parliament'. Every variant anomaly in Scots law had to be accepted by the English, 'no matter how much it may interfere with the symmetry of the general law of the United Kingdom' [*Confederation Debates*, 30-31].

Since Scotland contributed so little to the development of devolution overseas, we should hesitate before assuming that the Dominions provide the key to the future of the new Scottish parliament. In any case, the overseas commonwealth offers three distinct levels of legislative bodies as possible comparators. Will the Scottish parliament follow Ottawa, Canberra and Wellington, and move towards full national sovereignty? Will it behave like the second tier of provincial and state legislatures within federal constitutions, emulating Ontario or Queensland? Does devolution imply a constant struggle for additional powers, backed by threats of secession? Perhaps a third point of reference may be found in the unicameral and relatively weak provincial councils that fitfully operated within the predominantly unitary constitutions of New Zealand and South Africa. Or should each of these comparisons be dismissed as irrelevant because every legislature operates within its own unique social and political structure?

I

The legislature of the Dominion of Canada's was the first to be formally styled a 'parliament' in the British North America Act of 1867. The term 'Union Parliament' was used, a trifle grudgingly, in the abortive South Africa Act of 1877, but the Australian Commonwealth in 1901 was the second overseas country to receive a specifically named parliament. Notwithstanding the huge emotional pull of the memory of Grattan's Parliament, the Home Rule Bills of 1886 and 1893 referred only to a 'Legislative Body' or 'Irish Legislature'. Only in the Third Home Rule Bill was the term 'Irish Parliament' explicitly adopted. Indeed, the upstart legislature of Newfoundland was flatly warned by the colonial office in 1835 that if it persisted in its 'peculiarity' of referring to itself as 'the Colonial Parliament', its legislation would be systematically vetoed. While it might seem 'a matter of little or no importance by what title a Colonial Legislature thought fit to designate themselves', the imperial authorities refused to 'acquiesce in this deliberate and solemn use of a title' which might imply a claim to powers similar 'to those of the Houses of Peers and Commons in the United Kingdom' ['Government', 595]. In fact, not even the formal title necessarily conferred full parliamentary powers. In 1873, during a major political scandal, Canada's legislators empowered a parliamentary enquiry (so they thought) to take evidence on oath. The crown law officers declared this to be *ultra vires* because the British North America Act limited Ottawa's powers to those already exercised by Westminster. Of course the imperial parliament had the power to pass such a law, but, as it had never done so, no such authority could be exercised in Canada. In short, simply because Ottawa was called a parliament did not mean that it could exercise unfettered parliamentary power.

Yet colonial legislatures aped even the smallest eccentricities of the parliament they were forbidden to emulate. Almost all adopted the medieval format of parallel benches: New South Wales linked them into a horseshoe shape, without any notable addition to political consensus. All were presided over by a Speaker, complete with wig and robes (but not necessarily political neutrality) copied from Westminster. So derivative was the culture that French Canadians addressed the chair as Monsieur l'Orateur. Debates were published in 'Hansard'; the parliamentary dining room in Wellington is still called 'Bellamy's'. Charles Dickens in 1842 described the ceremonial opening of a new session of the Nova Scotia legislature as 'like looking at Westminster through the wrong end of a telescope' [Dickens, 13]. Variations were rare. Canada's legislators refer to all MPs as 'my honourable friend', foes included. Newfoundland alone broke with the tradition that government supporters sat on the Speaker's right, but that was solely because the stove was located to the left of the chair. In Newfoundland, the opposition was literally out in the cold. Queensland in 1922 briefly abolished the ritual of the division lobbies and permitted proxy voting: the government had a majority of one, and he was sick.

Of course, it was convenient for fledgling legislatures to model procedure upon Westminster. Some still do. 'In all cases not provided by the Standing Orders, sessional or other orders or practice of the House, the current practice of Commons House of the Parliament of the United Kingdom of Great Britain and Northern Ireland, shall be followed as far as it can be applied.' So states chapter one of the standing rules and orders of the New South Wales legislative assembly, as updated in 1996. The Cambridge Union took the same decision in 1823, but that did not turn a debating society into a parliament. Yet colonial politicians did not always conduct themselves with senatorial reserve. The Canadian parliament was notorious for heavy drinking: a marathon session to force through temperance legislation in 1878 degenerated into a legendary binge. Yet colonial legislatures took their collective dignity and privileges very seriously, probably because they were often ludicrously small: the assembly of Vancouver Island began in 1856 with seven members who represented just 43 voters. The first legislature of Prince Edward Island consisted of eighteen members who sat for ten days in 1773. They hired a doorkeeper, but on overhearing him refer to his charges as 'a damn queer parliament', they committed him to prison for contempt. The island's population in 1773 was about one thousand. In 1895 the Speaker of the Western Australian lower house appealed for support to the clerk of the House of Commons against the colony's nominated upper house, which had attempted to increase compensation payable to victims of railway accidents. He received the soothing reply that the Speaker at Westminster would have acted in precisely the same way had the Lords similarly misbehaved. At the time, Western Australia had the population of the Norfolk town of Great Yarmouth.

The new Scottish parliament starts life in an era when political institutions are held in less regard, and so prefers to stress its modernity. Moreover, it governs five million people - a population that the leading dominion, Canada, did not achieve until half a century after confederation. Some of its innovations are presentational: after all, the Presiding Officer is only a wigless Speaker. With 129 members, however, it is larger than the Canadian and Australian senates or indeed the parliament of New Zealand and so has the personnel to develop an effective committee system.

Most notably, the Scottish parliament differs from most of its overseas forebears in starting life as a single-chamber legislature. Most colonial legislatures began with two chambers, one of them feebly imitating the House of Lords. New South Wales in 1853 actually considered a semi-hereditary body, to be chosen by an electoral college of colonial baronets. Attempts to design alternatives ran into the problem that bedevils Lords reform in contemporary Britain: Canada's nominated Red Chamber is notoriously weak, Australia's elected senate that in 1975 proved far too strong. Ontario in 1867 led the way towards unicameralism by refusing to have an upper house at all. New Zealand scrapped its legislative council in 1950. Scottish debate has looked more to Scandinavia, where single-chamber parliaments are the norm. At a theoretical level, the 'Claim of Right' culture that informed the campaign for devolution assumes the organic unity of the Scottish people, while in practical terms the adoption of proportional representation provides some of the safeguards against unthinking majorities that have been traditionally expected from a revising chamber. In any case, there is no room at the Holyrood site for a second chamber. Perhaps, in an independent Scotland, the old Royal High School, brooding above on Calton Hill, might be pressed into service as an upper house.

In the first year of the Scottish parliament, there have been occasional echoes of the experience of the overseas commonwealth. The legal challenge to the validity of a bill to abolish hunting is a reminder that mere use of the term 'parliament' does not confer unrestricted powers. And the decision of the Presiding Officer to report leading Scottish newspapers to the press complaints tribunal suggests that it is still dangerous to poke fun at solemn legislators.

II

The fact that Canada and Australia are full members of the world community may suggest that devolution inevitably evolves into complete independence. Much depends on the definition of inevitability: Sydney Smith described thirty years as the political equivalent of eternity. The Dominions did not rush into independence. In fact, they usually found it convenient to avoid posing fundamental issues of sovereignty. In 1908, the Afrikaner chief justice of the Cape quashed a suggestion that the South African colonies might unite by passing concurrent local legislation. It was impossible 'to see how a scheme of union could be carried through without the assistance and intervention of the Imperial Parliament' since it was 'the only Legislature which in theory has the power of legislating for South Africa as a whole' [Hancock and van der Poel, 427]. In 1865, Westminster had passed declaratory legislation, the Colonial Laws Validity Act, reasserting full legislative control over the whole empire. The act however was primarily designed to deal with an obscure judge in South Australia who had invented a doctrine of judicial review which he used to strike down local laws that displeased him. In theory, colonial dependency was becoming an increasingly inappropriate status for rising new nations. In practice, most colonials saw themselves as overseas Britons, as they showed by rushing to the colours in 1914. Friction was rare and low-level: disagreements over copyright or bigamy are unlikely to provoke nationalist wars of liberation. Canadians felt let down by inadequate British support over the Alaska boundary dispute in 1903, but since full independence would simply have meant facing the Americans alone, it was hardly an attractive alternative. In 1923 a Canadian minister signed a treaty with the United States to regulate halibut stocks in the North Pacific. Imperial unity barely trembled.

On paper, the transition to legal Dominion independence occurred between 1926 and 1931. Canada's prime minister, Mackenzie King, felt that the refusal by the British-appointed governor-general to call a general election amounted to imperial interference in local politics. Lord Balfour cast an elder statesman's mantle over the problem, producing a definition that avoided reference to the loaded word 'independence' but insisted that Britain and the Dominions were co-equal members of the commonwealth, a body that apparently existed somewhere inside the British empire. This had no legal force, but it satisfied Mackenzie King.

In 1929 a conference on the operation of Dominion legislation considered such worthy topics as extra-territoriality. If a Canadian-registered merchant ship sailed three miles out to sea, was it bound by any law at all? To resolve these mysteries, in 1931 the British parliament passed the portentously titled Statute of Westminster, promising never to legislate for the Dominions unless at their express request.

Since all this happened barely a decade after the impressive display of imperial blood unity shown in the First World War, we might conclude that the severance of Scotland might happen equally suddenly. There was however an important counterpoint to the theme of Dominion nationalism. War had also stimulated powerful imperial sentiments overseas. An imperial war cabinet was established in 1917, and at the peace conference, Dominion representatives enjoyed walk-on parts with the top-table British empire delegation, but signed the treaty itself as quasi-independent units. For a brief moment, it seemed that the Dominions might make good the shortfall in British world power.

Whitehall however soon decided that the game was not worth the candle. The foreign secretary, Austen Chamberlain, complained in 1925 that it was impossible to negotiate with foreign governments while constantly pleading Britain must consult its distant and tiny Dominions. Thus, Dominion pressure for clarification of the relationship intersected with a British inclination towards disentanglement. The emotional grip remained strong, as was shown in 1939 when every Dominion but Ireland followed Britain into war against Hitler. Moreover, economic ties, such as the Ottawa trade agreements in 1932 and the formalisation of the sterling area, counterbalanced any political will towards secession.

The Statute of Westminster itself fell short of an unambiguous charter of independence. It took effect in each Dominion only when it was locally adopted: Australia waited until 1942; New Zealand until 1947. Newfoundland's experience of complete sovereignty was fleeting: in 1933 the colony faced bankruptcy and accepted direct rule from Britain. Although suspicious of Britain, Canadians were also distrustful of each other. They specifically reserved ultimate control over their own constitution to Westminster, where it remained, incongruously, until 1982. During the abdication crisis in 1936, it was simply taken for granted that the Dominions were deemed to have requested British legislation to remove their king.

The evolution of Dominion status probably offers few clues to the future of Scotland's parliament. The puzzling historical issue is to explain not why the Dominions broke away but rather why they tolerated their quasi-colonial limbo for so long. The Statute of Westminster was as much a declaration of independence from, rather than for, the Dominions, a British decision politely to cut loose from inconvenient encumbrances. In 1931 Britain was ruled by a prime minister from Lossiemouth. A future act of abnegation by Westminster might well be as much as product of little Englandism as a response to Scottish nationalism.

III

What of the federal second tier, Canada's provincial legislatures and Australia's state parliaments? Does double-decker government guarantee incessant conflict over jurisdiction and constant temptation to secession?

When the Dominion of Canada was created in 1867, it inherited a well-established civil service, and the grandiose Ottawa parliament building. The two new provinces of Ontario and Quebec had to create their own institutions: symbolically, the opening ceremony of the first Ontario legislative session was pervaded by the smell of sawdust. The Quebec civil service numbered just 92 full-time employees in 1869, obviously a far cry from the modern Scottish Office. The provinces received substantial grants from the Dominion government, calculated on a per capita basis which especially benefited thriving Ontario, and gave little motive for disputes with Ottawa. Indeed, Ontario and Quebec spent more time arguing with each other over the partition of their joint debt, a problem that was not finally buried until 1910.

Initially, Ontario and Quebec were closely supervised by Ottawa. In 1867 Macdonald effectively selected the premier of Ontario and kept him under close control, notably by threatening to disallow objectionable legislation. His French-Canadian lieutenant, George Cartier, not only hand-picked the first Quebec cabinet, but sat in the local legislature himself, one of 15 out of the 65 members of the first Quebec assembly who enjoyed a dual mandate, along with the influence that their political experience implied.

Macdonald's control of Ontario lasted longer than Tony Blair's over Wales, but in 1871 the opposition Liberals captured the province. The new regime quickly banned dual membership, and Quebec followed in 1874. It was Ontario and not Quebec that led the way in contesting Dominion supremacy. Behind their antipathy between Macdonald and his former law pupil, Ontario premier Oliver Mowat, lay rival conceptions of the Canadian constitution. The judicial committee of the privy council, supported Mowat's view that the Dominion was a true federation. The most notable case, Hodge versus the Queen (1883), ostensibly centred on the issue of jurisdiction over a table in a Toronto tavern. The judicial committee concluded that the provinces were in effect sovereign within the spheres of jurisdiction assigned to them by the British North America Act.

Increased power did not push Ontario towards secession. Rather, Mowat chose to harness the other provinces to his alternative concept of Canada. In 1887 dissident premiers proclaimed that the government in Ottawa was the creation of the provinces and so subordinate and answerable to them. This compact theory of the Canadian constitution is of dubious historical value, but arguably it has made political sense, since the original 'Macdonaldian' constitution was too rigidly centralised for such a vast country.

Thus, it seems wrong to assume that mere possession of a subordinate legislature encourages attempts at formal secession. Canada's ten provinces joined the federation at different times: Ontario in 1867, Newfoundland not until 1949. Aggregation of their memberships to the year 2000 produces a total of 1159 province-years. Since 1867, four attempts at secession have got as far as the ballot box, two through provincial elections in Nova Scotia and two by referendum in Quebec. The average of one constitutional upheaval every 290 province-years exactly equals the period separating the Act of Union in 1707 from the Scottish referendum of 1997.

The first Nova Scotian movement, between 1867 and 1869, was essentially a continuation of opposition to confederation, with some of the resentment directed primarily against the manner in which it had been imposed. Although candidates opposed to the new constitution captured 18 of the 19 Nova Scotian constituencies at the first Dominion general election, the very breadth of their movement contained seeds of disunity. Some insisted upon secession, which the British refused to consider, while others were prepared to settle for better terms, which Ottawa was very willing to grant.

The threat was revived in 1886, W.S. Fielding's Liberals won the provincial election on a platform of secession from Canada. Discontent was fuelled by regional economic decline, a problem beyond easy political solutions. Some Liberals were uneasy in their support for Fielding, and it was generally assumed that he would hoped to secure a repetition of the concessions of 1869. The neighbouring provinces were not interested in his preferred alternative of a union of the Maritime provinces. In the middle of the Irish home rule crisis, British politicians simply did not wish to know. The following year, Macdonald's Conservatives won two-thirds of the Nova Scotian constituencies in the Dominion general election and the movement collapsed. Fielding joined Mowat's anti-centralist front, and later switched to Ottawa politics, serving two long terms as Canada's finance minister. Had he beaten Mackenzie King in 1919 for the national leadership of the Liberal party, as he nearly did, Fielding would almost certainly have become prime minister of Canada. It was a remarkable career for someone who had tried to break up the country.

Australia's sole attempt at a formal break-away came in April 1933, when Western Australians voted by two-to-one in favour of becoming a separate British Dominion. (The secessionist movement called itself the Dominion League, a strategy comparable to the SNP slogan of 'Independence in Europe', but probably with greater emotional appeal.) Western Australia had reluctantly joined a federation that would obviously be dominated by the distant eastern states, and in thirty years the state had seen few benefits from membership. Although impressive, the referendum vote was primarily a cry for help in the Depression. At the same poll, voters threw out the incumbent right-wing parties and elected a Labor government opposed to secession. Two years later, the British parliament closed the door, arguing that the Statute of Westminster only permitted it to legislate for Australia on the advice of its Canberra counterpart.

More recently, there have been two formidable attempts to break up Canada by Quebec separatists. The referendum of 1980 registered a 40.5 per cent for the 'Yes' side, while it successor in 1995 produced a nail-biting 49.4 per cent in favour, including a clear majority of the province's majority francophone population. Despite the massive and growing literature comparing the two, it is probably safest to agree with the verdict expressed by Alex Salmond on the morrow of the 1995 vote, that Quebec is not Scotland. The prognosis that we may reach on the destiny of the Scottish parliament will be largely determined by the comparators that we choose. If we decide to see Scotland in the context of Quebec, then instability may loom in the crystal ball. If we look rather to the fifteen English-speaking Canadian provinces and Australian states, which probably provide closer cultural analogues, then we shall conclude that formal attempts at secession are abnormal episodes.

Quebec however raises questions about the use of the referendum and the enigma of what would happen in the aftermath of a 'Yes' vote. Both referendum questions in Quebec were cumbersomely worded and notable for their failure to use terms such as 'independence' or 'secession'. The 1980 proposition was almost one hundred words in length. The 1995 question lacked the ringing clarity of the Declaration of Arbroath, opaquely asking voters:

> Do you agree that Quebec should become sovereign, after having made a formal offer to Canada of a new economic and political partnership, within the scope of the Bill respecting the future of Quebec and the Agreement signed on June 12, 1995?
> [*Maclean's*, 12].

In 1980, voters were promised a second referendum to endorse any deal for 'sovereignty association' (itself a disputed concept) with Canada. It is widely believed however that in the event of a 'Yes' vote in 1995, the separatist provincial government would have moved quickly to assert full sovereignty, a risk-ridden course of action even in as perennially peaceable a country as Canada. The lesson from Quebec, or so the Canadian government now insists, is that voters must be asked a clear question, with ground-rules agreed in advance on the way forward in the event of a 'Yes' vote. Unhappily, the Quebec experience also suggests that the very fact of a powerful separatist movement means that the necessary goodwill between centre and periphery has already vanished. The close result in 1995 also underlines the point that referenda work best when they produce a clear consensus: Quebec voted 49.4 per cent for independence; two years later, Scotland registered a 48.6 per cent majority for devolution.

One final comic-opera case warns that tactical resort to a referendum can be disastrously counterproductive. The West Indies federation came into being in 1958 largely because it offered the only means by which small communities could move towards national independence. It was bedevilled by inter-island rivalries. Like Scotland, Jamaica lay distant from the federal capital in Trinidad. Like England, it accounted for over half the population of the nascent state and believed itself to be the predominant partner. Although captured by the pan-Caribbean vision himself, Jamaica's premier, Norman Manley, thought it prudent initially to stay out of the federal arena. As a result, the first prime minister of the West Indies, Sir Grantley Adams of Barbados, was generally regarded as a mere caretaker. Manley however easily crushed his cousin and rival, Alexander Bustamente, in the Jamaican general election of 1959, and the way seemed open for more explicitly federalist involvement. In May 1960, Bustamente's party unexpectedly refused to contest a federal by-election, and demanded that Jamaica should pull out altogether. Some suspected that the decision was prompted by the party's inability to finance a by-election campaign. By noon the same day, however, Manley had responded by announcing a referendum on Jamaican membership.

Unfortunately, this apparently brilliant political counterstroke unravelled to disaster. Legislation was required to create the necessary machinery for a referendum. Adams was understandably reluctant to offer incentives aimed at Jamaican opinion especially after Manley announced that he would regard a 'Yes' vote as a mandate to enter federal politics himself. (Some of his Jamaican admirers probably voted 'No' in order to keep him at home.) Although Manley had taken less than an hour to decide upon his referendum, it did not happen until September 1961, sixteen months later, by which time the habitual discourtesies of Caribbean politics had soured the Jamaican attitudes towards federation. Worst of all, Manley assumed that the 54.8 per cent vote that had given him victory at the 1959 election would translate into a referendum majority. In the event, he suffered a small swing of about five per cent, and Jamaica voted to pull out.

There are lessons to be drawn from Manley's gamble. Never call a referendum on your opponents' policy. Never call a referendum unless you can control the timetable. Never call a referendum unless you are certain of victory. Unfortunately, these lessons are so obvious that a historical example is hardly required.

IV

Reflecting the fact that the islands had been colonised in six separate bites, New Zealand's constitution of 1852 provided for a general assembly and six provincial councils - cumbersome enough government for 26,000 settlers. The provinces received a share of central revenues which they could supplement from local resources. Thanks to land sales and gold rush prosperity, Otago and Canterbury flourished but others ran into trouble, and one province collapsed altogether. An unusual and probably unwise provision allowed new provinces to be carved from the old merely on the petition of 150 voters. Three extra provinces emerged in this way, while others were undermined by threats of subdivision. In Marlborough, rival councils seated themselves at Picton and Blenheim. To the surprise of the Pictonians, the Blenheimites turned up one day to hi-jack their meeting, a coup that was only prevented by a heroic ten-hour filibuster.

The provincial system was killed by financial pressures. In 1867, the central government responded to the increasing cost of the Maori wars by bluntly telling the provinces to rely on their own resources. Since the wars were a North Island problem, there was some pressure to make the South Island a separate colony. This movement foundered, partly because the mountainous northern end of the South Island had closer ties with Wellington, but also because neither Christchurch nor Dunedin expected to become the new capital. (The campaign for devolution in Scotland would have been fraught indeed had Glasgow seriously contested Edinburgh's claims to the new parliament.) From 1870 New Zealand embarked on a programme of expansion financed by overseas loans. To maintain investor confidence, it was necessary to prevent the feckless provinces from borrowing. As a result, the weaker provinces acquiesced in abolition and in 1876, the general assembly swept them away altogether.

The provincial council of the Free Church settlement of Otago was the only parliamentary-style body between 1707 and 1999 to be primarily run by and for Scots. By artistic coincidence, it held its first meeting in 1853, the mid-point year between the old and new Scottish parliaments. Overall, it was the most successful of New Zealand's devolved governments, partly through the good fortune of its gold rush revenues. It survived both the short-lived secession of the Southland province and the demagogic leadership of the flamboyant Aberdonian, James Macandrew, whose vocal campaign against centralisation might have been summarised in the slogan: 'it's Otago's gold'. Otago Scots did not all rise to Macandrew's oratorical heights. The sole parliamentary speech of goldfields representative, Donald Macpherson, was phonetically rendered by a reporter as: 'Mr Speaker, the reek's comin' doon the lum' [Morrell, 294].

When the Union of South Africa was created in 1910, provincial councils were the price paid to satisfy the particularism of Natal, the only colony with an English-speaking majority among its white population. (In the Boer heartland, the Orange Free State tried to abandon its debt-ridden council in 1930.) From time to time, Natal's imperial loyalists dreamed of secession from the Afrikaner-dominated union, but these threats were contained by the local white elite. Durban's prosperity depended on trade with the rich Transvaal, and it would have been foolish for the small settler community to stand alone alongside the overwhelming Zulu majority. South Africa's provincial councils whimpered to an end in 1986, although they have reappeared and multiplied in the post-apartheid constitution.

In both countries, provincial councils were small and headed by independent executives, popularly-elected superintendents in New Zealand, centrally appointed administrators in South Africa. As a result, neither evolved local systems of ministerial responsibility. Their eventual eclipse in both countries should cause no alarm in Scotland's new parliament. In fact, it is hard to get rid of a devolved legislature. Defending his decision to accept home rule for Northern Ireland, Sir Edward Carson remarked that parliaments could not be knocked up and down like a ball. Settlers in Jamaica surrendered their legislature in 1865 after an uprising. Newfoundland last prime minister insisted that 'what we need now is a political holiday', when the island surrendered its right of self-government in the face of bankruptcy [Neary, 41]. It is hard to envisage these contingencies threatening the Scottish parliament. In any case, lost legislatures remain a powerful memory, and generally return in the end.

Parliaments operate within unique social and political contexts which complicate comparisons. For instance, one reason for the strength of second-tier legislatures in Canada and Australia can be found in the relative weakness of municipal institutions in both countries. In country districts of Australia, local government is generally weak, while effective city-wide institutions are lacking in Melbourne, Montreal and Sydney precisely because they would rival the local legislature. In New Zealand, the story was inverted, and provincial councils were weakened by pressures to establish county-level authorities. Similarly, attempts by Natal provincialists to widen their autonomy were undermined by the insistence of major local authorities on dealing directly with Pretoria. In the colonies, local government was generally the creation of the legislature and could be shaped as parliamentarians determined. Scotland is unusual in attempting to insert a devolved legislature as a mezzanine administrative level into a country which already has an entrenched and ideologically politicised system of local government. The convention of royal burghs sometimes overshadowed the old Scottish parliament; no Dominion legislature faced the challenge of establishing itself alongside a body like COSLA (the Convention of Scottish Local Authorities).

V

The operation of a legislature is affected by the nature of party politics and electoral systems. In smaller communities, party structures were often *ad hoc* or even non-existent: in New Zealand's Nelson Province, the local elite was nicknamed the Supper Party. Absence of a party system could produce sterility, as in Southern Rhodesia where Sir Godfrey Huggins was prime minister for longer than Walpole, or extreme instability, as happened in South Australia which endured 39 ministries in the first 36 years of responsible government. In modern Australia, where parties operate on sharply defined lines of class, voters tend to back the same party at both state and federal level. In Canada, on the other hand, several provinces have evolved local party systems of their own. The Ontario Conservatives and the Quebec Liberals are only loosely connected to the national parties bearing the same names: Jean Charest moved from leadership of the federal Tories to head the Quebec Liberals.

On the face of it, we might conclude that the four-party system resulting from the 1999 Scottish elections represents a transitional stage inherited from Westminster politics that should logically evolve into something like the two-party federalist-versus-separatist system of Quebec since the 1970s. This prediction however ignores the differing impact of class loyalties (Quebec's equivalent of the traditional Labour voter is more likely to be a separatist) and the likelihood that proportional representation will counter any pressures towards electoral tidiness. First-past-the-post is such an unreliable way of locating a majority that it seems remarkable that it has endured with so little challenge in so many systems. Canada in 1896, Britain in 1951, New Zealand in 1978 and 1981 and Quebec in 1998 provide instances where the party polling the most votes actually lost the election. New Zealand experimented with the second ballot between 1908 and 1913, and ventured upon a mixed member proportional system in 1996. Australia - and especially Tasmania - has gone furthest in the adoption of preferential and proportional voting. Overall, the Scottish parliament is a pace-setter in electoral reform and there is little to be learned from overseas precedents.

Even the architecture of a parliament can affect the way it operates. As a general rule, the more imposing the chamber, the less efficient the legislature. Anthony Trollope admired the fine Gothic architecture of the Canterbury provincial council But was told 'that it had one slight drawback. Those who spoke in it could not make themselves heard' [Trollope, ii, 376]. The Canadian House of Commons was also noted for poor acoustics: its orators were by definition those with the loudest voices.

One governor-general envied the facilities available to Canada's legislators: 'the accommodation would be thought magnificent by us Members of the English House of Commons. ... the fellows in these Colonies have been spoiled by all sorts of luxuries, large armchairs, desks with stationery before each man, & heaven knows what' [Knaplund, 143]. In fact, desks further intruded upon the parliamentary atmosphere: Canadian MPs perforce used them even during debates in lieu of offices, and the arrangement generated a whole sub-politics of desk-mates, who got to sit with whom and where.

Australia managed for sixty years with much-loved and very cramped temporary premises, until a permanent Parliament House was completed in 1988 at a cost of £500 million. In the largest construction project in the southern hemisphere, the new parliament consumed 25 times as much concrete as the Sydney Opera House. It contains 15 miles of corridors, 2500 clocks and a swimming pool. Symbolically, it was built into Canberra's Capital Hill and covered with an area of grass larger than the Melbourne Cricket Ground so that the people of Australia can literally tread their rulers under foot. While working conditions have improved, there is a general impression that the executive has become more remote from backbenchers. One politician complained of the new House of Representatives that members 'can't see the whites of their opponents' eyes' adding, 'I have been at crematoria that have been more fun' [Disney and Nethercote, 8]. The restricted site at Holyrood has been criticised, but it may prove to have advantages in fostering a live parliamentary culture.

VI

No longer a colonial politician but a Dominion statesman, in 1871 Sir John A. Macdonald decided to offer his thoughts on how to respond to the new movement for Irish home rule. Macdonald took for granted that full devolution was out of the question for troublesome Ireland. Even in Canada, there was 'great difficulty in keeping the subordinate legislatures ... from exceeding their powers'. Rather, Macdonald suggested, MPs 'from each of the four provinces of Ireland ... should form Grand Committees', meeting once a year in the different corners of Ireland. These committees would initially be granted limited powers of legislate and raise taxes, which might subsequently be increased. 'There would be little danger of their joining together in any concerted action.'

Since the House of Commons had enough to do presiding over the affairs of the empire, Macdonald thought his system might be applied more generally within the United Kingdom. England could be divided at the Humber 'and the ancient Principality [Wales] have a little Parliament of its own'. Best of all was the potential for Scotland. 'The Scotch members manage Scottish affairs at present in a committee-room at Westminster.' Why not formalise and (to use a later Canadian term) patriate the arrangement? It would 'gratify Edinburgh and the Scottish Lion if a Grand Committee, such as I have mentioned, with like powers, were to assemble there' [Pope, ii, 222-27]. More than a hundred years would pass before the Scottish grand committee turned itself into a road show, and by then it was too late to halt the campaign for full-scale devolution. Perhaps Macdonald's scheme would have renewed the old United Kingdom on proto-Blairite lines. A century later, however, it seems that the Dominion precedents offer Scotland more warnings than solutions.

References and Further Reading:
General: C.M.G. Himsworth and C.R. Munro, *Devolution and the Scotland Bill* (Edinburgh, 1998); Nicholas Mansergh, *The Commonwealth Experience* (London, 1969); D.B. Swinfen, *Imperial Control of Colonial Legislation 1813-1865: A Study of British Policy towards Colonial Legislative Powers* (Oxford, 1970).

Canada: *Parliamentary Debates on Subject of the Confederation of the Provinces of British North America* (Quebec, 1865); 'Government', in *Encyclopaedia of Newfoundland and Labrador*, vol ii, ed. J.R. Smallwood (St John's Newfoundland, 1984); *The Political Economy of Newfoundland, 1929-1972*, ed. P. Neary (Toronto, 1973); Charles Dickens, *American Notes* (London, 1868 ed.); M. Hamelin, *Les premières années du parlementarisme québécois (1867-1878)* (Quebec City, 1974); *Letters from Lord Sydenham Governor-General of Canada 1839-1841 to Lord John Russell*, ed. P. Knaplund (London, 1931); J.A. Pope, *Memoirs of the Right Honourable Sir John Alexander Macdonald* (2 vols., Ottawa, 1894).
Australia: *Parliament of New South Wales: Legislative Assembly Standing Rules and Orders* (Sydney, 1996); *The House on Capital Hill: Parliament, Politics and Power in the National Capital*, ed. J. Disney and J.R. Nethercote, (Canberra, 1996); E.D. Watt, 'Secession in Western Australia', *University Studies in Western Australian History*, 3 (1958), 43-86.
New Zealand: W.P. Morrell, *The Provincial System in New Zealand 1852-1876* (London, 1932); Anthony Trollope, *Australia and New Zealand* (2 vols., London, 1873).
Southern Africa: *Selections from the Smuts Papers*, vol ii, ed. W.K. Hancock and J. van der Poel(Cambridge, 1966).
West Indies: J. Mordecai, *The West Indies: The Federal Negotiations* (London, 1968).

11

The Home Rule Campaign in Ireland

CHARLES TOWNSHEND

The idea of Irish home rule was conceived as a middle way between the rigid defence of the Union and the open-ended demand for separation. It was foreshadowed as Daniel O'Connell's campaign for the repeal of the Union peaked in the early 1840s, and took distinctive form in the 1870s. Its originators, Sharman Crawford and Isaac Butt, were both Protestants and unionists, and though Butt came (via his legal work for the Fenian Amnesty Association) to embrace the Irish national cause he remained more sensitive than most nationalists to the potential for injustice to (and resistance by) the Irish Protestant community. Home Rule was deliberately designed as a compromise: in this lay its potential strength, and its ultimate weakness.

I

The home rule project
The essence of home rule or 'federalism' was and remained the contention that it could reconcile a just and acceptable measure of Irish 'national' autonomy with the maintenance, and indeed strengthening of the Union. Thus, the programme of the new Home Government Association in 1870 called for 'the restoration to Ireland of that right of domestic legislation, without which Ireland can never enjoy real prosperity or peace ... without breaking up the unity of the empire, interfering with the monarchy, or endangering the rights and liberties of any class of Irishmen.' An imperial parliament would 'preserve the unity and integrity of the United Kingdom as a great power among the nations of the world' [Thornley, 97]. This could be simply done, Butt suggested (in *Home Government for Ireland, Irish Federalism: Its Meaning, Its Objects, Its Hopes*, 1871):
> England, Scotland and Ireland, united as they are under one
> sovereign, should have a common executive and a common
> national council for all purposes necessary to constitute them, to
> other nations, as one state, while each of them should have its own
> domestic administration and its own domestic parliament for its
> own internal affairs.
Butt's key belief was that Ireland could achieve full nationhood within the empire. This was to be the persistent issue: would home rule satisfy Irish national aspirations? The question whether it could be accepted by the Union parliament depended in large measure on the answer.

Throughout its history, stretching over a half-century, the case for home rule was put in pragmatic as well as moral terms. It was important to emphasise its benefits for England, as for example Sir George Campbell did in stressing the need to relieve an overburdened parliament and meet the demand (British as much as Irish) for 'self-rule in the provinces', for which local government was not enough. 'What,' Justin McCarthy asked, 'can be said for a system which insists that the Imperial Parliament shall neglect the business which it alone can do, in order to undertake business which it can never do effectively?' [*Nineteenth Century*, March 1880]. The most vital argument, perhaps, was that home rule would secure or even strengthen the Union: as a government-inspired article in the *Fortnightly Review* of July 1885 put it, 'an alienated Ireland means a weakened England'.

The Home Government Association, for all its worthiness, caution, and moderation, was always in danger of falling between two stools: though home rule seemed congenial to the farmers' clubs, for instance, the Catholic bishops saw it as a suspect Tory stratagem - thus discouraging mass Catholic participation - while 'the Protestant Conservatives who had helped create the Association feared, particularly after the passage of the 1872 Ballot Act, that they would be entrapped and overwhelmed within a popular Catholic movement' [Jackson, 111]. In the notoriously indifferent (if not actually hostile) House of Commons, Butt's studied 'Englishness' was self-defeating - he introduced the home rule idea in 1874 with the remark that it remained to be discussed, and perhaps discussed for many years. Probably it would not even have been discussed for many years, but for the aggressive edge given to the Irish parliamentary group in the later 1870s by Joseph Biggar and Charles Stewart Parnell. The shock delivered to English assumptions by their ruthless exploitation of parliamentary procedures - 'obstruction' or - was vast and reverberant.

Under Parnell's unique style of leadership in the 1880s home rule outgrew its prosaic contours and acquired some of his mystique. The dynamism of the Land League was channelled into the parliamentary organisation of the National League, and secured the blessing of the Catholic hierarchy (most vitally, in respect of education under home rule). Both constitutional and revolutionary political traditions in Irish nationalism could combine around the carefully crafted ambiguity of Parnell's most resonant invocation of national destiny, delivered in January 1885:

> We can not, under the British constitution, ask for more than the
> restitution of Grattan's parliament. But no man has the right to fix
> the boundary to the march of a nation; no man has the right to say
> to his country, 'Thus far shalt thou go and no further', and we
> have never attempted to fix the *ne plus ultra* to the progress of
> Ireland's nationhood, and we never shall [*The Times*, 22 Jan.
> 1885].

This potent rhetoric gave the movement its maximum momentum in the 1886 election, the point at which the mainland political parties effectively ceased to exist in Ireland: only the Irish nationalists and unionists remained, the latter confined to Dublin University and Ulster seats. It was a triumph, but it carried a price, adding hatred and fear to the contempt with which Irish nationalism was regarded by its enemies.

The demand for home rule rested on an indefinite mix of promise and threat, as it had to if it was to contain national aspirations which were beginning to be radically recast (the demand for an 'Irish Ireland' accelerated with the creation of the Gaelic Athletic Association in 1884) while preserving the ultimate supremacy of England. But did it have any chance? Two main possibilities may be said to have existed: first, that the limited version of home rule - devolution - might have been taken up (as Butt hoped) by Conservatives using some variant of the 'colonial' model of subordinate 'legislatures' (or the more novel Canadian model). Or, failing that, the Liberals would adopt the more dynamic idea of an Irish 'parliament'. The two terms were technically synonymous, but carried a different symbolic freight.

The first was always improbable, though a fringe of Conservative thinkers embraced the federalist approach, and it became intellectually more attractive as the divisions over home rule sharpened. Gladstone himself seems to have believed that a Conservative solution was not only desirable but possible. A more authentic view, however, was expressed by Lord Salisbury: 'One issue there is which ... is absolutely closed. The highest interests of the Empire, as well as the most sacred obligations of honour, forbid us to solve this question by conceding any species of independence to Ireland' ['Disintegration', *Quarterly Review*, Oct. 1883]. For Salisbury, this 'would be an act of political bankruptcy, an avowal that we are unable to satisfy even the most sacred obligations, and that all our claims to protect or govern anyone beyond our own narrow island were at an end.'

The prospect of the Liberals taking up home rule was always more plausible. It is often suggested that Gladstone was 'converted' to the principle in the mid-1880s, but it seems more likely (as Colin Matthew argues) that there was no discontinuity in his thinking. His long-standing 'mission to pacify Ireland' involved a progressive exploration of remedial measures, and the underlying moral validation of home rule was apparent in the analysis he offered to W.E. Forster in April 1882, at the time when coercive legislation was prominent in his government's response to the land war. He blamed the failure of pacification on 'this miserable & almost total want of the sense of responsibility for the public good & public peace in Ireland; & this responsibility we cannot create except through local self-government.' And significantly he added:

> If we say we must postpone the question till the state of the country is more fit for it, I should answer that the least danger is in going forward at once. It is liberty alone, which fits men for liberty. This proposition like every other in politics has its bounds; but it is far safer than the counter-doctrine, wait till they are fit' [Matthew, 200].

Early the following year Gladstone provided an equally sophisticated analysis of the negative or business argument for home rule, writing to Granville on 22 January 1883:

> Under the present highly centralised system of Government, every demand, which can be started on behalf of a poor and ill-organised country, comes directly on the British Government and Treasury; if refused it becomes at once a head of grievance, if granted not only a new drain but a certain source of political complication and embarrassment, the peasant proprietary - the winter's distress - the state of the labourers - the loans to farmers - the promotion of public works - the encouragement of fisheries - the promotion of emigration - each and every one of these questions has a sting, and the sting can only be taken out of it by our treating it in correspondence with a popular and responsible *Irish* body - competent to act for its own portion of the country [Kendle, 34].

Of course, once Gladstone decided that Irish home rule was an idea whose time had come, he brooked no delay or opposition in pushing it forward, and his haste may have fatally damaged the chance of manoeuvring it through parliament. Though he was not blind to the fast crystallising issue of Ulster (less so indeed than his successors a generation later), his very sophistication led to a misreading of the forces against him. As Colin Matthew points out, he 'did not share that potent Imperial-State worship which for many unionists in the late-Victorian period became a substitute for the Church-and-State Toryism of the past', and his underestimation of its strength played an important part in his decision to initiate legislation in 1886 [Matthew, 212].

II

The first home rule struggle
The 1886 Home Rule Bill, very much Gladstone's personal creation, was presented as a means of bringing social order to Ireland, extracting Britain from its demoralising reliance on coercion, and giving the law a domestic instead of a foreign

character. The fundamental fault of the present administrative system, he argued, was that the motor muscle was English and not Irish. The best and surest foundation for future peace was the will of the nation. But behind these Liberal nostrums lay major problems (both of detail and of substance) with representation, finance, and the protection of minorities. The last of these was most easily dealt with, on paper at least, by giving the proposed Irish legislative body two 'orders' which could sit together or separately. The first would have 28 elected Irish peers, and 75 members elected on the £75 property franchise, to reassure the old ascendancy class. The second would have 204 (or possibly 206) members elected on the parliamentary franchise. The restriction on Irish legislative powers, excluding the crown, defence, and foreign affairs, with control of the police reserved for two years under the viceroy, was uncontentious in Britain. The thorniest problem to dog all home rule proposals was a volatile mix of two related issues: Irish representation at Westminster and British fiscal supremacy. Gladstone first went for the removal of the Irish MPs, which exposed his bill to the charge of taxation without representation, since Ireland would have to continue paying an 'imperial contribution' for the reserved powers. Later home rule bills never succeeded in resolving this problem, since the alternative path of maintaining Irish representation at Westminster (as in the second Home Rule bill) provoked English charges of Irish power without responsibility. (The 80 Irish Westminster MPs of the 1893 bill were to be cut to 40 in 1912, and finally removed again in 1920).

Predictably, most of the participants in the Commons debate on the first Home Rule bill 'lost sight of the essential issue and wandered off into personal attacks on the Irish or their own interpretation of Anglo-Irish history' [Kendle, 51]. But amongst these meanderings a core set of arguments against home rule emerged, and these remained fairly constant over the next generation. The lines were drawn up well in advance, as when E.A. Freeman in 1874 rejected federalism as unworkable, asserting that 'total separation would be a less evil than such a scheme of federation, or whatever it is to be called, as is now proposed' [Kendle, 18]. Joseph Chamberlain, by contrast, was sympathetic to federalism on the US model, but not to home rule. He accepted that Ireland had 'a right to local government more complete, more popular, more thoroughly representative, and more far-reaching than anything that has hitherto been suggested.' But 'I can never consent to regard Ireland as a separate people with the inherent rights of an absolutely independent community' [Kendle, 26, 25]. The powers Parnell

> claims for his separate Parliament are altogether beyond anything
> which exists in the case of the State legislatures of the American
> Union, which has hitherto been the type and model of the Irish
> demands; and if this claim were conceded, we might as well for
> ever abandon all hope of maintaining a United Kingdom. We
> should establish within thirty miles of our shores a new foreign
> country, animated from the outset with unfriendly intentions
> towards ourselves' [Kendle, 29-30].

This was a crucial argument with a grim corollary: 'if nationalism means separation, I for one am prepared to resist it. ... Sooner than yield on this point I would govern Ireland by force to the end of the chapter' [Kendle, 25]. The implications of separation were dramatically spelt out by the *Spectator* as an early domino theory - 'The contagion of disintegration will spread rapidly' [26 Dec. 1885].

The most sustained attack was mounted by England's dominant constitutional lawyer, A.V. Dicey, already a declared enemy of federalism, which, he argued in the *Contemporary Review* in July 1882, would not only 'by undermining parliamentary sovereignty, deprive English institutions of their elasticity, their strength, and their life', but which also 'holds out no hope of conciliation with Ireland' [Kendle, 22]. Dicey was convinced, as he wrote to Bryce in January 1885, that 'The alternative for good or bad is ultimately between Union & separation (complete independence)' [Kendle, 23]. Like Freeman, Dicey insisted that federalism could only work when it was a step towards unity, not away from it. In *The Law of the Constitution* he warned the nation of the 'tendency of federalism to limit on every side the action of government and to split up the strength of the state among coordinate and independent authorities' [Kendle, 24].

Dicey marshalled his whole battery of argument against the 1886 bill in *England's Case Against Home Rule,* augmenting it further against the 1893 bill in *A Leap in the Dark.* Home rule was an illusion (whether deliberate or deluded) based on a misconception of sovereignty; and Dicey scornfully dismissed Gladstone's invocation of trust. 'You cannot give your trust simply because you wish to give it ... The Irish Home Rule leaders as a body cannot inspire trust, for the simple reason that their whole policy and conduct prove them untrustworthy.' This chimed with the characteristic Protestant view of Catholic politics voiced, for instance, by the historian W.E.H. Lecky (writing to *The Times* on 5 May 1886):

> I do not believe - and I do not think the people of Great Britain will
> believe - that the government of Ireland can be safely entrusted to the
> supported by the votes of an ignorant peasantry, whose passions it
> has been their object for many years to inflame.

Goldwin Smith put it more curtly yet: 'The Celts of Ireland are as yet unfit for parliamentary government' [Kendle, 21].

Last but not least, even in 1886, came the first manifestations of the Ulster problem, identified by Sir George Campbell in 1880 in blunt terms. 'Ireland is in a condition ... analogous to one of the South African colonies, in which only British authority prevents collision between a colonist minority and a native majority' [Kendle, 19]. That warning became a strident threat when the imminence of home rule in 1886 pushed liberal and reactionary Protestants into a common front. Lord Randolph Churchill, cynically playing the 'Orange card' in February 1886, audaciously accused Gladstone of opportunism when he planned: 'to hand over coldly, for the sake of purchasing a short and illusory Parliamentary tranquillity, the lives and liberties of the Loyalists of Ireland to their hereditary and most bitter foes'. Churchill invoked a new extreme of argument - 'Ulster at the proper moment will resort to the supreme arbitrament of force; *Ulster will fight, Ulster will be right*' [Rhodes James, 234].

After the Home Rule bill's defeat (by 343 votes to 313) on 8 June 1886, all these arguments, especially the last, returned at higher pitch when the second Home Rule bill was carried through the Commons in February-September 1893. The second bill (drawn up by a cabinet committee rather than by Gladstone himself) closely paralleled the first, though with a simplified bicameral legislature (a legislative council of 48 and an assembly of 103). The extensive exceptions to the devolved powers (crown, war and peace, defence, army, navy, foreign treaties, treason, aliens, external trade, coinage, currency, etc.) were preserved. The u-turn on the principle of Irish representation at Westminster brought in complex rules for the voting powers of the 80 Irish members of the imperial parliament, and even more complex financial provisions. Dicey fulminated that the retention of the Irish members would break up the whole system of cabinet government and undermine the whole system of government. He reiterated the vacuity of the entire scheme of home rule: in trying to give the weak power against the strong (arguing that Dublin would be made supreme over Belfast, and ignorance given dominion over education), it defied reality. No institution could stand which did not correspond to the nature of things.

After an extended but narrow-minded parliamentary debate -there were 85 sittings with constant use of the guillotine - the bill carried the Commons by 307 to 267; but it was inevitably lost in the Lords by 419 to 41 a week later. By 1893, the home rule movement had been wrecked by the Parnell split. Gladstone's commitment to home rule survived Parnell's fall in 1891, but the movement in Ireland itself did not recover the febrile intensity its strange leader had given it. Though the Irish Nationalist party machine was rebuilt (the split was formally healed at the turn of the century) and its authoritarian disciplinary culture faithfully maintained by Parnell's old lieutenants, Dillon and Redmond, the long period of political impotence during the ascendancy of Salisbury and Balfour, sworn enemies of devolution, produced a change of atmosphere. The eventual doom of the Home Rule party should not be projected too far backwards: public disengagement from home rule activism did not necessarily mean that the objective was being abandoned. Rather a generation emerged which assumed that home rule was inevitable, and looked ahead to wider issues concerning the quality of national life. The Irish literary revival, and even the 'Irish-Ireland' movement, were not necessarily incompatible with home rule. But the growing conflict over Irish identity had profound, indirect political effects. The steady strengthening of Catholic assertiveness simultaneously reduced the Nationalist party's room for manoeuvre on the issue of concessions to unionism, and intensified unionist determination to resist 'Rome Rule'.

How far this had gone by the early 1900s was revealed by the 'devolution crisis' of 1903-4, when a renewed discussion of mild federalism between Lord Dunraven's Irish Reform Association (whose report of August 1904 condemned the present system of financial administration as wasteful and inappropriate to the needs of the country) and the Irish under-secretary, MacDonnell, sketched a semi-elected viceregal council embodying a mixture of political and commercial interests, and important minorities. Even this cautious proposal, when it leaked out, caused a ferocious Conservative spat which ended the political career of the dedicated chief secretary, Wyndham, shortly after his historic resolution of the agrarian question through the 1903 Land Act. The persistent dominance of hardliners, led by Balfour himself, was ominous.

The Liberals returned to power in 1905 bruised by their experiences with home rule, and influenced by Lord Rosebery's retreat from the 'Irish alliance'. The Irish Council bill drafted in 1906 could be seen as the beginning of home rule by instalments - or the reverse, as John Dillon argued to John Morley (on 18 December 1906):

> This idea appears to me to break up the Irish party machine and
> dominance in Irish politics and get a kind of Indian Council
> composed of that favourite abstraction of amateur solvers of the
> Irish problem - non-political business men - and so turn Ireland
> into a loyal peaceful country, very subservient and manageable,
> purged of politics, and devoted to the breeding of pigs and the
> making of butter [Kendle, 100].

Home rulers clung on to the fundamental moral argument about national freedom. Even the temperate John Redmond insisted, in 1907, that no ameliorative reforms, no number of land acts, no redress of financial grievances, no material improvements or industrial development, could ever satisfy Ireland until Irish laws were made and administered in Ireland by Irishmen. For American official consumption, however, Redmond, in the USA in late September 1910, was prepared to say that 'By Home Rule we mean something like you have here, where Federal affairs are governed by the Federal government, and state affairs by the State government' [Kendle, 116].

By the time home rule came back into the arena of practical politics, twenty years too late, it had been outflanked on both nationalist and unionist sides. The British constitutional crisis of 1910 removed the entrenched unionist bulwark of the Lords, but in doing so it heightened the desperation of the die-hard opponents of home rule. Physical resistance had been openly hinted at in both the first two home rule episodes, and, with the growing scale of unionist organisations in the early twentieth century, it became a virtual certainty. The steady refusal of the Liberals to prepare for it may appear in retrospect to be almost incredible. But it is surprising how little they had prepared at all to implement this long-standing and (for most) still fundamental objective.

III

The 'Ulster' crisis
The third Home Rule bill was drawn up in an oddly complicated way, with an 'expert' committee on financial relations having no contact with the cabinet committee dealing solely with constitutional issues. Despite borrowing heavily from the 1893 bill, this group made remarkably slow progress. By September 1911, Herbert Samuel noted to Herbert Gladstone that the bill was 'in being but with a good many blanks and square brackets' [Kendle, 141]. When after nearly a year the expert committee reached the awkward conclusion that Ireland was rapidly losing the possibility of becoming self-sufficient, Samuel took another six weeks to draft the bill's hugely complicated financial clauses. These threatened to become a major constraint on Irish independence - and moreover could not be adapted for the exclusion of Ulster counties, so denying the government the flexibility it soon came to need as opposition to home rule intensified.

Resistance to the bill burgeoned to dramatic and alarming proportions. In December 1909 the circumstances in which Asquith had announced his party's return to the home rule policy were a gift to the unionist denunciation of the 'corrupt bargain' to buy Irish support; and grassroots unionist organisations had multiplied over the years since 1886. Even before the bill was published monster marches were held across the northern Ulster counties, and in September 1911 Carson framed the loyalist challenge in the most radical terms possible: 'We must be prepared, the morning Home Rule passes, ourselves to become responsible for the government of the Protestant Province of Ulster.' 'To tell me', he protested, 'that the small farmers and labourers of the South and West of Ireland are in a position to frame Acts of Parliament for the guidance and governance of this great community of the North of Ireland, is really to turn Parliament into a pantomime and nothing else' [Bew, 37]. A year later, as the bill made its way through parliament, the spectacular 'Ulster Day' demonstration witnessed the mass signing of the new Ulster covenant and the beginning of a grass-roots paramilitary movement. By the autumn of 1913 the Ulster Volunteer Force was an ostentatiously efficient organisation of over 100,000 men who took every possible opportunity to display their military skills.

Despite a growing queasiness amongst the Liberal ministers, they and the nationalists kept each other up to the mark by reiterating that all this was a bluff. Whether the cabinet had the stomach to call the bluff, however, remained to be seen. Any real hope of heading off unionist resistance rested on an attempt to key home rule in with the vestiges of the old UK-federalist idea which still survived on the fringes of the Conservative party. J.L. Garvin urged Balfour, on 17 October 1910:

How then can we who have worked the economic revolution in Ireland say that we will not recognise the possibility of any Irish administrative change in the direction of limited self-government perhaps no more inimical to the Parliamentary Union of the United Kingdom - perhaps no less advantageous to it - than is the local autonomy of Quebec to the Parliamentary Union of Canada [Kendle, 120].

The federalist stalwart, F.S. Oliver, once again dangled the tempting prospect that 'Closure, the destroyer of parliaments, might disappear, the powers of caucus might be abated ... congestion in the House of the Commons might be relieved, and cabinet government might be restored' [Kendle, 119]. But Dicey was ready as ever to puncture the federalist balloon, asking whether Mazzini would for a moment have accepted a federal government under which Italy would become a province of a federated Austrian empire? In October 1910 the idea was comprehensively dished by Balfour, who remained deeply suspicious of the Irish, and dismissive of the 'fuzzy thinking and vague generalities of the federalists' [Kendle, 123]. Though Asquith seemed to hint at it when he first presented the Home Rule bill, nothing more was heard of it from the government side. Maybe there had never been anything in it; though Austen Chamberlain went on worrying (to F.S. Oliver, on 6 March 1914) that 'If Asquith had acted on the hints thrown out by Lansdowne, Carson and myself, and had confronted us with a definite proposal to cooperate in that solution, I think it might have been carried, but a large section of the Party, from Balfour downwards, abhorred it' [Kendle, 170]. Lionel Curtis more realistically concluded that 'A scheme of federalism was only an incident in a vain attempt to get some settlement which would stave off the impending nightmare of civil war' [Kendle, 172].

The failure of federalism left some form of Ulster exclusion as the only way of averting that threat. The moral ascendancy of home rule for Liberals was gradually undermined by creeping doubts about the morality of imposing it on a resistant minority. The criteria that could be used to decide whether the minority's dissent was justified were disturbingly vague. (It had been difficult enough after all to establish the credentials of the Irish nation.) The initial reaction to Ulster intransigence followed party lines. The Liberal ideologist, L.T. Hobhouse, faced with the question why Ulster could not claim to be a nation, answered it by reducing the core of loyalism from Ulster to Belfast and some adjacent counties, and asserting that loyalism did not claim nationality, but only desired to hang on to the ascendancy system. 'With this demand Liberalism can have no sort of sympathy', Hobhouse sternly concluded - adding characteristically that 'If Belfast would condescend to put her case with a little more moderation, and a little allowance for the two sides of the question, it would be easier to meet her views' ['Irish Nationalism and Liberal Principle', Morgan, 309].

When Belfast stuck to its guns, the Liberals realised belatedly that they were running out of constitutional road. The underlying fear was that the British electorate would not support the coercion of people who wanted to remain 'British'. Erratically, but symptomatically, proposals emerged to undercut the case for armed resistance. As early as August 1911 the Irish minister, Augustine Birrell, outlined the idea that became known as the 'county option', suggesting that only two counties might actually opt out of home rule if offered the chance. A formal proposal of an option for 4 (or all 9) Ulster counties was put as a backbench Commons' amendment in June 1912. Horace Plunkett offered the reverse idea, that Ulster should be included for a trial period, then be able to vote itself out (earlier if authorised by an independent tribunal, e.g. the judicial committee of the privy council). In November 1913 Lloyd George suggested to a small inner cabinet group that temporary exclusion of 'Ulster' for five or six years, with automatic inclusion then, would knock all moral props from under Carson's rebellion, and either make it impossible for Ulster to take up arms, or, if it did, it would put the Liberals in a strong position with the British public whenever the Liberals chose to suppress it. Finally, a six-year exclusion period was offered by Asquith in the Commons, on 9 March 1914, only to be rejected by Carson with the extremist language now typical of the whole crisis: 'Ulster wants this question settled now and forever. We do not want a sentence of death with a stay of execution for six years' [Stewart, 141]. If the government had any remaining hope of calling Ulster's bluff, it disintegrated during the spring with the twin crises of the Curragh mutiny, when British cavalry officers refused to coerce Ulster, and the large-scale UVF gun-running at Larne. The six-year limit to exclusion was removed by the Lords on the third reading, on 14 July 1914, and replaced by Lansdowne's amendment excluding all nine counties permanently.

The impasse was complete, and when the last-ditch Buckingham Palace conference of 21-24 July broke down, there appeared to be no way out. When the Commons debate, postponed after the Irish Volunteers' Howth gun-running, was superseded by the outbreak of European war, Asquith's relief was palpable. Although home rule appeared to come tantalisingly close to realisation in 1914, the fear of civil war was decisive. For the Liberal party, home rule was not so much a moral crusade as a pragmatic solution to the problem of governing Ireland. Though it was partly couched in moral terms, its persuasive power rested on the assumption that doing justice to Ireland would make Ireland more peaceful, not more violent. The events of spring 1914 were a terrible and ultimately fatal blow to the viability of the entire home rule concept.

The home rule movement was in decline through the first three years of the war, though the exact rate of its decline is hard to determine. Paul Bew has recently stressed the continuing vigour of Redmond's party at least until 1916, arguing that the republican rebellion was a reaction to the strength rather than the weakness of the constitutional movement. The war itself provided powerful testimony of the commitment of the younger leaders of the last home rule generation, such as Thomas Kettle, to the cause. The party exploited as best it could the fact that home rule was on the statute book, but the triumph look increasingly threadbare as the war stretched on. (And Kettle himself was killed in battle.) The failure of Lloyd George's negotiations in the aftermath of the republican insurrection at Easter 1916 inescapably underlined the intractable conflict between nationalist and Ulster unionist positions, while the very terms of the negotiations did heavy damage to Redmond's political position in Ireland. The insurrection was a priceless gift to unionist intransigence, instantly wiping out the credit built up by Redmond's loyal support for the war effort.

Even now the government might have recognised that the only way of saving moderate nationalism was to force through home rule (with temporary exclusion) immediately. Its strength was immeasurably greater than it had been before the war; and an army mutiny on the issue was hardly possible. But the presence of Carson in the war cabinet underlined the fact that 'party' policies had to remain on ice for the duration. Tory attitudes were unreconstructed: as Lord Lansdowne protested to the cabinet on 21 June 1916, if home rule were conceded, even 'in the guise of an interim arrangement', 'the triumph of lawlessness and disloyalty would be complete' [Mansergh, 96]. The government's inability - or disinclination - to force a resolution was shown in the resort to a long drawn-out constitutional convention which diverted such attention as Britain could muster from the erosion of home rule's public support in Ireland. As a political project, home rule was mortally imperilled by the reconstruction of Sinn Fein in 1917, though mainstream nationalist opinion did not become republican, or even Griffithite, overnight. It took another catastrophic British policy intervention, the futile attempt to impose military conscription on Ireland in the spring of 1918 with a renewed (but vacuous) offer of home rule, to send the great party into free fall. At the end of the year it was practically annihilated in the general election. The one area (outside Trinity College, Dublin) where it survived was Ulster.

IV

The Government of Ireland Act
The government had not lifted a finger to save the home rule party - indeed all its actions and messages tended in the opposite direction. To home rulers it seemed bent on manufacturing Sinn Feiners. In fact, it seems to have had no inkling that home rule might be disappearing from its menu of options. When it eventually returned to the business of preparing a fourth home rule bill, the task was assigned to Walter

Long, an old Tory with a hesitant leaning to federalism (though as Carson witheringly said to Oliver, he 'never knows what he wants, but he is always intriguing to get it' [Kendle, 192]) and a firm belief in the potential of coercion to produce moderation. The result was a year's delay in framing the legislation, during which Long made two enduring contributions to Irish policy: the creation of the 'Black and Tans', and the creation of Northern Ireland.

Although Long's committee was presented (by Edwin Montagu) with a forceful restatement of the argument for all-Ireland home rule, with a renewable option of exclusion by county, it decided - all too reasonably - that the likely excluded areas would be administratively unworkable, and that the plebiscites involved would inflame sectarian passion and do more to entrench Irish divisions than would any externally imposed partition. Moreover exclusion, by leaving parts of Ireland 'under British rule' would violate the principle of self-determination (a nod to the rhetoric of the new world order) provoking nationalist resentment and foreign criticism. On the other hand, the establishment of a quasi-federal structure of two home rule parliaments would both 'meet the fundamental demand of the overwhelming majority of Irishmen since the days of O'Connell', and 'enormously minimise' the partition issue [Mansergh, 124]. The catalogue of sanguine self-delusion was completed by the committee's idea that if the whole province of Ulster were excluded - far the most convenient dividing line - the appearance of religious division would also be minimised.

This fantasy persisted until the final stages of drafting, and certainly helped to bolster the overall argument in favour of dual home rule. Ultimately it was abandoned in favour of a six-county area; but even so, for all the embarrassing asymmetry of the two units, and the obvious salience of religious ethnicity in the division, the scheme retained a certain elegance on paper, with some of the reserved powers now used as an inducement to the two to cooperate via a Council of Ireland. (As the mild federalist Austen Chamberlain noted during the parliamentary debate on 29 March 1920, 'it is a paradox that the only hope of union in Ireland is to recognise her present division' [Mansergh, 138].)

In practice, it was a dead letter before it passed into law. Long's idea that resolute coercion ('restoration of order') could eventually bring moderate nationalists to accept 26-county home rule was stymied both by Lloyd George's impatience and by the traditional constraints of the British system. If anything nationalist opinion hardened around the core of republican armed resistance, and the Irish Republican Army was able to dictate the result of the elections in May 1921 to the 26-county southern parliament. The proportional representation system - multi-seat constituencies with single transferable vote - ostensibly designed to provide protection for the double-minority that the Government of Ireland Act created, may have been intended to save the remnant of the old parliamentary party as well. But the sad end to the great home rule movement was the assembly in Dublin of just four Trinity College MPs (with the 15 senators nominated by the viceroy) on 18 June. The contrast with the parliament of Northern Ireland, already equipped with its executive machinery, was striking. In the end, home rule worked only for its most inveterate opponents.

References and further reading :
Paul Bew, *Ideology and the Irish Question. Ulster Unionism and Irish Nationalism 1912-1916* (Oxford, 1994); Alvin Jackson, *Ireland 1798-1998* (Oxford, 1999); John Kendle, *Ireland and the Federal Solution. The Debate over the United Kingdom Constitution 1870-1921* (Montreal, 1989); Nicholas Mansergh, *The Unresolved Question: the Anglo-Irish Settlement and its undoing 1912-72* (New Haven, 1991); H.C.G. Matthew, *Gladstone 1875-1898* (Oxford, 1995); *The New Irish Constitution*, ed. J.H. Morgan(London, 1912); Conor Cruise O'Brien, *Parnell and*

his Party 1880-90 (Oxford, 1967); Alan O'Day, *Irish Home Rule 1867-1921* (Manchester, 1998); Senia Paseta, *Before the Revolution. Nationalism, Social Change and Ireland's Catholic Elite, 1879-1922* (Cork, 1999); Robert Rhodes James, *Lord Randolph Churchill* (London, 1959); A.T.Q. Stewart, *The Ulster Crisis* (London, 1969); David Thornley, *Isaac Butt and Home Rule* (London, 1964); Charles Townshend, *Ireland: The 20th Century* (London, 1999); Alan J. Ward, *The Irish Constitutional Tradition* (Dublin, 1994).

12

The First Home Rule Movement in Scotland
1886-1918

GRAEME MORTON

'The ball is now at our foot, and the wind in our favour, if we have
only the pith to kick the ball into the goal ahead of us' [Theodore Napier,
Forfar Herald 10 April 1896].

Romance, valour and daring are so vital to national identity. In Scotland, the land of
mountain and flood, we find the heather and the hills, the kith and the kin, and the
dislocation of emigration used to inspire songs and stories which juxtapose beauty
and bleak desolation in equal measure. Such evocations inspire a sense of
Scottishness, yet the most remarkable aspect, projected from the early history of
modern nationalism, was the straightforward practicality of the demands. It has been
a distinctively boring movement, rarely making its appeal through the eloquence of
inspirational entreaties or the self-sacrifice of civil disobedience. It has not lacked
appeal 'for the nation', and constitutional proposals have been suitably broad, not
specific. But the rationale was an administrative one: the better government of
Scotland. Birthright to self-determination was not absent, just readily downplayed.
    Nationalism in Scotland is a phenomenon of the second half of the twentieth
century. Its roots are varied and uncertain, with no shortage of organisations existing
to politicise national identity since the springtime of nations in the 1840s.
Throughout, the demand to restore a state to this nation has been slow-burning, one
of three constitutional solutions on offer. In the 1850s the National Association for
the Vindication of Scottish Rights (NAVSR) re-emphasised Scotland's equality with
England from the time of the Union of 1707. By stressing how successful that union
had been, and would continue to be, if Scotland was treated as an equal with
England, an oxymoron, Unionist-Nationalism, explains a national identity that
wanted more union with England, not less. Demand for a Scottish parliament was
dismissed in favour of greater powers to the localities - the town and county councils
- to resist the centralisation of government at Westminster or, instructively, in
Edinburgh. From the mid-1880s the Scottish Home Rule Association (SHRA)
pushed a solution for Scotland's better government through a devolved parliament
within a British federal structure. The concept had been around since the 1830s, but
now was the age of 'home rule'. From the 1920s and 1930s, the argument for
devolution sat alongside that of the separatists and their proposal that Scotland's
parliament be re-established on the principles of independent nationhood: it was a
constitutional mix which saw out that century.

I

The concern of this chapter is the first home rule movement in Scotland. Nationalist
parties have struggled to dominate the electorate in Scotland, never gaining a majority
of votes, so we should not expect too much from its beginning. The dilemma facing
this study is the almost complete political failure of the SHRA. It was on the fringes

of Scottish politics and its origins - too - were external to Scottish politics. After a burst of activity from its formation in 1886, the Scottish Home Rule Association slipped from public view about the time when the Young Scots Society was established in 1900, petering out until it was re-formed in 1918 by Roland Muirhead. By then its politics were distinctly Labour rather than Liberal. By 1920 the association had over one thousand members and 138 organisations were affiliated. It concentrated on trying to influence the views of prospective parliamentary candidates, asking them to affirm their support for home rule. That it was still an organisation on the coat tails of a parliamentary party was a large part of the reason behind the formation of the National Party of Scotland in 1928. The same was also true of the Young Scots Society, the successful exponent of 'New Liberalism' at the time of the 1906 general election and, only after 1909, a firm supporter of Scottish home rule. During, but especially after, the 1910 general election, the Young Scots Society was then extraordinarily active, distributing thousands of pamphlets and holding hundreds of meetings. These organisations were not alone: the International Scots Home Rule League was formed in 1913 and the Scottish National League (SNL) followed the re-formation of the SHRA, in 1919-20. The SNL was pro-independence, the breakaway Scottish National Movement (1926) was less sure. The very number of overlapping pressure and political groupings, split by personality as much as doctrine, ensured there was no simple path to the formation of the Scottish National Party in 1934. Nor does it represent a straightforward hardening of the demand from better local government in the 1850s to home rule in the 1880s to independence in the 1920s. But it indicates that the constitutional debate had moved on. What role, then, should we assign to the first home rule movement?

II

The argument for discontinuity
Three pieces of evidence support the distinctiveness of the years 1880 to 1918. The claim for a devolved parliament was not just upping the rhetorical stakes. It has been the period - before or since - marked most by a series of measures for devolution presented before Westminster. A total of 13 resolutions were debated between 1890 and 1914, on eight of these occasions the House of Commons championed the principle and at 11 of these votes the majority of Scottish MPs gave their support. None of the Bills ever made it to the committee stage; too often they were hindered by their half-hearted presentation to ensure Scotland's claim would not be forgotten in the debates upon Ireland, rather than submitted with conviction.

This period is also marked by the creation of the Scottish Office in 1885, the outcome of a fight championed by Rosebery against the neglect of Scottish affairs. For Rosebery, this new arrangement, not home rule, was a sufficient response at this time, and he remained far from whole-hearted in aligning himself with the aims of the SHRA. Even with the admission of the secretary to the cabinet in 1892, upgraded to a secretary of state in 1926, and throughout a long fought-for increase in the number, seniority and pay of its staff of civil servants, the Scottish Office was a remarkably low-key government department. The invisibility of the Scottish secretary and his staff in the proposals for home rule orchestrated by the SHRA is striking when one considers its corporatist interventions during the 1920s and 1930s which marked its role in Scotland's governance. When the Scottish Home Rule Association was formed in May 1886, there was no mention of the Scottish Office as its springboard. Rather, it was founded a few months after Gladstone presented the first Home Rule Bill for Ireland. That the SHRA was spawned from political expediency, not long-standing principle, is one point to bear in mind. Another is the non-appearance of the SHRA, or an equivalent, in 1870, to rival the moderate Home Government Association in Ireland. This time-lag, until reacting to Gladstone's first

Home Rule Bill, provides some credence to both the discontinuity of this period from the 1850s, and the view that we are dealing with a party-political orientated organisation.

III

Liberal Politics
The debate over constitutional change comes to dominate the Liberal party from the 1870s and continued throughout the 1880s. The search for a solution to the long-running tension with Ireland became the final passion of Gladstone from his second until his fourth ministry. What was going on in Ireland - and not going on in parliament because of the disruption of Irish MPs - weighed heavily in Gladstone's thinking, rather than the concerns of Scotland. But his contemplations upon better government tantalised and ultimately frustrated the home rulers. The first titbits came from the Midlothian campaigns of 1879-80, 1885 and 1890. Most fundamentally, it was while staying with Rosebery at Dalmeny during the campaign to retain his seat at the 1885 general election, that Gladstone committed to paper his conversion to the cause of home rule for Ireland. In October 1885 he made it known to his advisers that he wished to consult the Canada Acts of 1840 and 1867, suggesting the possibility of granting Ireland similar Dominion status. The final conversion was sudden, but the issues had been debated for over a decade. Gladstone had made grudgingly positive noises supporting home rule in a speech in Aberdeen in 1871. Then, in the opinion of the *Economist*, he made plain that 'the whole Union has the right to say whether a union or separation will best promote the interests of all' [30 Sept. 1871]. Without being convinced himself, he developed in earnest a debate on constitutional reform during his first campaigning visit to Midlothian for the 1880 general election. At the Corn Exchange in Dalkeith, in front of a crowd of three thousand, Gladstone expounded a version of federal government for the United Kingdom, the themes of which were to become known as home rule all round:

> I desire, I may almost say I intensely desire to see Parliament
> relieved of some portion of its duties. I see the efficiency of
> Parliament interfered with not only by obstruction from Irish
> members, but even more gravely by the enormous weight that is
> placed upon the time and the minds of those whom you sent to
> represent you. We have got an overweight Parliament: and if
> Ireland, or any other portion of the country, is desirous and able so
> to arrange its affairs that by taking the local part of some local part
> of its transactions off the hands of Parliament, it can liberate and
> strengthen Parliament for Imperial concerns, I say I will not only
> accord a reluctant assent, but I will give a zealous support to such a
> scheme. ... I will consent to give to Ireland no principle, nothing that
> is not to be upon equal terms offered to Scotland and to the different
> proportions of the United Kingdom [*Midlothian Campaign* , 44].

Despite this warming to home rule, of the dozen or so speeches made in the Midlothian campaign of 1879 to 1880, only the second speech, at Dalkeith, gave full attention to Scotland. The other speeches were otherwise confined to the broad issues of foreign and colonial affairs. Gladstone presented a precise dissection of the morality of government and, as if to emphasise all that the SHRA would argue in the following decade, he littered his orations with commentary upon parliament's dealings with matters overseas. He clearly signalled that these, not local matters, were the issues of real importance to the imperial parliament. Coupled with a ready tendency to label the empire and Britain's influence overseas as 'what England has undertaken' [*Midlothian Campaign*, 24], Gladstone seemed unaware of the contradictions evident to the nationalists. Yet his speeches were popular enough to result in large sales once re-drafted and published, and the campaign did much to invigorate Liberalism in Scotland.

Gladstone's zealous support to a home rule scheme which would reduce the burden on the imperial parliament developed from analyses rooted in the nationalist arguments of the 1850s. His initial reason for opening up debate on Scotland's governance was to highlight the inadequate parliamentary representation of Scotland at Westminster. If Scotland were represented proportionate to its population, it would have 70 MPs, not 60, and, if relative revenue were taken as the criterion, Scotland should be sending 78 MPs to Westminster. Gladstone blamed the framers of the Reform Bills of 1867 and 1868 for this situation [*Midlothian Campaign*, 35]. His proposal for devolution was premised on local government as the constitutional solution: 'If you ask me what I think of Home Rule, I must tell you that I will only answer when you tell me how Home Rule is related to local government' [*Midlothian Campaign*, 44]. Both are arguments straight from the National Association for the Vindication of Scottish Rights in the 1850s [*A Citizen of Edinburgh*, 6-30]. Neither pre-dated the federalist rationale of the SHRA.

Gladstone presented a petition in favour of home rule for Scotland to the House of Commons on behalf of the electors of Midlothian in July 1890. He had been persuaded of the harm Scottish home rule would do in England, fearing regional rule, and, more importantly, worried that it would hinder the case of Ireland. The lord advocate, J.P. Robertson, had been quoted in *The Scotsman* of February of that year declaring the SHRA was a 'step backwards' and 'that anything more dismal or bleak than the prospect of life in Scotland under a Scottish Parliament he could not conceive' [*The Scottish Home Rule Debate*, 4]. It was clear to the SHRA that, by 1892, Gladstone was determined not to be drawn publicly on Scotland's grievances in relation to those of Ireland, having accepted the view of his chief whip, Edward Marjoribanks, that the creation of a Scottish grand committee (established two years later) would be sufficient to deal with Scottish business. When he failed even to mention Scottish home rule in his address to the electors of Midlothian during the general election campaign of 1892, the SHRA's officials immediately sent a letter outlining their grievances. During the next week of the campaign, Gladstone again ignored the issue at the hustings in Dalkeith, despite being sent an address signed by five hundred Midlothian electors. For this neglect he was then hustled into dealing with appended questions on the issue by John Romans. Dissatisfaction from William Mitchell, the SHRA's secretary, was deep: Gladstone's responses were his 'finest examples of his electioneering subtlety. But the verbosity to which he resorts on such occasions forbids quotation from his speeches' [Mitchell (c.1893), 88-9]. Romans, JP and county councillor for Midlothian, resigned as convener of the Liberal committee of Newbattle parish because of Gladstone's intransigence, and the Liberal party's failure to adopt Scottish home rule. Romans was a member of the NAVSR in the 1850s and one of the founders of the SHRA in 1886. Because of the ensuing crisis with the home rule cause in 1893, he felt the need to put country before party.

IV

Scottish Home Rule Association
Although claiming to act only as a mouthpiece of Scottish national aspirations, the argument that the SHRA was the first parliamentary political Scottish national movement is supported by a further range of evidence. Its objectives were defined in an ABC on Home Rule in 1887, published in *The Union of 1707 Viewed Financially*:

A. To secure to the Government of Scotland, in the same degree as
it is present possessed by the Imperial Government, the control of

her Civil Servants, Judges, and other officials, with the exception of those engaged in the Military, Naval and Diplomatic Services, and in collecting Imperial Revenue.
B. To promote the establishment of a Legislature sitting in Scotland, with full control over all purely Scottish questions, and with an Executive Government responsible to it and the Crown.
C. To maintain the integrity of the Empire, and secure that the voice of Scotland shall be heard in the Imperial Parliament as fully as at present when discussing Imperial Affairs.

Interestingly, in the retrospective *Prospectus* of 1892, point 'C' - the maintenance of the empire - is transposed with point 'A' to become the first priority. A fourth objective was then added: to foster the national sentiment of Scotland, and to maintain her national rights and honour. This brought it much closer to the unionist-nationalism of the NAVSR and of its heraldic concerns. But the disjunction between the movements was greater at first, and from the mid-1880s the union was presented as an arrangement that was now outdated. No longer was the union the source of prosperity, but, rather, it was the people of Scotland who were the cause. The SHRA was preoccupied with supporting bills for home rule all round presented to the houses of parliament, and opposing home rule only, or first, to Ireland. It campaigned within the Liberal party but the SHRA's aggression and insensitivity were unpopular with the Scottish leadership. The SHRA produced a range of pamphlets, sent letters of persuasion to parliamentary candidates (wanting them to declare their support for Scottish home rule as part of their own election platform), and inundated the Scottish newspapers with letters and statements. The last of its campaigning tactics - letters to the newspaper - illustrates how, when denied party-political power, this organisation was able to drag the debate on Scotland's governance into the public domain.

V

Making Public Opinion in Civil Society
In April 1896, in response to the failure of the English Liberal Association meeting in Huddersfield to add home rule for Scotland to the party's stated aims, a series of letters were penned by Charles and James Waddie, John S. Waddie and Theodore Napier, stating the case for home rule all round. Often these letters were published within days of each other, as a concerted campaign, appearing in a remarkably wide range of regional newspapers over the next four years. Many were signed and were written on the association's behalf, although a goodly number were simply designated as 'contributions' to the newspapers - tactics previously used by James and John Grant, the co-secretaries of the NAVSR in the 1850s. The disappointment of the Huddersfield congress was a year on from the resolution in favour of home rule all round carried in the House of Commons by a majority of 25, which had convinced James Waddie that the opinion of the country was settling on federation. The dashing of such optimism was made all the more painful since the SHRA leadership saw themselves as natural Liberals who had been betrayed by their leadership in England. The Liberals were in government for only three years in the 1886 to 1905 period, and they were accused of failing to develop any policies for Scotland during their years in opposition and of offering no reward for the Scottish votes which had previously kept the Liberals in power for 40 of the last 60 years . The Liberal success in gaining three by-election victories in 1896, with home rule support, in Aberdeen North, Wick (and Frome), prompted much letter writing on the current appeal of home rule all round to the electorate, but still it failed to have the desired effect on party policy.

Denied influence in parliament, a range of arguments making plain the case for Scottish rights was then presented to the reading public. Like the publications of the NAVSR, perceived financial loss was to the fore. The disproportionate spending on English dockyards, highlighting the £1.9 million spent to extend Devonport Dock and the cost of the upkeep for the London parks, were typical issues. There were also accusations that Scotland was losing upwards of eight million pounds each year from its share of probate, customs & excise grants, while the inland revenue returns for 1896 were quoted in order to show that Scotland was paying nearly half as much more as England per head of the population. However reminiscent these debates were of the nationalist organisation over forty years earlier, what marks this period out is that this loss was no longer attributed just to the inequities of a parliament dominated by English-based MPs, the crux of Gladstone's Midlothian argument. Now the analysis had broadened: the system of government was cumbersome and expensive for all portions of the United Kingdom. Scotland, it was calculated, lost about eight million pounds each year through having to go to London for every local bill, and, 'inevitably, England, Ireland, and Wales lose in proportion' [*Fifeshire Advertiser*, 4 April 1896]. Home rule all round was presented as a patriotic question for all the nationalities, because it was a utilitarian question to reduce the cost of legislation in order to increase the wealth of all, and relieve the imperial parliament of work it was quite unable to do. The four nations of the United Kingdom were being poorly governed because there were now too many demands placed on parliamentary time. It was noted that even the Isle of Man and the Channel Islands had home rule, so why not extend the principle. Of the hundreds of local bills not three per cent were passed, and much criticism was advanced over the recent loss of 12 clauses in the Scottish County Councils Bill for Scotland, despite Scottish MPs voting in favour of it. The quadrupling of the population of the British Isles was offered as evidence that the work to be done was now too complex and unwieldy for a union parliament created in the eighteenth century. Inevitably, it seemed, Scottish issues would be denied time for debate: 'An hour or two in the small hours of the morning three or four times a session, with MPs from England not appearing in the House until the Division Bell sounded and then they would vote along Party lines' [*Perthshire Courier*, 7 April 1896]. Even the Tory press was concerned when a whole parliamentary session was about to end without any Scottish business conducted, because Westminster was seen to be in a hopeless state of arrears, dealing with a South African question, a Venezuelan question, an Egyptian question, an Armenian question, plus a host of other imperial questions. Scottish fears were the underlying agenda, but the presentation was on British terms.

Common complaints over parliamentary exclusion did not stop the SHRA being hostile to Irish home rule, despite earlier attempts at co-operation. The antipathy was based on political and constitutional grounds, but included a touch of religious bigotry and racism, too. There was delight at the failure of Gladstone's first Irish Home Rule Bill to get through the Commons, while the success of the second bill was attributed to the personal influence of this most popular statesman, implying an element of sympathy, not to be shared by the Lords, and not likely to be gained again. The proposition of home rule all round was always the reply to plans for Irish home rule, described as impossible, impracticable and illogical, principally because it would allow 80 Irish members to comment on English, Scottish and Welsh matters, while the Irish had sole control over their own affairs. Charles Waddie analysed such piecemeal constitutional change as mere folly, indicating that 'logic does not seem to be a strong point in the Irish character' in 'the most backward of the whole four nations of the United Kingdom' [*Ayrshire Post*, 10 April 1896; *Methodist Times*, 28 May 1896]. He suggested that Englishmen did not like Irishmen, whereas the average Englishman had the greatest respect for a Scotsman. Whereas the Presbyterians of Scotland were in full sympathy with the nonconformists of

England, religious differences had stopped the Scottish and Irish nationalists from working together. More secular difficulties were also laid bare with the belief that both Parnellites and anti-Parnellites were hostile to home rule for Scotland or home rule all round, and were resolved to vote against such a scheme if proposed by the Liberal party. Refusing to make common-cause with Ireland's claims, the home rule movement in Scotland lost an important opportunity of securing greater political support.

VI

Home Rule All Round and (Dis)Continuity
With so much discord, the concept of home rule all round remained on the fringes of Liberal policy up to 1914. Even if co-operation between Scotland and Ireland could have been achieved, any scheme was too easily dismissed as deficient because of the difficulty in finding a realistic plan for England. The proposal for a federal structure based on equal powers faced the problem that England was just too big in relation to the other countries, and would be difficult to sub-divide, even if there was such a desire, which there was not. James Mitchell has emphasised the importance to the intellectual debate of A. V. Dicey's *England's Case Against Home Rule*, published in 1886, which highlighted the legal obstacles and practical difficulties of offering devolution to one part of the United Kingdom - Ireland - without advancing commensurate measures for the remaining portions [69]. Charles Waddie downplayed Ireland's needs by pointing out that England suffered most from the congestion of business [(1895), 2]. The urban theorist Patrick Geddes embarked on his own solution to the problem of over-centralisation, co-editing a series, *The Making of the Future*, which included C. B. Fawcett's thesis, *Provinces of England*, which advocated a balanced measure of home rule all round. The size of England, which had over three-quarters of the total population, would, he argued, mean an English parliament dominating a British parliament, if England were not divided further along regional lines, based on natural and topographical boundaries and sustained by local patriotisms and traditions [23-4].

Federation was new - at least at this level of discussion. But it did not escape the debates of the previous half century. John Waddie argued that home rule ran deep in Scottish minds. He recalled there has 'always been a sporadic vindication of Scottish rights' and that 'a greater movement in this direction was lost in the tragedy of the Crimean War' [*Montrose Review*, 10 April 1896]. In other contributions he summoned up the spectre of government over-centralisation in London, the vary basis of the NAVSR's analysis of Scotland's ills. This line was developed most obviously by John Romans, a former member of the NAVSR. He warned that 'The centralising system has been the aim and object of British statesmen since the Union' [*Home Rule for Scotland*, 40]. In 1898, while chairman of the association, Romans, and Charles Waddie, sent an address to the Lords and Commons on *The Evils of Centralisation and its Cure* . There were other bridges between the two periods. Thomas Carlyle's speech in spring 1848, in reply to O'Connell's demand for repeal of the union between Ireland and Britain, was reprinted in 1889. W.E. Aytoun's 'Scotland since the Union', originally published in *Blackwood's Magazine* in 1853, was reprinted in 1891. Patriotic songs were common, but were now more jingoistic than forty years earlier. A song for the 600th anniversary of the battle of Stirling Bridge was published in a dozen Scottish regional newspapers and over 40 newspapers in the United States.

There was a great difference in the SHRA's anti-unionism: 'Let us be united to undo the wrong inflicted upon our country in 1707, and approve the far seeing wisdom of our ancestors who advocated federation, of which Home Rule all round is simply the modern phrase to express the idea', declared Charles Waddie

[*Dumbarton Herald*, 8 April 1896]. Theodore Napier was equally forthright: 'The Incorporating Union of 1707 is not only obsolete and unsuited to modern requirements, but has proved an absolute failure' [*Dumbarton Herald*, 23 April 1896] and the Union of 1707 was the result of 'shameful bribery' of Scottish members by English gold and against the express wish of the Scottish nation [*Border Advertiser*, 29 April 1896]. Even the selfish actions of the church were blamed for using the union for its own ends. Waddie claimed that the kind of union he wanted was defined by what he termed the proper sense of the word, as 'our patriotic ancestors of 1707 advocated' [Waddie (1895), 16]. By that he meant a federal union.

Like the NAVSR's commitment to the Union, the anti-unionism of the Scottish Home Rule Association was not intended to break up the United Kingdom or the empire. Theodore Napier made clear that their plans were not separatist because their reforms were to benefit the whole Empire: 'It is the Unionists who are real separatists' [*Forfar Herald*, 10 April 1896]. Gladstone was even told off for using the confusing language of Scottish nationalism, when the term home rule for Scotland was well established. It was the language of administration. For Napier it meant a local national parliament, while home rule all round meant 'local National Parliaments for Scotland, England, Ireland and Wales for the transaction of the local affairs of each nationality' along with a federal parliament [*Scottish Highlander, 16 April 1896; Dumbarton Herald*, 23 April 1896]. John Waddie used the term 'purely national and local' as being the remit of 'national Legislatures in the four historic divisions of the United Kingdom' [*Montrose Review*, 10 April 1896]. Local meant national - and how administratively neutral is the language of divisions! When the local issues were defined, they were some of the biggest social problems facing the United Kingdom: unemployment, housing of the poor, old age pensions, land laws, local veto, disestablishment, fishery laws and access to the countryside. Whereas local issues were a matter of municipal reform in the 1850s, now they were the concerns of a local national Scottish parliament.

VII

Logical Solution, Political Impasse
Both politicians at Westminster and the SHRA recognised that a logical constitutional answer for Ireland was home rule all round, but that it was politically impracticable. The Irish problem was not going to be solved by means other than a workable political fix and, with the rejection of home rule and the lack of any intellectual coherence to the constitutional proposals, the Scottish cause was weakened. The SHRA was playing a political game, but one it could not win. The SHRA therefore had to promote Scottish national identity in other ways if it were to continue with its campaigning. The newspapers, the pamphlets and the meetings were part of this strategy. The dominant role of a few prominent individuals kept the movement active. Charles Waddie turned to staging historical plays on the life of Wallace in order to break through the political impasse in 1898. David Macrae, an SHRA vice-president, published his history of Wallace in 1905, in the same year that Lord Rosebery's speech at the 1897 celebration marking the 600th anniversary of the battle of Stirling Bridge was reprinted. Lewis Spence, founding member of the Scottish National Movement in 1926, published his *Story of William Wallace* in 1919 and used the occasion to tell of his part amongst a small gathering who met on 5 August 1905 on the 600th anniversary of Wallace's betrayal and capture. None, however, equalled the charisma of Theodore Napier. As well as penning so many letters to the press on behalf of the SHRA, Napier was a member of the Scottish Patriotic Association, one time President of the Scottish National Association of Victoria, and a campaigner for 24 June - the day of Bannockburn - to be proclaimed Independence Day and a public holiday. Napier was also vice president of the

Legitimist Jacobite League of Great Britain and Ireland, founded in 1891. Napier, who was born in Melbourne, took to wearing the dress of a Highland chieftain and to paying homage annually to Culloden and Fotheringay Castle. On behalf of the SHRA he acted as honorary secretary of the Scottish Petition to Queen Victoria, highlighting the inappropriate use in official terminology of 'England', when 'Britain' was the correct term. He obtained 40 thousand signatures by June 1897 and claimed 104,647 signatures at the close of the campaign. The official reply from Colin Scott Moncrieff was dismissive and the petition was as ineffectual as a similar appeal had been in 1853. Napier was singular in many ways, but his actions were indicative of a movement which could not win the party-political argument.

Politically the SHRA was relatively powerless until after 1918. Then it was much more successful at creating an organisational structure, with enough pressure on electoral candidates in Scotland to cause a stir. Yet, we are looking for roots, not endpoints, and the SHRA did mark a change from what had gone before. The SHRA tried to influence party policy-making: taking that as its path of preference. It was in symbiosis with Liberal party policy and Gladstone's orations. A devolved parliamentary structure was proposed for the first time in any committed and consistent way. Both points are demonstrated by the number of resolutions presented before parliament. The SHRA was highly critical of the Union of 1707 and showed little explicit loyalty to the monarch. This anti-unionism, with federalism as its solution, marked the SHRA at the start of the intellectual debate contained within modern nationalism. Despite this break with the 1850s, there was still explicit support for the coherence of the United Kingdom and the empire in each period. Gladstone used arguments from the 1850s in his case for Scotland, paying lip-service later to home rule all round, but remaining wary of undermining Ireland's reform. The SHRA focused on similar campaigns as the NAVSR - financial and heraldic relations between England and Scotland, for instance - but these would surface again later in the twentieth century. The SHRA was dominated by a few key individuals - or, more rightly, characters. It was forced to mobilise public opinion when its activities as a pressure group seeking to influence the Liberals were unsuccessful. But the attempt had been made at a party-political alliance. Concurrent with the themes of anti-unionism and home rule all round, as a contradictory but complementary constitutional arrangement, the argument for discontinuity from the 1850s is made. The Scottish Home Rule Association was worthy of its name, but Scottish nationalism was only just beginning to stir.

References and further reading :
A *Citizen of Edinburgh, A Vindication of Scottish Rights, Addressed to Both Houses of Parliament* (Edinburgh, 1854); Robert John Akroyd, 'Lord Rosebery and Scottish Nationalism, 1868-1896', unpublished PhD thesis(University of Edinburgh, 1996); Vernon Bogdanor, *Devolution in the United Kingdom* (Oxford, 1999); David Brooks, 'Gladstone and Midlothian: The background to the first campaign', *Scottish Historical Review*, 44 (1985), 42-67; Stewart J Brown, '"Echoes of Midlothian" Scottish Liberalism and the South African War, 1899-1902', *Scottish Historical Review*, 71, (1992), 42-67; C.B. Fawcett, *Provinces of England: A study of some geographical aspects of devolution* (London, 1919); Richard J. Finlay, *Independent and Free: Scottish Politics and the Origins of the Scottish National Party, 1918-1945* (Edinburgh, 1994); Richard J. Finlay, 'Continuity and Change: Scottish politics 1900-1945', in *Scotland in the Twentieth Century*, ed. T.M. Devine and R.J. Finlay (Edinburgh, 1996), 64-84; Richard J. Finlay, *A Partnership for Good? Scottish Politics and the Union since 1880* (Edinburgh, 1997); Michael Fry, *Patronage and Principle: A political history of modern Scotland* (Aberdeen, 1987); I.G.C. Hutchison, *A Political History of Scotland 1832-1924. Parties, Elections and Issues* (Edinburgh, 1986); James G.

Kellas, 'The Liberal Party in Scotland 1876-1895', *Scottish Historical Review*, 44 (1965), 1-16; J.E. Kendle 'The Round Table Movement and "Home Rule All Round"', *Historical Journal*, 11 (1968), 332-53; Ian Levitt, 'Scottish Sentiment, 'Administrative Devolution and Westminster, 1885-1964', in *Scotland, 1850-1979: Society, Politics and the Union*, ed. Michael Lynch (London, 1993), 35-42; David McCrone, 'The Unstable Union: Scotland since the 1920s', in ibid., 43-49; *Midlothian Campaign. Political Speeches delivered in November and December 1879 and March and April 1880 by the Right Hon. W. E. Gladstone, MP* (Edinburgh, 1880); James Mitchell, *Strategies for Self-government: the campaign for a Scottish Parliament* (Edinburgh, 1996); W. Mitchell, *Is Scotland to be sold again?* (Edinburgh, c.1893); Graeme Morton, 'Scottish rights and 'centralisation' in the mid-nineteenth century', in *Nations and Nationalism* , 2 (1996), 257-79; Graeme Morton, *Unionist-Nationalism: Governing Urban Scotland, 1830-1860* (East Linton, 1999); John Romans, *Home Rule for Scotland* (Edinburgh, c. 1894); Scottish Home Rule Association, *The Scottish Home Rule Debate of 19th and 20th February, 1890* ; Charles Waddie, *The Federation of Great Britain* (Edinburgh, 1895); Charles Waddie, *The Bi-centenary of the Union of the Scottish and English Parliaments. A brief Historical Account of how it affected the Welfare of Scotland* (Edinburgh, 1907).

13

Civil Society, Protest and Parliament:
Housing and Land in Modern Scotland

EWEN A. CAMERON

The idea is frequently expressed that Scotland's post-Union national identity is based on the survival of a distinct civil society based on the legal system, the Presbyterian church and the education system. This notion presents an overly simplistic impression of Scottish national identity and, more importantly for the purposes of this paper, elides a number of complexities in the history of Scottish civil society in the period since the Union. Arguably, the legal system and legal code has underpinned the distinctiveness of Scottish society since 1707; this was especially important in questions of land and property, both urban and rural. The Scottish legal code gave almost untrammelled power to landlords in interactions with tenants. This was a key factor in the modernisation and commercialisation of lowland Scottish agriculture in the late eighteenth century. The same powers allowed landowners in the Highlands to transform their estates through a series of evictions which revolutionised the tenurial and economic structure of the region. In urban Scotland the relationship between the legal system relating to land and the social structure was also crucial in an era of rapid change: Scottish towns, especially industrial towns, had grown very quickly in the late eighteenth and throughout the nineteenth century, and the demand for housing was intense. Due to this rapid urbanisation and the feudal nature of land tenure in Scotland the pattern of housing developed in a distinctive manner.

The ramifications of such distinctiveness were not confined to the legal system or to social relations between landlords and tenants of various kinds, but spilled over into incidences of protest and into more conventional political activity which marked Scottish radicalism with a particular brand of anti-landlordism. This paper will look at the interaction between the Westminster parliament and two areas of Scottish society which reflect this underlying distinctiveness: namely, housing and the land question. Legislation on these questions has had a profound impact on the Scottish rural and urban landscape. A discussion of these two issue serves as a reminder of the diversity of the political agenda in Scotland: although home rule has been an important part of that agenda it has not dominated it. The most subtle advocates of home rule and independence have been able to relate the constitutional question to wider social issues. The trajectory of these issues differs, however, as they become subject to the dictates of the Westminster parliament. In the case of the Highland land question, distinctive legislation was passed in 1886 and 1897 which meant that tenurial relations in the seven most northerly Scottish counties were different from the rest of rural Scotland. Further legislation in 1911 and 1919 attempted to extend Highland land legislation to Scotland as a whole, but this was never wholly realised. Thus, land legislation for the Highlands was distinctive, even in a Scottish context. A comparison with Ireland, however, reveals the application of similar policies, most notably in the shape of the Irish Land Act of 1881, upon which the Crofters Act of 1886 was based. In many ways the land question represents unfinished business on the Scottish political agenda; this has been recognised since 1997 with the establishment of the Land Reform Policy Group [LRPG] and the proposals for legislation to be scrutinised by the Scottish parliament which have emerged from their deliberations.

The history of legislation on the housing question is quite different: Scottish events were crucial to the wider pattern of British housing policy. This can be seen in the passage of the Rent Restriction Act of 1915, a response to the rent strikes of that year; and the 1924 Housing Act which established provisions for government subsidy to local authorities to build houses for rent. The 1915 act, in particular, has been held to be vital in the development of British housing policy in the twentieth century: F.M.L. Thompson has gone so far as to argue that it was 'arguably the most decisive single stroke of policy in the present century' [Daunton, 'Housing', 247] This act was passed after considerable agitation over the housing question in Glasgow. John Wheatley, who had long campaigned on the housing question during his time as a Glasgow city councillor and had been involved in the 1915 rent strikes, was the minister of health in the first Labour government and piloted the 1924 Housing Act through parliament. A theme which brings these two areas of public policy together is the fact that both were the occasions of considerable protest. The rent strikes in Govan and Partick in 1915 foreshadowed the Rent Act; and the Crofters Act of 1886 was passed after four years of protest in the Scottish Highlands: protest which continued in bursts until the 1920s.

The Crofters Act has remained the basis for most subsequent Highland land legislation; departures from its principles, such as legislation of 1897 and 1976 which provided facilities for crofters to become owner occupiers (a popular change of status in Ireland), have proved largely ineffective. The ideas of the LRPG do not propose fundamental alteration of the code of crofting legislation. In the case of housing, the regime established by Wheatley and other inter-war housing ministers has been almost completely dismantled during the 1980s. The policy of Margaret Thatcher's Conservative governments to encourage council tenants to become owner occupiers has had a profound effect in west central Scotland, an area which traditionally had a very high proportion of population living in accommodation rented from local authorities. A final comparative point is that these are two areas of policy where governments have acted to interfere with property rights, those of Highland landowners in the case of the Crofters Act, and urban landlords in the case of the Rent Restriction Act of 1915. Radicals of the late nineteenth and early twentieth century viewed these issues through the same lens: men such as John Ferguson and Michael Davitt urged that they could be solved together with the introduction of Henry George's 'single tax' on land, or through the straightforward nationalisation of land.

I

Land and Politics

The background to the passage of the Crofters Act of 1886 can be found in the series of protests which spread across the Scottish Highlands in the 1880s. The main effect of the act was to make evictions by landowners more difficult through the granting of security of tenure to crofters; the rents of crofters were to be subject to arbitration by a new court established by the act - the Crofters Commission; and crofters were given the right to claim compensation for their improvements and could not be rented on such improvements. Since the famine of the 1840s the level of eviction had been running at a much reduced level. This is not to say, however, that landowners had ceased to resort to coercive tactics to ensure the payment of rent or compliance with other estate regulations, most notably the prohibition of subdivision of holdings. The forces which had driven eviction to such high levels in earlier periods, the profitability of the sheep farming industry and the fear of social breakdown during the famine, were no longer present. Indeed, the falling prices and high overheads, associated with sheep farming in the 1860s and 1870s, had seen the expansion of commercialised sport, especially deer stalking, as an alternative use of land in the Highlands. There had been periodic protests against the encroachment of these forms of land use onto territory which had formerly been available to the crofting community for grazing. The fact that such land could be taken over by estate managers without any compensation for improvements carried out by the crofters (although these were rarely highly valuable) was a source of resentment.

Early examples of protest took place at Bernera, a tidal island off the west coast of Lewis, in 1874; and at Leckmelm in Wester Ross in 1879. The latter event saw the beginnings of political agitation on the Highland land question. The focus of events moved to the island of Skye after the controversy over the Leckmelm evictions had subsided. Protest occurred in 1881 on the estate of Kilmuir, where crofters instigated a rent strike. The political dimension of the growing problems in the Highlands became prominent after disorder at Braes, near Portree, in April 1882. The politics of this stage of the crofter question were characterised by a dispute between the Home Office and the commissioners of supply for Inverness-shire, over the costs of policing such remote areas in troubled times. Initially, the problem of parliamentary sovereignty and the crofter question was an academic one as the government was determined not to, as they saw it, give encouragement or concession to rebellious Highlanders. Mid-1882 was perhaps not a propitious moment for agrarian agitators, coming at the culmination of three years of agitation in the west of Ireland and immediately after the Phoenix Park murders. The unfortunate commissioners of supply for the county of Inverness had to shoulder the burden of policing the ongoing crofters' agitation. This strategy of aloofness by government could not be sustained as the agitation worsened, and marines had to be sent to Skye during the winter of 1882-83. The government was forced to yield to pressure in the spring of 1883, when they appointed a royal commission, under the chairmanship of Lord Napier, to investigate the grievances of the crofters. Although the commission made wide-ranging recommendations, those on the land question were considered by the government to be impractical.

The government turned to other sources in an attempt to deal with ongoing disorder in the Highlands: a further military force was despatched to Skye during the winter of 1884-85 and in early 1885 attempts were made to present voluntary concessions by landowners as a solution. These expedients, especially the latter, were recognised as insufficient and in the spring of 1885 an attempt was made to legislate on the crofter question. Debate centred not on the question of interference with the sanctity of property rights, but on the precedent of legislating for a particular group of people in a particular region of the country. This question was debated in correspondence between Gladstone and his home secretary, William Harcourt (prior to the establishment of the Scottish Office in late 1885 the Home Office was responsible for most government business relating to Scotland). The debate was resolved by Gladstone's suggestion that crofting legislation could be confined to parishes with an established history of common pasturage. His justification for this was intriguing: he argued that the rights of property in the Highlands were not absolute, the historic title of the people to the land had been usurped by landowners in pursuit of material gain. He argued that the rights of property in the Highlands were not absolute, but came with 'engagements' in the shape of this traumatic history:

> For it is, after all, this historical fact that constitutes the crofters' title
> to demand the interference of Parliament. It is not because they are
> poor, or because there are too many of them, or because they want
> more land to support their families, but because those whom they

represent had rights of which they have been surreptitiously deprived
to the injury of the community [Cameron, 33].

Thus, what can be seen in this case is an initial denial on the part of the
government that the crofters required special legislation to deal with their grievances,
but, later under the influence of protest, there was a resort to such legislation. This
process was expedited by a number of factors: the continuing agitation in the
Highlands, which on occasion required military intervention, and would continue to
do so until 1888; the fact that the much more organised and politicised agitation in
Ireland lay in the background to Highland events; and the growing political
awareness of the crofters, especially after their enfranchisement in 1885 and the
election of crofter candidates in preference to official Liberal candidates at the election
of that year.

The importance of the Crofters Act can be seen in a brief overview of the
subsequent history of the history of Scottish land legislation. The great fear
expressed by opponents of the 1886 act was that this cruel and unusual measure
would spread to the Lowlands. This would be especially injurious to landlords
because of two conditions which applied to Lowland farming: the system of long
leases and the fact that landlords, as opposed to tenants, provided most of the
investment in improvements. Conservative policy in the 1890s was, like Liberal
policy in the previous decade, modelled on the contemporary Irish example.
Attempts were made to identify areas where the Highland economy could be
developed, the infrastructure of the region improved, and the concept of land
purchase was imported from Ireland. It was thought that the responsibilities of
ownership would wean Irish small farmers off their nationalist proclivities: in
Scotland the aim was rather more prosaic, to create, in the words of the duke of
Argyll, in a letter to the secretary for Scotland, Lord Lothian, 'a very desirable
Conservative middle class of proprietors' [Cameron, 83]. In Ireland small tenants
proved amenable to the idea of ownership but declined to abandon home rule in
return. In Scotland the record of the Congested Districts Board, the organisation
established in 1897 to carry through this policy, was more mixed than that of its Irish
counterpart, especially as crofters declined to accept the responsibilities of
ownership.

II

Housing and Politics
Over the period from the mid-nineteenth century until the end of the Great War
housing climbed up the Scottish political agenda. The speed of Scottish urbanisation,
allied to feudal aspects of property relations had produced significant overcrowding
in Scottish burghs. This fact, along with traditional practice and the relatively high
price of land in urban areas, meant that the Scottish urban landscape was composed
of tenement buildings containing multiple dwellings, a pattern more familiar to
European cities such as Paris or Berlin, than to English industrial centres such as
Leeds or Manchester, where self-contained cottages or terraced houses were the most
common form of dwelling. A further result was very high levels of overcrowding in
Scottish urban areas: as late as 1901 over 70 per cent of Glasgow's dwellings were
of one or two rooms. Even European cities such as Paris or Berlin, with 57 per cent
and 45 per cent in this category respectively, were not comparable; London, with
only 35 per cent of dwellings limited to one or two rooms, was another world
[Daunton, 197]. There had been attempts to deal with these problems, but in the
nineteenth century they were mostly carried out on a local scale. Slum clearance
schemes in the 1860s saw the demolition of substandard housing and its replacement
with higher quality, and more expensive, buildings; buildings which those cleared

from the slums could not afford to rent. These initiatives served to relocate, rather than eradicate, social problems.

By the 1880s the expansion of the economy masked underlying problems in the housing market in Scotland and the royal commission which reported in 1885 underestimated the extent of the difficulties. Nevertheless, there were a number of structural problems which could not be elided. The first of these was the relationship between wages, prices and rents in Scotland in the late nineteenth century: put crudely, wages were comparatively low whereas prices and rents were comparatively high. Second, the system of letting was highly inflexible: most lets were for twelve months from 28 May (Whitsunday) but the bargain was concluded some four months before, on 2 February (Candlemas). The rigidity of these arrangements placed tenants at a disadvantage if their circumstances changed in the middle of a let. Finally, landlords had, through the doctrine of hypothec, almost complete security in the recovery of unpaid rents, an important influence in sustaining high rents in Scotland. Landlords also had at their disposal considerable powers to remove tenants for rent arrears or other breaches of a lease. It is ironic that in the same year as the Liberal government passed the Small Landholders (Scotland) Act, which purported to offer an improvement in the position of crofters and small tenants, they also passed the Housing, Letting (Scotland) Act which speeded up the already rapid process of urban eviction.

These inequalities in the relationship between tenants and landlords were the cause of deep resentments and conflict, especially during the Edwardian period when the industrial economy was in recession and the extent of house building in the Scottish burghs collapsed. Importantly then, the protests which occurred in 1915 did not stem solely from wartime conditions, but also from a legacy of resentment and political activity on the housing question. This issue was seized on by local Labour politicians and the housing question became central to the development of the Labour party in the west of Scotland.

The rent strikes of 1915 were part of a much wider pattern of protest on Clydeside during the Great War. These events are now interpreted by most historians as part of a movement of skilled workers to protect their status and bargaining power from their employers, rather than an anti-war agitation. Nevertheless, the rent strikes posed a threat to the war effort and to the stability of important munitions areas such as the Clyde. This fact can be seen by the rapidity of the response of the government and the employers when faced with the problems posed by the strikers. Activists such as John Wheatley were vocal when the combination of high interest rates, shortage of houses and intense demand due to the swollen industrial workforce, led to upward pressure on rents and increased levels of eviction. The intensity of the struggle was increased by the publicity afforded to cases where the families of serving soldiers were subject to eviction. Wheatley drew particular attention to the threat of eviction hanging over the family of Michael McHugh, a wounded soldier from Shettleston.

The eviction was due to take place in June 1915 but a large crowd prevented this from happening. Protest was also evident at the home of the factor responsible for the property, as he was burned in effigy. Just as crofters sought to protest without compromising their patriotism, a Union Jack was nailed across the door of the close where the McHugh family lived. Wheatley even appealed to Lord Kitchener on the iniquity of the threat of eviction hanging over the families of serving soldiers. The strikes spread throughout the working-class areas of Glasgow: to Shettleston, which contained many men who worked at the foundries in the east end of the city, and to the more westerly districts of Partick on the north bank of the Clyde and Govan on the south, which were dominated by shipyard workers. Patrick Dollan estimated that 10,000 people were withholding rent by the autumn of 1915. Women were at the forefront of this movement, as they had been on certain occasions during protests in the Highlands. Although many of those involved in the organisation of the strikes were politically motivated, and although the Labour party was active on the issue, there was a considerable amount of apolitical motivation as well. The struggle could not have been successful, as it undoubtedly was, without being able to transcend political and religious divisions. Activists such as Mary Barbour and the radical, feminist and wife of the manse, Helen Crawfurd, skilfully exploited the culture and raucousness of the streets to sustain the strikes and to develop strategies for the humiliation of the factor.

As with the land question in Ireland and the Scottish Highlands in the 1880s, the government's response to protest was to investigate the issue through a committee, the Hunter-Scott Committee of 1915, and to follow this up with the introduction of rent control in urban areas. There were, however, a number of differences in the two cases: first, in the urban case, rent was the grievance. Although the rent strike had been used as a tactic in the Irish Land War and the Crofters War, rent levels were only one of a range of grievances in the former case, and only a serious problem in isolated areas in the latter. Although the Glasgow rent strikers used tactics similar to those of their rural counterparts in a previous generation, most notably the humiliation of factors, they were agitating over a very specific issue, that of artificially high rent levels due to shortages of housing. Second, wartime conditions were central to the rent control which was imposed by the government in late 1915. Walter Long, the president of the Local Government Board, was clear about this in his introduction of the Rent Restriction Bill to the House of Commons on 25 November 1915. His awareness of the fact that this was exceptional legislation interfering with urban property rights and coming between bargains made between landlords and tenants, was justified, perhaps uneasily, by the continuation of the war: '.if it were not for the fact we are at war ... I do not think I should propose legislation of this kind' [*Hansard*, LXXVI, col. 42]. He went on to point out that the legislation was introduced not for reasons of social justice but to remove an obstacle to the war effort: two of the most common arguments which were used to justify high rents during the war, namely high wages and a shortage of housing due to the cessation of building, were specifically rejected by Long.

Whereas the Crofters Act and the Irish Land Act had established courts to arbitrate on the level of rents, the 1915 Rent Act froze rents at August 1914 levels. Tenants were also to be given a degree of security of tenure, conditional on the payment of rent and the upkeep of the property. The act was to apply for the duration of the war and for six months thereafter, although in the event it proved difficult to end rent restriction. At the end of the war it was recognised that the enduring problem of excess demand in the housing market meant that rent could not be immediately deregulated without recreating the same difficulties which had arisen in 1915. This fact, and the failures of the Addison and Chamberlain Acts to stimulate private building, helped to create a climate for the public sector to take over from the private builders who had manifestly failed to meet the needs of the situation in the west of Scotland.

The Great War was the most important factor in the background to the 1915 Rent Act, rather than the justice of the case of the rent strikers, or the long history of difficulties faced by tenants in urban Scotland. The historicism which was such an important factor in the passage of the Crofters Act was entirely absent in the case of housing, perhaps because the historical grievances were of too recent a date. The war had a different effect on the land question; the Small Landholders Act of 1911 was evidently ineffectual by 1914 and land settlement activity was suspended when war broke out. Recruiting levels in the Highlands were very high, the Board of Agriculture also found that its staff was affected by military service and transfer to other more important areas of administration. In one aspect of the Highland land question wartime conditions did have a positive impact, this was the use of the

Defence of the Realm Act to create new temporary holdings for crofters on land which had been formerly used as deer forest, with the objective of increasing the level of food production. This worked well during the period of conflict but proved to be problematic after the armistice when a number of crofters declined to relinquish their holdings.

III

A Land Fit for Heroes?
A further comparison which deserves exploration is the fact that both the land question and the housing issue were important aspects of the attempts by Lloyd George's coalition government to implement a programme of reconstruction after the Great War. The 1919 Land Settlement (Scotland) Act effectively created provisions for the nationalisation of land in the Highlands. Although its provisions covered the whole country, land settlement activity in the Lowlands was reined in after the cuts in government expenditure in 1922. Although this piece of legislation worked better than the 1911 Small Landholders Act it was a ponderous and bureaucratic beast and a source of frustration to land-hungry crofters. As a result of this, and other specialised local factors, protest was renewed. Most protests took the form of land raids, the act of staking a claim to a very specific piece of land by occupying it. Examples were seen on the islands of Skye, Lewis, North and South Uist, and Tiree in the years immediately following the Great War. The Board of Agriculture made valiant efforts not to direct their operations in response to raids but this principle proved difficult to sustain. By the mid-1920s this phase of protest was exhausted; land settlement had also run out of steam due to a shortage of available land and restrictions on government expenditure. A further feature of this period in the Highlands was the return of emigration as an element in the equation of land, population and resources in the Highlands. The Empire Settlement Act of 1922, combined with dire economic conditions, led to the departure of large numbers of emigrants, especially from the island of Lewis in 1923 and 1924.

The legislation on the housing question in the post-war period showed a similar pattern of large ideals and grandiose plans not entirely fulfilled by legislation. The Housing and Town Planning (Scotland) Act of 1919 made provision for local authorities to quantify housing shortages and to provide plans for their eradication. Limited Treasury funding was available to assist these projects but the act was widely perceived to be a failure with only about 25,000 houses constructed, and only 2000 of them in Scotland. Neville Chamberlain's Housing Act of 1923 was a little more successful with its provisions for local authorities to subsidise private building and then to claim compensation from the Treasury. The most important act in this burst of legislation, however, was the Housing Act passed during the term of office of the first Labour government in 1924. The principal architect of this act was John Wheatley, who, as we have seen, had regarded the housing question as fundamental since his days as a Glasgow city councillor before the Great War. There were three important elements in Wheatley's approach which marked the 1924 Act as distinctive. First, the act provided for a subsidy of £9 per house (slightly more in agricultural parishes) to both local authorities and private builders. Second, this subsidy was only payable to private builders if they built houses for letting at rents no greater than those being charged by the local authority for an equivalent house. Third, the subsidy was only payable if the house to be rented met certain qualitative standards. Thus, Wheatley's act returned the emphasis to the public sector and bound in the question of quality to the government's subsidy of house building. One area where the act was deficient was in the question of slum clearance: it is doubtful whether those who endured the worst housing conditions received any immediate benefit from the new act.

Slum clearance was turned to by the next Labour government when an act of 1930 established a programme which paid a subsidy for each person re-housed. Nearly 16,000 houses were built in 1933 and 1934 to replace condemned properties, whereas only 20,000 such houses had been constructed during the period 1919 to 1932. Nevertheless, despite this weakness, and the fact that the subsidy was reduced in 1927 and abolished entirely in 1933, a substantial number of houses were built under Wheatley's provisions. Across the United Kingdom a record 273,000 houses were constructed in 1927, and in Glasgow alone over 20,000 two- and three-apartment houses, or 42 per cent of all government subsidised houses in the inter-war period, were constructed under the provisions of the 1924 act. Thus, the inter-war period saw a profound change in the provision of housing in Scotland. Prior to 1914 most houses were built by private builders for rental: between 1919 and 1939 public sector construction exceeded that of the private sector by 235 per cent. This trend continued in the period from the end of the Second World War until the mid-1970s. Public expenditure cutbacks under the Labour government and the ideological considerations of the Conservative government in the 1980s have shifted the emphasis back to the private sector.

IV

Conclusion
As noted above, the regime which was established by the rural land legislation discussed here has been enduring. The principles of the 1886 act remain at the heart of crofting legislation today. Further attempts to reform crofting in the 1950s, after the report of the commission of enquiry into crofting conditions in 1953; and in the late 1960s, after proposals by the crofters commission, raised the spectre of tampering with the 1886 regime and encountered opposition for this reason. The 1976 Crofting Reform Act, which provided facilities for crofters to purchase their holdings, has, like its predecessor of 1897, been unsuccessful - with only a small number of crofters choosing to exercise the purchase option. Recent developments in the Highlands have confirmed the continuing loyalty to those principles: when the Assynt Crofters Trust Ltd purchased the North Lochinver estate in 1993 they did so in the expectation of continuing to run the estate on the tenurial principles established in 1886. It should also be noted that they threatened, as a secondary tactic which did not prove necessary, to use the right-to-buy clauses of the 1976 act to destroy the estate as a saleable commodity. By contrast, the structure of Scottish housing established by the legislation of the inter-war years, which subsidised the construction of homes by local authorities, has been fundamentally altered in recent years.

As late as 1981 55 per cent of Scotland's housing was in the public rented sector, the comparable figure in England and Wales was only 26 per cent. In Glasgow over 60 per cent of the housing stock was in the public sector, and in certain areas the figure was even higher: Clydebank, Monklands and Motherwell District Councils had over 80 per cent of housing in the public sector; Cumnock and Doon, West Lothian, and Cumbernauld and Kilsyth, had figures of over 70 per cent. Concomitantly, relatively few Scots owned their own houses: in 1981 only 35 per cent of Scottish households owned their homes, a much lower figure than the 58 per cent of English and Welsh households who did so. Thus, 'the strong government commitment to home ownership, therefore, faced a much greater uphill struggle in Scotland, and represented a more extreme reversal of policy' [Rodger, 177-80]. This orthodoxy was profoundly altered in the 1980s with the sale of council houses and the reduction in exchequer funding for the construction of local authority housing. Over 40 per cent of council houses were constructed with such funding in 1977, a proportion which had fallen to only seven per cent. The census of 1991 recorded that 52 per cent of Scottish homes were owner occupied; 38 per cent were rented from local authorities; and only five per cent were rented privately. These statistics demonstrate clearly the evolution of this aspect of Scottish society from the position in the nineteenth century, when the private sector dominated; and the change which took place during the 1970s and 1980s which saw the erosion of the public sector as a provider of homes to the Scottish population.

This essay has sought to explore the ways in which protest on two key Scottish issues impacted upon parliament and helped to induce important pieces of legislation which have had an important influence in shaping the Scottish landscape in the twentieth century. It is noticeable that these incidences of protest were essentially limited rebellions on the question of property rights, something to which the Scottish legal code gave jealous protection. Parliamentary interference with such rights in the shape of the Crofters Act of 1886 and the Rent Restriction Act of 1915 were justified on the grounds of dealing with a special case, that of the crofters; or, in 1915, responding to an emergency situation during wartime. A link between these two issues would not have been seen as contrived by Victorian radicals who conceived of the social problems created by unequal relations between landlords and tenants in a holistic manner. With this in mind, it is ironic that although the land question, and associated anti-landlordism, has proved to be an enduring rhetorical device in the Scottish Labour movement, it was the Liberal party which erected most of the legislative landmarks in this territory. Housing was crucial to the development of the Labour movement in a local context in the west of Scotland before, during and after the Great War, and Wheatley's Housing Act of 1924 laid the foundations for the domination of the Scottish housing market by the public rented sector. Thus, although the origin of these two problems have a certain similarity, and although both were the occasion of protest, the geographical impact of the resulting legislation has been quite different.

The crofting legislation was confined to a carefully defined part of Scotland, although Irish legislation was drawn on in its composition. Although John Wheatley's ideas were inspired by the housing question in Glasgow, and although he was in favour of the idea of Scottish home rule, he was firm in his belief that housing was a social problem which should be dealt with by principles which could be applied throughout the United Kingdom. This is not to say, of course, that the results of such legislation did not have a particular impact in urban Scotland. Westminster could be influenced by protest, but perhaps only when that protest became general, as it may have seemed to the government was happening over the land question in Scotland and Ireland in the 1880s; or when it occurred in conditions, such as those prevailing during wartime, which necessitated a rapid response by government. A final point concerns the nature of the Scottish political agenda, working backwards from the events of the late 1990s can lead to assumptions which exaggerate the importance of the home rule issue. This rather limited case study of parliamentary action on two key areas of Scottish politics has demonstrated that simplistic notions of abject neglect of, or sensitive consideration for, Scottish peculiarities by the United Kingdom parliament at Westminster cannot be sustained.

Further Reading :
Ewen A. Cameron, *Land for the People? The British Government and the Scottish Highlands, c.1880-1925* (East Linton, 1996); Samuel Cooper, 'John Wheatley: A Study in Labour History', unpublished PhD thesis (University of Glasgow, 1973); Martin J. Daunton, 'Housing' in, *The Cambridge Social History of Britain, 1750-1950*, vol 2, *People and Their Environment*, ed. F.M.L. Thompson (Cambridge, 1990), pp. 195-250; Clive Dewey, 'Celtic Agrarian Legislation and the Celtic Revival: Historicist Implications of Gallstone's Irish and Scottish Land Acts 1870-1886', *Past and Present*, no 64 (1974), 30-70; James Hunter, *The Making of the*

Crofting Community (Edinburgh, 1976); I.M.M. MacPhail, *The Crofters' War* (Stornoway, 1989); *Housing, Social Policy and the State*, ed. Joseph Melling (London, 1980); Iain J.M. Robertson, 'Governing the Highlands: The Place of Popular Protest in the Highlands of Scotland after 1918', *Rural History*, 8 (1997), 109-24; *Scottish Housing in the Twentieth Century*, ed. Richard Rodger (London, 1989); Ian S. Wood, *John Wheatley* (Manchester, 1990).

14

Legislative and Executive Autonomy in Modern Scotland

I.G.C. HUTCHISON

The history of the extension of administrative home rule to Scotland is relatively clear, although the motives for each major step varied, with a mix of efficiency, the desire to stave of nationalist pressure and fairly basic vote-winning calculations being present in varying amounts. The first stage came in 1885, and thereafter proceeded steadily, so that in 1969 the head civil servant at the Scottish Office was able to inform the Kilbrandon Commission on the Constitution that virtually complete executive devolution had been achieved.

I

In 1885 a Scottish secretary was appointed and the Scottish Office was situated at Dover House, in London. This change, restoring an office abolished after the 1745 Jacobite rising, came as the result of widespread discontent with the handling of Scottish legislation in the mid-Victorian era. The individual effectively responsible for dealing with Scottish business in the government was the lord advocate. But there were numerous problems with this arrangement. The lord advocate was primarily a legal officer, who dealt with judicial promotions and frequently appeared in important court cases. He thus had little time for wider administrative work. Moreover the lord advocate's political career was usually short-lived: it was the norm for him to claim the first judicial vacancy which arose. As, moreover, the lord advocate had no seat in the cabinet, his influence in governmental decision-taking was highly marginal. As a result, it was widely believed that in parliament Scottish issues were not allocated adequate time to be fully aired. The problems of getting an education act for Scotland passed - a process which took nearly twenty years, finally getting on the statute book in 1872, and then two years after the equivalent measure for England - seemed to sum up the neglect of Scottish matters. The failure of the government to respond effectively to the problems faced by the Scottish universities in the early 1880s confirmed this perception. Accordingly, a public meeting held on 16 January 1884, attended by leading Tories such as Lord Lothian as well as prominent Liberals, demonstrated the united desire among Scots to have a minister directly responsible for Scottish business.

But for some thirty years thereafter the appointment was of only limited import. It was not until 1892 that the minister had an automatic cabinet seat, and it was only in 1926 that the post was raised to its eighteenth-century standing of a secretaryship of state - but even then it was took a further eleven years before the salary commensurate with the job's status was paid. Nor was the period from 1885 to 1918 characterised by marked activity by Scottish secretaries. Very few legislative measures flowed from the Scottish Office until the tenure of John Sinclair (Lord Pentland), when important land and education acts were put through. Indeed, before 1905, most holders of the position sat in the Lords, so the lord advocate remained responsible for Scottish matters in the Commons.

Until 1928, moreover, the Scottish secretary had rather limited oversight of Scottish administration, as most fields - local government, prisons, agriculture, etc. - were administered by boards, nominally under the Scottish Office, but in reality pretty well independent. This set-up was denounced by two government reports (MacDonnell in 1914 and Haldane in 1918) as archaic, for several reasons. First, there was no clear chain of ministerial responsibility, so MPs could not question their operations in parliament. Second, appointments to the boards' staff were not on a competitive basis, as had been instituted for the British civil service after the Northcote-Trevelyan reforms of 1853, but still rested on patronage. Third, there was no framework of administrative class civil servants, the all-rounder so beloved of Whitehall, and instead narrow experts were the norm. Finally, the boards were also charged with adopting a dilatory approach to deciding matters, which made for inefficiency in the public services. The abolition of most of these boards in 1928 was justified on grounds of efficiency, and public bodies and the press generally endorsed this action.

In 1939, consequent upon the Gilmour Report of 1937, the next major change took place. The work of the Scottish Office had hitherto been mainly carried out in London at Dover House, in order to facilitate dealings with parliament and to maintain close liaison with the rest of Whitehall. But now the work of the Scottish Office was, as far as possible, transferred to Edinburgh, and at the same time the remaining boards not abolished in 1928 wee wound up. St Andrews House was built as a symbol of this change, with the offices of departments hitherto scattered across Edinburgh now gathered into one single site. The Scottish Office was divided into four departments, with the permanent secretary in overall charge of co-ordination, so that it now conformed very closely to the Whitehall pattern.

These changes were partly justified on efficiency grounds, but also represented a response to anti-centralising feelings voiced at the time of the abolition of the boards. These had been based in Edinburgh, allowing pressure groups and interested bodies direct and immediate access, and the removal after 1928 of their replacements to London was resented in many quarters. Additionally, the growth of interest in Scottish nationalism in the early 1930s worried the Tories, as much of the support for the Scottish party came from right of centre individuals. Accordingly, the move to Edinburgh was conceived as a means of placating these elements. The widespread alarm about the deep economic and social problems afflicting Scotland in the 1930s and the sense that Scottish matters were neglected in parliamentary proceedings further encouraged the 1939 reforms.

The course of further extensions of home rule in administration continued after World War II, but only after a tussle within the mandarinate at the end of that war. A Machinery of Government committee, composed of leading civil servants, was set up to assess the lessons of war-time administrative machinery. At the outset, the extent of devolution given to the Scottish Office was queried. Sir Arthur Barlow argued that the proper approach to be adopted was that separation of administrative authority on a territorial footing should occur solely in fields where the Scottish and English systems were fundamentally different. To give way to separatist sentiment in areas where the problems and functions of government were similar across Britain would be to invite administrative disaster. He queried, for example, whether Scotland really needed a separate department of agriculture, since the similarities between Scotland and England far outnumbered the differences. The argument was resolved when the Scottish secretary, Tom Johnston, intervened to insist on a large degree of Scottish devolution rather than a highly unified centralised system, which, he contended, would simply encourage nationalist discontent. Thus, Johnston adroitly played the card which successive Scottish ministers have found invaluable in extracting concessions from Westminster and Whitehall. [This episode can be followed in: NAS, SHHD MSS, HH 1/2574 (which contains Johnston's memoranda), 36/18, 46].

Thereafter, the way was open for the Balfour Commission of 1953, which was set up by the Tories partly to respond to the nationalist mood evinced by the Scottish Covenant Movement, and partly to capitalise on Scottish hostility to nationalisation, which had removed control of much of the Scottish economy to London. The Balfour report urged that, as far as possible, control of Scottish administration should be located in the Scottish Office. The government agreed to this, with concentration of most transport functions in Edinburgh being the immediate consequence, and the construction of the Forth and Tay road bridges were acclaimed as the direct fruits of this devolution. Later in the 1960s and 1970s substantial responsibility for economic planning was devolved to the Scottish Office. Hence across almost a century a vast swathe of administrative authority was handed over to the Scottish Office in a cumulative process.

II

Given this substantial and ever-expanding degree of administrative self-government conferred on Scotland, the absence of any degree of legislative devolution is surprising. In contrast to Northern Ireland, which achieved both types of devolution simultaneously in 1921, a Scottish parliament only arrived in 1999, over a century after the Scottish Office had been established. The only significant concession to democratic oversight was the Scottish Grand Committee of the House of Commons. Made permanent in 1907, it was accorded greater powers in 1948, and again in 1957. The reasons for this slow trajectory lie partly in internal problems associated with home rule, but also with wider influences acting against legislative devolution.

The campaign for Scottish home rule was highly sporadic. There were phases of agitation, soon followed by extended periods of quiescence. In the later 1880s, many petitions for home rule flowed in to the Scottish Office, but the files are empty for some twenty years from about 1890 until some four years before the Great War, when another upsurge occurred. The first six or seven years after 1918 were also high points, but thereafter the issue became insignificant for the rest of the inter-war period, a short flurry in the early 1930s excepted. The post-1945 Scottish Covenant campaign perfectly epitomised this evanescence: for some six years in the late 1940s and early 1950s it drew enormous support, the government itself estimating that a remarkable one and a quarter million - some 40 per cent of adult Scots signed the petition. Yet by 1952, the movement was effectively finished, and the Scottish Office files on the home rule movement contained very little material for the rest of the decade. An attempt to resuscitate the Covenant campaign at the start of the 1960s failed through a total lack of public interest. Until 1967, indeed, it appeared that the question was in abeyance. This episodic pattern is of course starkly different to both Ireland, where the nationalist agitation was a continuous presence for half a century from the early 1870s, and India, where an ever-present campaign began in the 1880s. British governments were accordingly not likely to be impressed with the patchy Scottish performance.

A further drawback was that frequently the calls for home rule came from marginal groups, or were associated with a crankish element - what Anthony Crosland apparently used to refer to as 'the green ink brigade'. As to the former category: the bulk of the demands in the later 1880s emanated from branches of the Highland Land League, e.g. Rogart, and in the early 1920s they came mostly from local branches of the Independent Labour Party, the Co-operative Women's Guild and the Liberals. The governments for these periods were overwhelmingly Unionist, and so were hardly prone to be swayed by demands from opposition groupings. The movement in the 1910-14 era was spearheaded by the Liberal ginger group, the

Young Scots, who were less easily dismissed as minority faddists, the more so as the Liberals were in power at the time. The Covenant Movement after 1945 also posed a more significant challenge, but as we have seen, neither persisted.

Many who lobbied the government could be treated as unrepresentative, not to say slightly dotty. This was a pronounced aspect of the decade or so after 1945, the most extreme instance being an announcement by an octogenarian medium, claiming to have been in communication across the ether with the sixth earl of Eglinton (1588-1661). The earl revealed that, after consulting with a group of famous Scottish noblemen (including Argyll, Mar, Lothian and Sutherland), they were agreed that the best form of government for Scotland was that there should be a separate Scottish parliament, with twelve to twenty Scottish MPs in the imperial parliament - conclusions remarkably close to those proposed by many at the time [Ibid., HH 1/796, P. Allen to secretary of state for Scotland, 13 Mar. 1952]. Even estimating the significance of demands was perplexing. In 1890, the convention of royal burghs voted solidly, by 52 to 11, in favour of Scottish home rule. The next year, the convention decided equally firmly, by 57 to 10, against.

Against these flimsy forces advocating home rule was a broad front composed of many powerful hostile agencies. Businessmen were virtually universally opposed, particularly the Confederation of British Industries and its predecessors, and of course these wielded great influence with the Conservative administrations who were in office for the bulk of the century after 1885. So, when nationalist pressure seemed to be mounting in the early 1930s, a member of the Weir family, perhaps the most influential dynasty of industrialists at the time, contacted the Scottish secretary, offering to lead a counter-campaign. The Scottish TUC rather lost interest in home rule in the late 1920s, and in 1950 voted heavily against the measure. So, when asking the cabinet to approve the appointment of the Balfour Commission the Scottish secretary, James Stuart, could be reassuring about the outcome:

> I would expect industrial and commercial interests, local authorities
> and trade unions, when giving evidence to the Commission, to
> come out strongly against any separatist ideas and against any
> proposal for change which would not lead to greater efficiency
> [Ibid., HH 41/1391, 24 June 1952].

Again, the two leading Scottish newspapers were adamantine against separatism in the period down to World War II. *The Scotsman* ran a series of editorials in the late 1920s insisting that 'it is still true beyond fear of contradiction there is no real demand for Home Rule among the people of Scotland', so that the clamour for it came form 'a few small but highly vocal bodies'. It explained that 'Scottish Home Rule would almost 'certainly be a costly experiment' [31 Oct. 1928, 25 Jan. 1929]. The *Glasgow Herald*, the voice of the west of Scotland business community, reiterated these themes with even greater vehemence.

After 1945 this anti-home rule alliance was somewhat fractured: *The Scotsman* switched to advocating devolution with increasing vigour, while the Church of Scotland also added its support to the demand. Nevertheless, opinion still seemed mostly critical: a 1949 Scottish Office survey of local press responses to the Covenant Movement found that only seven of the 35 journals examined carried editorials on the matter, and just one of these seven championed home rule.

The difficulty of devising a workable scheme of devolution also deterred governments. In part, the incoherence on the part of home rulers complicated matters. On occasions the demand was for Scottish Westminster MPs to sit in Scotland, at other times it was proposed that there should be separately elected representatives, while yet again some wanted the Scottish Grand Committee to meet regularly in Edinburgh, rather than London. The difficulties which were encountered in the 1970s in trying to settle on a workable devolution framework had exercised politicians and civil servants from the 1920s. On the one hand, if Scottish MPs elected to Westminster were to constitute the Scottish parliament, it was difficult to envisage how they could find the time to discharge satisfactorily both jobs.

But the alternative, an Edinburgh parliament composed of separately elected members, was no more straightforward, with seven areas identified as problematic. Alarm was expressed at the resultant loss of Scottish influence at the heart of the British government, and the Balfour Commission encapsulated this: 'it would inevitable reduce the prestige and standing of Scotland and her representation in parliament at Westminster and would thereby weaken her voice in Britain and world affairs' [Balfour Commission, 53]. More specifically, the assumed removal of the Scottish secretary from the cabinet (as was the case with Northern Ireland) would mean that no voice could be raised at the highest decision-making levels to argue Scotland's case for special consideration. Allied to this was the claim that, without a strong Scottish voice at the core of Whitehall and Westminster, Treasury generosity to Scotland, inasmuch as payments in excess of the Goschen formula were frequently made to meet special Scottish needs, might very well disappear and a routine application of the strict arithmetical ratio would operate instead.

It was, furthermore, doubted whether there was enough talent and ability in Scotland to fill all the positions which would be generated by constitutional change. This cut two ways. In a period when there was a plethora of outstanding Scots, it was held that they would surely wish to be involved in British politics, rather than be confined to the narrow spectrum of Scottish affairs. As Lord Advocate Cooper put it in 1937: 'I should not like to see the Imperial Parliament dissolving into a handful of glorified Town Councils each clustering round a different Parish Pump' [NAS, SHHD MSS, HH 1/1229, To Scottish secretary of state, 29 Sept. 1937]. At other times, it was claimed that there was a dearth of talent: it must be remembered that between 1945 and 1985, no Conservative Scottish MP held any cabinet post except the Scottish Office, and the same holds broadly true for Labour, with very few exceptions (notably, George Thomson in the late 1960s and John Smith briefly at the end of the Callaghan administration). In these circumstances, it was doubtful whether a separate Scottish parliament would be well led.

The stresses created by the quite feasible position of different parties being in power in London and Edinburgh was also highlighted. In these circumstances, a Scottish secretary could not possibly sit in the 'Imperial' [i.e. British] cabinet. Policy implications were also worrying: what would be the outcome, it was asked, if one government was committed to denationalisation, while the other wished to retain the existing state ownership structure? In the light of these factors, it was very difficult to see Labour after 1959 agreeing to any diminution of the number of Scottish seats in Westminster, as the party was heavily dependent thenceforward on its Scottish contingent if it were to hold office.

Beyond the specific issues centred on home rule, there were wider considerations. One significant factor was the ideological cast of the two main parties. The Tories were, apart from occasional wobblings, the party of the union, as their long-standing title in Scotland indicated: until 1965 they stood as Unionists. The deviations from this were brief dabblings in electoral trafficking rather than any serious intellectual conversion. In the inter-war years the party reckoned that giving administrative devolution would stifle broader nationalist demands, and there were two later flirtations. One episode came just after 1945, and another at the end of the 1960s, but once installed in office the party pointedly did not act to implement pre-election policies.

Labour, which had, at least notionally, been supportive of Scottish home rule in the early part of this century, lost interest and then became hostile. For some, such as Tom Johnston, the apostasy arose from a belief nurtured in the 1930s that only a centralised command economy could bring about socialism, so that devolution would be inimical to this goal. But there was also a strong opinion in left circles from the 1930s that identified European nationalism as a major factor in fascism. Hence after 1945 there was still hostility to separatist tendencies, and the Attlee cabinet justified its rejection of legislative devolution for Scotland by remarking on the integrationist process at work in western Europe, to which separatist demands ran counter.

More speculatively, it may be surmised that the substantial amount of support prevalent in Scotland from the early 1930s for a corporatist approach to economic and social policy proved a negative force against home rule. Corporatism tended to prefer to operate out of the glare of democratic scrutiny, opting instead for deals concocted in back-rooms and shielding decisions from wider accountability. Because this approach was seen by many influential Scots as broadly successful for the half century from the 1930s, the incentive to call for a Scottish legislature may have been diluted.

Concern about the viability of a Scottish parliament hinged partly, as we have seen, on doubts about the pool of political talent available. But there were for a long period also reservations about the calibre of the Scottish Office civil servants who would handle the full panoply of legislative devolution. The professional civil service on the Whitehall model, it must be emphasised, was introduced to the Scottish Office on a widespread basis only after the 1928 reorganisation. Many politicians and senior Whitehall mandarins regarded the Edinburgh bureaucrats as either fledglings or less able and lacking depth of expertise. It was noticeable that bright Scots entering the top administrative class often looked to London, not Scotland, for positions: John Hume, who became a senior Scottish Office figure, applied in 1946 to three departments, with the Scottish Office listed as his third choice. The Machinery of Government committee, composed of top civil servants, pinpointed this weakness as the main defect of the Scottish Office which justified their desire to claw back devolved administrative functions. Hume worked mainly in health, and recounts that all the major policy initiatives and developments were instigated and researched into by his counterparts in the Whitehall Health ministry. He explains that they had far deeper expertise in the various fields, because there were so many of them, while he, covering a range of responsibilities, could not accumulate such knowledge [Hume, 40-1]. Again, it may be significant that one head of the Scottish Office moved to be in charge of the Home Office, yet there is no instance of someone moving in the other direction: this indicates the balance of prestige.

Whitehall staff may not have been favourably impressed by the pace and mode of the conduct of business in St Andrews House. On his arrival there in 1946, Hume was informed that in the 1930s work had finished by about 4 p.m., so that, as he observes, one could complete a round of golf before dinner. The Balfour Commission quizzed the pre-World War II Scottish secretaries as to whether civil servants had taken decisions without the prior knowledge and consent of their political masters. While two ministers, Lord Alness and Ernest Brown, denied this, two others, Lord Clydesmuir (John Colville) and Tom Johnston, accepted that this had indeed happened. Johnston added, as a sort of exculpation, that it had occurred only in the Department of Agriculture! This sort of conduct was of course a major breach of the fundamental code of relations between ministers and civil servants, and must have appalled Whitehall. It is also interesting to speculate about the impact on Whitehall and Westminster of the case of the very senior Scottish Office civil servant George Pottinger, who was jailed for corruption as part of the John Poulson affair in the early 1970s. Pottinger was unique in that certainly since 1918 no top civil servant had been convicted of such an offence. It may have confirmed to many that the Scottish Office was not on the same plane as Whitehall, and that relations between Scottish civil servants and those they dealt with were too close in a small country for pure, impartial administration. (Of course, the alternative interpretation was that an elected Scottish parliament could well have scrutinised the executive for just such cases of professional misconduct.)

One aspect was that the Scottish Office lacked the glamorous departments such as the Treasury and the Foreign Office which attracted high-fliers. Indeed, several of the very areas which bulked largest in Scottish administration were regarded in Whitehall as possessing the least cachet: education, housing and agriculture being instances. Nevertheless, when the head of the Scottish Office, Sir Douglas Haddow, assured the Kilbrandon Commission in 1969 that he was confident his staff could cope with parliamentary devolution, and added that there was now no problem in recruiting good quality personnel. Somewhat gnomically, he remarked that all St Andrews House lacked was a Treasury department. Since that was of course the core of the Whitehall machine, his comments are a little ambiguous.

It is also possible that civil servants in St Andrews House were less than keen on parliamentary devolution. This would have meant closer scrutiny than the occasional examination by the Scottish Grand Committee. Parliamentary questions to the Scottish secretary were not very penetrating, mainly because of the range of topics for which ministers were answerable, so that MPs could rarely get to close engagement on detailed issues. It is broadly accurate to say that while Scottish Office civil servants were positive about acquiring additional tranches of administrative self-government - as their strong resistance to the Machinery of Government committee proposals revealed - their memoranda on legislative devolution tended to emphasise the obstacles (although of course this chimed in with the inclinations of the politicians).

Within government, the question of enhancing Scottish devolution was complicated by the case of Wales. The interconnections exercised both politicians and civil servants, and the Welsh-Scottish interaction proved a two-way relationship. In the 1930s and 1940s further Scottish self-government was sometimes resisted because politicians feared this might exacerbate Welsh susceptibilities, and stiffen that country's bid for home rule. So, when in 1937 the Scottish secretary asked the prime minister to appoint an extra junior minister to share the growing volume of Scottish Office work, he was turned down on the grounds that such a move would cause difficulties with Welsh opinion. The Attlee administration resisted efforts by Scottish secretaries to have any full-blown inquiry into the government of Scotland, partly because it was felt that this would stimulate Welsh demands. Welsh Labour MPs were evidently very worried about inciting nationalist opinion in their country, and Aneurin Bevan was particularly vocal in pushing this argument within the cabinet.

In the mid-1950s, the focus of concern shifted. Welsh calls for the creation of a Welsh Office were being voiced with greater force. Scottish Office civil servants expressed deep unease at the Welsh proposals. First, the projected Welsh devolution package would create dangerous anomalies, for the extent of home rule being claimed for Wales in certain matters was substantially less than that already possessed by Scotland. The Scottish Office was worried that Whitehall might use the Welsh model as a pretext to standardise matters by retrieving devolved areas from St Andrews House. Second, it would weaken the bargaining influence of the Scottish secretary if there were also a Welsh minister in cabinet, pressing that country's claims to special treatment. The upshot, as a top Scottish Office figure argued, could be that '[the Scottish secretary] would become one of two territorial gadflies which the English minister would avoid as much as possible, and treat as nuisances when he failed'. Third, co-ordination of policy between three separate ministries would create very great difficulties and slow down the pace of government, since 'triangular liaison is likely to be as embarrassing officially as it is in private life [Ibid., HH 1/2904 Memorandum, 'Government Administration in Wales: Note on C.(57) 10', no date; HH 1/2905, C.C. Cunningham to (Scottish) under secretary of state, 20

Nov. 1956]. Lastly, in an ironic inversion of the argument offered against Scottish self-government a decade earlier, Scottish Office civil servants now fretted that any Welsh devolution might spark an upsurge of more extreme Scottish nationalist demands.

The operations of the Scottish Grand Committee did little to suggest that the Scottish MPs were interested in or ready for legislative devolution. Often only a handful of members involved themselves wholeheartedly in the committee's work. When Tom Johnston, as Scottish secretary in World War II, arranged to hold meetings in Scotland of Scottish MPs as a sort of surrogate parliament (a proposal he had been suggesting in the 1930s), he had to confess to getting only limited response. Of the twelve meetings convened, only one attracted half of the eligible MPs, and for the rest, barely a quarter turned up. Admittedly war-time exigencies may have affected turn-out, but an irate SNP branch official wrote to Willie Ross twenty years later to complain that only thirteen MPs were present for the Grand Committee's debate on housing, an issue of particular concern to Scotland. Indeed, as Hume remarked, members who did attend the meetings of the committee often did so with no real interest in the proceedings. Many Scottish Labour MPs had no proper office accommodation, so they were in the habit of using the large table round which the committee sat to deal with their constituency paperwork and correspondence, displaying scant attention to the committee's deliberations [Hume, 28-9].

When the members did participate in committee work, the results were not very encouraging. In 1961, the Scottish Secretary, John Maclay, reported to R.A. Butler that it was difficult:

> to dampen the excessive loquacity of certain Scottish members. ...
> [I]n recent years the Chair has almost given up the struggle except
> when obvious obstruction goes on. One comment has been that it
> is extremely difficult to tell from what they are saying whether
> certain members are 'deliberately obstructing or not' [Ibid., HH
> 41/2096, secretary of state to leader of the Commons, n.d. (draft)].

The necessity of packing the committee with English members after 1959, when the Tories had fewer Scottish MPs than Labour, may have suggested to some politicians that the tensions arising from having different parties in power in London and Edinburgh under legislative devolution would be profound.

Politicians adopted a Janus-like approach to home rule. On the one side, the nationalist movement posed no serious electoral threat before 1967, for the Scottish National Party's sole parliamentary victory before then - at Motherwell in 1945 - arose, as James Mitchell notes in his paper, from exceptional circumstances. Throughout the 1930s prime ministers stressed the absence of any support for the movement. Reneging on pre-election pledges to expand self-government brought no electoral retaliation. Labour did nothing to implement its promise in 1945 to give more home rule, yet the party actually increased it poll in 1950, and in 1951 drew the largest popular vote in Scotland it has achieved before or since. Likewise although the Tories in government from 1951 did not honour their manifesto commitment to expand Scottish ministerial appointments and to grant greater control to Scotland of its own affairs, nevertheless the best result ever for the party came in 1955, when it made electoral history by being the only party since 1918 to the present to secure more than 50 per cent of the total vote.

Yet politicians were constantly unnerved by the fear of a nationalist surge. In 1932, when the Scottish Nationalists were polling poorly, the Scottish secretary and the chancellor of the exchequer agreed that a study should be carried out to demonstrate that Scotland was receiving her fair share of government spending, while another survey tried to show that Scottish affairs were not neglected in the Commons. After 1945, this edginess returned. Arthur Woodburn, the newly appointed Scottish secretary, alerted the cabinet late in 1947 to 'a powerful upsurge of Scottish opinion at the moment ... [which] could cut through political parties ... [T]he great dividing issues are settled, leaving the cleavages between the parties less deep-rooted and intense.' Herbert Morrison responded to Woodburn's idea of a commission of inquiry into Scottish devolution by warning :'You may set afoot an agitation for concessions on a lavish scale which you will not be able to control' [Ibid., HH 1/1231, undated (but 1947) draft by Scottish secretary; H. Morrison to Scottish secretary, 13 Nov. 1947]. Again, as in the 1930s, it was agreed to produce data to convince Scots that their country was being given a proper allocation of state funds.

Linked to these uncertainties was a factor which may have made politicians more uneasy, *viz.* the apparent ignorance of the Scottish public about the extent of devolution. This was alluded to in 1949, when the government produced a pamphlet outlining the structure of administration in Scotland, and was reiterated in the Balfour Commission report. A graphic illustration of this ignorance came at a sitting of the Kilbrandon Commission in 1969, at the height of massive publicity on Scottish self-government, stimulated alike by J.P. Mackintosh's seminal book on devolution, published in 1968, by Mrs Ewing's dramatic victory at Hamilton and by the Tories' 'Declaration of Perth', advocating home rule. An interesting exchange took place between Sir Douglas Haddow, the head of the Scottish Office, and one of the assessors to the commission, Ian Millar. The assessors were prominent people in Scottish public life: Millar ran one of the largest building firms in Scotland and subsequently became lord provost of Edinburgh. Sir Douglas told the commission:

> I think the average man in Scotland does not know that people like
> Mr McGuiness [another civil servant] and myself exist - which is
> perhaps a good thing ...
> *Mr Millar*: I was enormously impressed by the amount of   devolution
> we have , and I really did not know about it.
> *Sir D. Haddow*: This is very common, if I may say so ... It is quite
> extraordinary the extent of the ignorance in Scotland of the stage to
> which Scottish devolution has gone. The number of letters
> complaining about Scottish affairs which come even from Members
> of Parliament to English ministers, which have to be passed on to the
> Scottish Office, is really remarkable [Kilbrandon Report, Evidence,
> Vol. II, qq. 42, 62-3].

Likewise, the polling undertaken for the Kilbrandon Commission showed limited knowledge among Scots both of the degree to which administrative autonomy had been devolved and of the areas which fell under the Scottish Office's remit. Flawed though political and social scientists may insist these data are, they do suggest greater ignorance in Scotland than in Wales.

III

After 1966, much of the inhibiting brakes on legislative devolution were removed: in particular, the challenge of the Scottish Nationalist Party was continuous. Also, a clearer design for a home rule parliament emerged, in good part thanks to the Kilbrandon Commission, ironically initially intended to defuse the demand for self-government by deliberating until, as the Labour government anticipated, the heady nationalist momentum after the Hamilton by-election had dissipated, as had always happened previously. Yet some peculiar problems remained, most notably the failure of the 1979 referendum to deliver a decisive majority in favour of devolution, despite the long-standing indications in the opinion polls that most Scots wanted this. The emphatic margin in favour in the 1997 referendum looks to signify a major shift in the mood of the Scots. While Professor Mitchell's essay gives systematic consideration to many of the most important factors involved, one or two additional points may be raised here. Widespread Scottish repudiation of the policies and methods adopted after 1979 by the Conservatives governments unquestionably had a major impact, and the following is not intended to undermine that factor.

It may be that the speedy and total demise of the corporatist approach which accompanied the advent of the 1979 Conservative administration had an influential impact in Scotland. As noted earlier, corporatism had been systematically and enthusiastically adopted from the 1930s. But corporatism, essentially a secretive process, had not been able to survive the withdrawal of government backing after 1979. Its passing may have induced many to feel that permanent democratic institutions, such as a devolved parliament, might offer a more secure guarantee for the prosecution of specific Scottish interests.

A significant element may have been the timing of the two referenda, for it is commonplace that voters in a plebiscite may have other scores to settle beside the precise issues focused on in the vote. The 1997 referendum followed very shortly after the general election, which had seen the Tories obliterated in Scotland. The chance to have, so to speak, a second vote against that hapless party must have been very a strong motive, and the sustained afflatus behind Labour's huge win showed the vital significance of timing - hence the Blair government's reluctance to have a referendum on the single currency, at least until after a second election victory (as they hope). By contrast the 1979 vote came at the end of the 'Winter of Discontent', when public disaffection with the Callaghan administration was high, and it may be that Scots used this as a sort of national by-election to chastise Labour.

Furthermore, the absence of detailed scheme in 1997 may have obviated the problems posed in 1979: in the former there was no pettifogging detail to disturb and distract the voter. It was the raising of difficult technical issues which partly diverted support away from devolution in 1979, but in 1997 there were no specific proposals on to which the opponents could latch. The failure of the recent Australian referendum on the monarchy was lost because voters, although not broadly favourable to retaining the queen, greatly disliked the alternative offered in the vote. Even the separation of the vote on taxation powers from the general principle of devolution adroitly avoided giving any hostages to the 'antis' in 1997.

References and Further Reading:
NAS SHHD MSS: [Edinburgh] National Archives of Scotland, Scottish Home & Health Department MSS; *Report of the Committee on Scottish Administration* [Gilmour Committee], PP 1936-7 (Cmnd 5563); *Report of the Royal Commission on Scottish Affairs* [Balfour Report], PP 1953-4 (Cmnd 9212); *Report of the Royal Commission on the Constitution* [Kilbrandon Report], PP 1973 (Cmnd 5460); John Hume, *Mandarin Grade 3* (Edinburgh 1993); J. Burns, 'The Scottish Committees of the House of Commons, 1948-59', *Political Studies*, 8 (1960), 272-96; G.E. Edwards, 'The Scottish Grand Committee, 1958-70', *Parliamentary Affairs*, 25 (1972), 303-25; J.S. Gibson, *The Thistle and the Crown. A History of the Scottish Office* (Edinburgh, 1985); H.J. Hanham, 'The Creation of the Scottish Office', *Juridical Review*, 10 (1965), 205-44 ; H.J. Hanham, 'The Development of the Scottish Office', in *Government and Nationalism in Scotland*, ed. J.N. Wolfe (Edinburgh, 1969), pp. 51-78 ; James Mitchell, 'The Gilmour Report on Scottish Central Administration', *Juridical Review*, (1989), 173-88; Lindsay Paterson, *The Autonomy of Modern Scotland* (Edinburgh, 1994).

15

Home Rule and Devolution in Ulster

PAUL ARTHUR

'Only connect' - if ever there was a suitable aphorism for a study of the devolution experiment in Northern Ireland this is it. In a different setting it calls to mind Tom Nairn's critique of the history of theorising about nationalism where he identified two dramatic faults:

> One is a tendency to treat the subject in a one-nation or one-state frame of reference: so that each nationalism has to be understood, in effect, mainly with reference to 'its own' ethnic, economic, or other basis - rather than by comparison with the 'general historic process'. The second (and obviously related) tendency is to take nationalist ideology far too literally and far too seriously [Nairn, 93].

An awareness of both these faults will run through this narrative. Context will be all. It is all too easy to be both descriptive (because the story is too well known), and prescriptive - because it serves as such a spectacular case of mismanagement. This paper may fall between these two stools. The topic invites a broad brush approach. It is as well then to begin with some health warnings.

The first concerns nomenclature:

> The political figment called 'Ulster', less a geographical expression than a value, was brought into prominence as a pawn in English party manoeuvre, but it had an existence outside the insubstantial world of high politics. It became a bearer for the collection of symbols which reciprocally expressed and shaped the identity of Northern Protestant groups [Townshend, 182].

These remarks were set in the context of the debate in British politics in the 1880s, but they draw our attention, too, to the 'mytho-logics' entailed in shaping identities. They stress that political activity is not static nor can it be wholly insular. More than a century later 'The Agreement Reached in Multiparty Negotiations' was signed in Belfast on Good Friday 1998. I give the official title, its place of birth and the (religious) date of its signature in that order because all three titles are adopted - 'The Agreement', the 'Belfast Agreement' and 'The Good Friday Agreement' - as a form of ethnic shorthand. Whatever title we adopt we cannot get away from the obvious that we have moved well beyond 'Northern Ireland' or 'Ulster'.

That leads us into the second caveat. We should not confine our remarks solely within the territory that became Northern Ireland, and within a time-frame that begins with partition. A useful starting point is a discussion of 'British' historiography as 'the various peoples and nations, ethnic cultures, social structures, and locally defined communities which have from time to time existed in the area known as "Great Britain and Ireland" [and which] acted so as to create the conditions of their several existences but have also interacted so as to modify the condition of one another's existence' [Pocock, 317]. The Unionists of Northern Ireland have been too defensively introspective (especially in the Stormont years when they were left largely to their own devices) to recognise the significance of interaction. They failed to develop a 'security community' - that is a set of interrelationships in which there is a real assurance that the members of the community will not fight each other physically, but will settle their disputes in some other way. They did not make the connection between political obligation and the security community, a distinction which Pocock makes between 'zones of law' and 'zones of war'. The former is defined by settled government, and the latter is one in which the king or his subjects can make his or their presence effective only in arms. It is conceivable though that he may rule 'a bifurcated realm or a realm having two faces: it is theoretically possible to distinguish between the "domain" where his writ runs and his clerks of justice assert his sedentary authority, and the "march" where his power is the sum of his relations with powerful military figures, feudatories or tributaries, subjects or aliens' [Pocock, 322]. Ulster (and later Northern Ireland) was a 'march' in search of a 'domain'.

A third point was that devolution was imposed - and that is not too strong a term - as a form of political and administrative convenience. It was designed to answer the necessities of a desperate political situation. Originally Ulster's politicians were divided on a policy of separation from, or integration with, Great Britain. Devolution was foisted upon it by Westminster and was accepted (in the words of its first prime minister) only as 'the supreme sacrifice' to secure the peace. There were doubts as to whether the Government of Ireland Act (1920) was designed for permanent effect. Its provisions:

> were dictated with a view to political pacification rather than
> administrative efficiency. When Southern Ireland broke away from
> British rule, the Act was amended in form so as to be rendered
> applicable to Northern Ireland alone. But it was not amended in
> substance. As a consequence, powers were delegated to Northern
> Ireland which had been drafted to meet quite a different situation. No
> regard was paid to the needs of the six counties as a political and
> economic unit [Mansergh, 314].

Whatever criticisms can be levelled at the Scotland Act and the Government of Wales Act neither comes within this danger zone because, ultimately, the new arrangements (of the 1920 act, that is) solely suited the Westminster government. Devolved institutions in Belfast provided, in the sober words of the Kilbrandon Report more than forty years later, 'every inducement to the Government in London to keep Northern Ireland out of United Kingdom politics' [Cmnd 5460: 1973, para 1303].

As a corollary we need to bear in mind the state of domestic British politics when the act went through. One needs to be aware of the sheer effort in trying to manage - let alone govern - Ireland. If the Act of Union (1800) had been designed to enable British politicians to devote less, not more, of their time to Irish affairs, then it failed, so that developments over the Irish question had, by 1911, thrown very grave doubt on the political system's capacity to contain irreconcilable conflict between each of the main parties. This at a time when the Chief of the Imperial General Staff was writing: 'In no single theatre are we strong enough ... not in Ireland, not in England, not on the Rhine, not in Constantinople, nor Batoum, nor Palestine, nor Mesopotamia, nor Persia, nor India'. He was writing in the midst of a period (1919-23) when expenditure on the army was cut by a half each year from £395 million to £45 million, and when Bonar Law was announcing that Britain could no longer be policeman of the world. That reminds us that Britain had ruled over a world system and, in that respect, the 'Irish troubles are useful to us because they form a kind of intersection between the problems of empire and the problems of domestic British politics' [Gallagher, 98, 96-7 and 86-7].

If we can extract any lessons from the above they should be the emphasis on security; the value of a non-insular approach; an underlying concern about identity; and the dubious utility of the 'Ulster' model.

I

The 'Dual Polity' as administrative convenience
We are less concerned with the minutiae of devolution in practice than with general themes which arose as a result of the Northern Ireland experience. Our starting point will be on the debate on territoriality and identity which was never far below the surface in Ulster politics. Jim Bulpitt's simple definition of the historic structure of power in the United Kingdom will serve as our guide. He calls it the Dual Polity: 'a structure of territorial politics in which Centre and periphery had relatively little to do with each other [which] until recently the Centre sought not to govern the United Kingdom but to manage it'. In terms of its management of the domestic environment the centre 'will attempt to construct what can be labelled an external support system, that is to say, it will attempt to minimise the impact of external forces on domestic politics, or ensure that these forces are favourable to the maintenance of domestic tranquillity'. He acknowledges that the political settlement worked out for the United Kingdom in the years following 1688 was 'highly ambiguous', and that Northern Ireland was the most extreme example of duality in the United Kingdom [Bulpitt, 160,238,59].

In relation to Northern Ireland the dual polity worked because Unionists were ideal collaborators 'stable, quiescent, efficient, and yet fundamentally weak in their relations with the Centre [they were] sustained by the Centre's indifference, not by peripheral strength' [Ibid., 146]. In the beginning one can understand the centre's indifference. Devolved institutions relieved congestion. At a stroke, the 105 Irish MPs were reduced to 46, and then to 13 Ulster MPs. In 1922 a convention was established whereby Ulster affairs could not be discussed on the floor of the Commons because Northern Ireland had her own subordinate legislature where such matters could be discussed. After that, very little time was spent on Northern Ireland affairs: Nicholas Mansergh calculated it at one hour and fifty minutes in a period of just over a year in 1934-35, and Richard Rose estimated that the Commons devoted less than one-sixth of one per cent of its time to discussion of Northern Ireland questions between 1964-69. Essentially the London-Belfast relationship was benign, if not soporific.

The Unionist government extracted a price for this virtual fifty-year respite for Westminster. At the beginning Sir James Craig suggested that there had to be 'a dignity about our Parliament ... so that no opponent dare come forward at any time and say of that great structure ... "that is only a small affair and we can easily sweep it to one side"'. It was not a small affair. In the house elected in 1933, 27 per cent were in receipt of official salaries - comparable figures for the Dail and Westminster were just over ten per cent and about eight per cent respectively - some of which were identical with those of their London counterparts; and this at a time when the minister of agriculture had been told that one afternoon a week would suffice for his duties [Mansergh, 176 and 179; O'Neill, 49]. Parliament buildings, completed in 1932, were of Ozymandian proportions. The architectural historian of Belfast diplomatically describes it as one of 'two architectural monuments of consequence, both too recent to be easily judged' - although, in placing it alongside other public buildings in the city, he writes that architecturally 'they constitute the corporate expression of embattled Unionism, and an effort (perhaps largely unconscious) to convert a brash and sprawling industrial centre into a politico-religious capital city' [Brett, 65]. Others are more sardonic.

Architectural grandeur was matched by replication of procedure and ceremonial. Stormont proceeded as if it was Westminster across the water. This cannot be dismissed as mere persiflage, because it led Unionists into delusions about the nature of their polity, a fact which was to have serious consequences after 1969 when the Labour government began to pay much closer attention to Northern Ireland affairs, and loyalists began to resent British 'interference'. Northern Ireland's last prime minister criticised the illusions around devolution because it 'created unspoken separatist tendencies. It also meant that it hit an unprepared Westminster right between the eyes' [Faulkner, 26].

One can understand the illusions of separatism. Despite the fact that constitutionally Stormont had limited powers 'the Parliament and Government of Northern Ireland were in practice given greater autonomy (than the 1920 act permitted) in the running of all Northern Ireland affairs other than in respect of financial matters' [Palley, 388]. In these circumstances the reluctant devolutionists of 1920 became strong advocates of regional government. The Ulster Unionist Council (UUC) Report of 1936 warned that the cry 'back to Westminster' was fraught with great danger. The 1920 act had envisaged that Northern Ireland would have sufficient revenue to finance the transferred services and to furnish a substantial contribution towards the cost of the 'imperial contribution', that is those services still operated by the United Kingdom government. Stormont was to be given a comfortable income and left to its own devices. Soon it was clear that this arrangement would not work. Cabinet papers from the first government reveal that Unionist politicians believed that Ulster was being driven into a united Ireland by the imposition of financial penalties. But Westminster came to Ulster's aid without seeking the consent of Dublin. The Colwyn Committee of 1923 went a long way towards undermining two of the underlying principles of the 1920 act: it provided a strong disincentive to the exercise of Northern Ireland's power to vary its own taxes; and it envisaged that the imperial contribution might be reduced to vanishing point.

A trend had been set in which Westminster's control over Stormont expenditure was minimised: 'Payments to Northern Ireland ... were covered by permanent statutory authority. They were made out of the Consolidated Fund, and the annual approval of Parliament was not required. The only exception to this were agricultural payments' [see the *Kilbrandon Report*, 1272-1314 for a succinct and lucid explanation of the financial arrangements]. Gradually Stormont built on these gains through the Unemployment Insurance Agreement (1926), the acceptance of the principle of parity (1938) and of leeway (1954) as well as the Social Services Agreement in 1948. Much of the credit must go the first prime minister, Sir James Craig, who acted less at times as Northern Ireland's prime minister, than as its ambassador to Britain. At home he built up a reputation as a profligate spender with electoral considerations in mind because he insisted that Westminster had a moral duty to bail the province out of any financial difficulties. This was not to the liking of the Treasury, a point to which we shall return.

II

The 'Dual Polity' as political convenience
The changing financial relationship suggests an extension of Ulster's autonomy. We are not pretending that this was always conscious and persistent. Unionism never did develop a positive political philosophy nor even a distinctive Ulster identity. Even while one distinguished commentator was writing that 'Britain was simply receding as an idea' [Marr, 68], another was commenting that only 'among Ulster Unionists, where the reasons for self-awareness are different, special and steeped in the potent forces of blood and religion, does the label of "British" (for the majority) supersede all else' [Heffer, 15]. Unionists were reactive. The early years of devolution were ones of testing their determination against the reluctance of London to intervene again in Irish affairs. Once it became obvious that Whitehall was pursuing a policy of letting sleeping dogs lie, the Northern Ireland government set its own seal on policy within the province. As early as 1922, when Stormont passed a bill which proposed

the abolition of proportional representation for local council elections, Westminster capitulated after a two month stand-off.

After that there was little resistance. In 1925 the Northern Ireland government introduced an amendment which made provision for religious instruction and allowed the religion of candidates for teaching posts to be taken into account in direct contravention of the 1920 Act which had prohibited the state endowment of religion. The Home Office contented itself with expressing private reservations, a stance it adopted again in 1928 and in 1930 when further controversy arose in this area [Birrell and Murie, 237-8]. Indeed, the record suggests that the Home Office enjoyed a complaisant relationship with successive Unionist governments - a fact confirmed by the permanent under-secretary for state in 1954 when he concluded smugly: 'Personal contacts which have been established between Home Office officials and their Northern Ireland colleagues have led to mutual understanding and good will in the handling of thorny problems, despite occasional differences of opinion' [Newsam, 172]. Others cite instances of complicit Home Office reactions in the 1930s, the 1940s; and the 1960s.

That is not to say that Unionists could afford to be complacent. Anglo-Irish negotiations in 1938 were a case in point. These negotiations concerned, *inter alia*, trade and the question of the treatment of the northern minority. Both were sore points with the Unionist government and it struck such a hard bargain so that, 'as part of the price of Northern Ireland's acquiescence in the Anglo-Eire settlement of 1938 did the imperial government eventually accept, and then only in principle, the idea of a minus contribution' [Buckland, 92]. The chancellor of the exchequer considered Northern Ireland's fears exaggerated and its demands outrageous. The permanent secretary at the Treasury was even more forthright:

> The real issue is whether Northern Ireland is to be allowed to veto
> a settlement between us and southern Ireland ... Blackmail and bluff
> (oddly enough called 'loyalty') have for many years been the
> accepted methods of Northern Ireland. It is high time these
> parochial die-hards were made to face up to a touch of reality
> [McMahon, 278-9].

The fact of the matter was that so long as Northern Ireland wished to remain within the UK it was politically convenient to let sleeping dogs lie.

The return of a Labour government in July 1945 presented a more enduring danger, with fears that partition might be ended and that the Stormont government would be compelled to adopt 'very strong socialist measures'. In November the prime minister, Sir Basil Brooke, listed the various options in his diary: 'Stay as we are with possible chaos; join Eire - unthinkable; back to Westminster - dangerous; dominion status, might lower living standards. It was that last option, dominion status, that was being examined by Unionist ministers, backbenchers and officials even during the last two years of the Labour government. But the Brooke government had three things in its favour: its wartime record; its strategic importance; and Eire's decision to secede from the Commonwealth and become a Republic [Barton, 1-20]. In any case the cabinet soon realised that the British government was staffed by 'practical and experienced men who are personally friendly to Ulster'. They recognised that their strength lay in their regional identity and that they had secured the best of all possible worlds within the constraints imposed by economic dependence on the rest of the United Kingdom [Harkness, 106-8].

Indeed, it has been asserted that Northern Ireland developed
> many of the characteristics of an independent state. Although it
> received continued and increasing financial and economic support
> from Westminster, it retained its own parliament, its own Civil
> Service and its own security forces, and it was able to pursue policies
> distinctly different from Britain in many politically controversial

areas. Westminster supervision was slight, and ... it is arguable that
in practice the status of the Stormont government was closer to the
federal model than the devolution model - that is, that the two
governments were almost co-ordinate in powers with each other,
each with its own sphere of influence [Birrell and Murie, 28-9].
Unionist MPs may have considered that they had the best of all possible worlds: the
vast majority of Northern Ireland MPs at Westminster took the Conservative whip -
hence the illusion of integration; and a devolution which appeared to brook little or
no interference from Westminster. In those circumstances it might not be that
surprising that in 1956 the Maltese sought union with the United Kingdom on 'an
Ulster basis', a proposal supported by 74 per cent of those Maltese who voted in a
referendum in February 1956. But the plan was dropped since the turnout had been a
mere 45 per cent.
     All of the above lends weight to the suggestion that the relationship was closer to
the federal model. The most sober analysis of the devolution experience needs to be
quoted in full:

>   The evidence considered in this study supports the view that, in
>   spite of the very real constraints, Northern Ireland and its
>   government could and did diverge substantially from the standards
>   and legislation operating in Great Britain and at Westminster.
>   Independent action, different policies and substantially different
>   legislation did emerge. Nor can this simply be explained as a
>   freedom to do less. Even where identical policies were adopted in
>   Northern Ireland it is demonstrably not true that they were adopted
>   in a compliant or compulsory environment. These were real
>   political decisions and choices made at every stage, and the steps
>   taken were not always those which involved least conflict with
>   Westminster or 'rocked the boat' to the smallest extent ... The
>   whole history of devolution since the Second World War is one of
>   pushing back the constraints and creating room to exercise choice.
>   It may be that this was not done vigorously enough. However, to
>   imply that there was a fixed and permanent Stormont-Westminster
>   relationship and that what could be done was predetermined by
>   Westminster ignores the evidence about the process of government
>   and policy-making [Birrell and Murie, 266].

Unionists, then, could claim to have overcome diversity and to have shaped a
distinctive political entity. Yet one of their most noted qualities has been their lack of
self-confidence. A cursory glance at the titles of recent studies examining the
Unionist and Protestant tradition is revealing: *A Precarious Belonging* [by John
Dunlop]; *God Save Ulster!* [by Steve Bruce]; *The Edge of the Union* [by Steve
Bruce]; *Ulster's Uncertain Defenders* [by Sarah Nelson]; *The Faithful Tribe* [by
Ruth Dudley Edwards]; and *Under Siege* [by Arthur Aughey] - the list could go on.
The biblical overtones and the sense of siege have Weberian undertones. It was Max
Weber who wrote that 'the sentiment of ethnic solidarity does not of itself make a
"nation"'. But to the degree 'that it represents a step in the process of nation-
formation, it testifies that a group of people must know ethnically what they are not
before they know what they are' [Connor, 377-400]. To this could be added that a
sense of ethnic honour, and belief in the excellence of one's own customs and the
inferiority of alien ones, emerged in Northern Ireland. In place of the nation, Ulster
Protestants gathered behind a sense of ethnic honour. They had assumed (without
too much introspection) that they were British, and they compared their lot -
especially after they were put in control of their own affairs - with the alien (and
inferior) Catholic Irish. They failed 'only to connect'.

Since at least the time of the first Home Rule Bill (1886) there had been an 'Ulster entity'. But how to define it? In the course of modernisation the Ulster Protestant community developed feelings of nationality which were, at best, confused, ambivalent and fragile. It was during these years that there emerged a Protestant state and a Protestant lack of a genuine feeling of co-nationality with the British people. In more recent years Unionists have returned to introspection and analysts have attempted to categorise Protestant Ulster. Peter Gibbon, for example, allows for the emergence of an embryonic Ulster nationalism. Applying social-psychological criteria, Richard Rose asserts that a case can be made for the 'creation of a nation-state' of Northern Ireland. Nairn writes exasperatingly of the 'peculiar fractured development of the Ulster-Protestant nationality' which is like 'a "mad" variable which falsifies every reasonable strategy of escape ... there is only one direction in which this change can now occur - that is, towards the formulation of more than a nominal "Ulster nationalism"' [Nairn, 240-1]. The checklist can be extended. For the moment it serves a specific purpose: it demonstrates the difficulties encountered by policy-makers at a critical time in categorising one of the major actors.

Unionism *appeared* to be a monolith until, that is, Westminster did begin to 'interfere'. So light had been Westminster's supervision that the first full debate in the Commons on Northern Ireland's position did not occur until 1 June 1950. There was no serious attempt to deal with minority grievances, bipartisanship was maintained and the motion was not put to a division. The government through the home secretary, Chuter Ede, contented itself with the thought that 'Northern Ireland is in a slightly different position from that of a self-governing Dominion. I think it would be unwise of this House to exercise too meticulous a control over an area to which it has given self-government'. But it is worth pointing out that during negotiations on the Ireland Bill (1949) Clement Attlee had on several occasions reminded Unionist ministers that the United Kingdom parliament was sovereign and that it could not 'bind its successors'. During the same negotiations Chuter Ede stated bluntly that 'he did not like and would be unable to defend the electoral methods of the Northern Ireland government'. (It should be said that as early as April 1946 Chuter Ede had characterised the Northern Ireland cabinet as being the 'remnants of the old ascendancy class, very frightened of the Catholics and the general world trend to the left'). At the end of the day no individual opinions carried any real weight because as one minister wrote to Ernest Bevin: 'Because this is such a troublesome political question in Britain, and because you all have so much to do there is a natural tendency to shelve it' [Barton, 1-20]. That is precisely what happened and procrastination became the name of the game. So when Labour was next returned to power it had little idea of what were the financial relations between London and Belfast. Richard Crossman recorded in his diary (on 12 September 1968) when he attended a meeting of the Steering Committee on Economic Policy (SEP): 'At this point I said, "I am an ignoramus; may I be told what is the exact financial arrangement?" Nobody could say. Neither Jack Diamond nor the Chancellor knew the formula according to which the Northern Ireland Government gets its money.'

That was written less than a month before the rioting in Derry which began the current round of political violence. The ostensible reason for the outbreak was minority concerns with electoral irregularities. But that concealed a much deeper malaise. Violence had been a feature of political life in every decade of Northern Ireland's short life. In a particularly apt phrase Wright comments that in place of what 'metropolitans call peace' Northern Ireland enjoyed at best 'a tranquillity of communal deterrence' [xiii]. It manifested itself in an intimidatory political culture; and when it reappeared in the form of the IRA in 1969 one commentator noted that the whole process was so *natural* as to beyond comment. Attitudes were more important than weapons, and that was to be the key to republican strategy: 'Nothing had to be imported, nothing fashioned by ideologues, nothing sold to the people, nothing secretly arranged because of events. All that was needed was to exploit the existing reality' [Bell, 41]. In essence, Northern Ireland had developed into a society without empathy. Reduced to the level of individual relations, communal deterrence took the form of civility whereby matters of religion and politics were not discussed in 'mixed' company lest they offend. It encouraged what Seamus Heaney calls 'a potent monocular vision', an ignorance of the other side and hence a lack of self-understanding. Heaney describes it in his poem *An Ulster Twilight*, recalling a more innocent time when his Protestant neighbour brought a Christmas gift:

> And knew that if we met again
> In an Ulster twilight we would begin
> And end whatever we might say
> In a speech all toys and carpentry
>
> A doorstop courtesy to shun
> Your father's uniform and gun
> But - now that I have said it out -
> Maybe none the worse for that.

Contrast that with Tom Paulin's *Settlers*, a family account of the 1912 UVF gun-running seen through the eyes of the manager of the Belfast iceworks:

> Some mornings, walking through the company gate,
> He touches the bonnet of a brown lorry.
> It is warm. The men watch and say nothing.
> 'Queer, how it runs off in the night,'
> He says to McCullough, then climbs to his office.
> He stores a warm knowledge in his palm.
>
> Nightlandings on the Antrim coast, the movement of guns
> Now snug in their oiled paper below the floors
> Of sundry kirks and tabernacles in that county.

Evasion and complicity - the watchwords of a divided society. The price of shelving this troublesome political question was monumental. The collapse of the old order was visible to see. Between April 1969 and March 1972 no less than three prime ministers were replaced. The home affairs minister, William Craig, was sacked in December 1968 for contemplating UDI. He had challenged Westminster's right to intervene. Northern Ireland's constitution was 'more than a mere act of Parliament', he declared: it represented an 'agreed settlement' - 'the settlement made when our grandfathers and fathers made their historic stand'. He went on to form the Vanguard Unionist movement. It produced a pamphlet after the imposition of direct rule in March 1972 which argues that Ulster loyalists are 'an old and historic community', for whom union with Britain had never been 'an end in itself', but 'was always a means of preserving Ulster's British tradition and the identity of her loyalist people'. British politicians, by 'dismantling Ulster's capacity for resistance to friend [*sic*] or foe' had 'unwittingly forged a nation that cannot entrust to them its security or national destiny' [Miller, 153-4]. We are back in a 'zone of war' as well as stretching the concept of devolution and of autonomy. To a people who never connected, independence seemed the logical outcome. We return to the growth of factionalism, to an intense exercise in navel contemplation, to reinforcing 'Ulster' as the Albania of western Europe hermetically sealed from the outside world. It was a return to quests for identity but, as Porter asserts, '[W]restling with political issues of identity is not in itself a sign of abnormality - though wrestling with virtually nothing else is' [8].

The other side of that particular coin allowed for no ambiguity. Political violence was to be both a cleansing thing (in the Pearsean sense) and an end thing. It would deliver Irish unity (or Ulster autonomy). But its results were twofold. One is examined with eloquence and quiet dignity in the 3637 stories of the men, women and children who have died as a result of the Northern Ireland troubles. The other was the impact of the *Green Book* (the IRA's training manual) strategy on liberal democracy:

> The *Green Book* strategy failed. It did so, however, only after causing British politicians to be surrounded by armed police, bullet-proof glass and barriers. This has not been good for the understanding of our politicians. It produced courts which regularly fell below the standards of the much-prized British legal tradition and, on several notorious occasions, shamed Britain around the world by huge miscarriages of justice. It has been a prime modern excuse for an almost obsessive state secrecy and for a powerful domestic secret service. Abroad, it has damaged Britain in the eyes of its most important twentieth-century ally, the United States. This is a formidable list of effects on the British state [Marr, 82].

Perhaps previous governments should have paid more attention to the poets. In *Ode*, written in 1934, Louis MacNeice warned that 'bottled time turns sour upon the sill'.

III

Making connections
It is tempting to condemn much of the period of direct rule as a missed opportunity - politicians and statesmen moulded in conventional constitutionalism, wedded to the Woodrow Wilson model of the nation-state with the United Kingdom as a slightly aberrant, but essentially healthy, patient; devolution as political containment - power devolved is power retained. But direct rule was in essence a huge learning curve for the British and Irish governments. They needed several years to overcome their mutual ignorance. In any case they carried their mutually exclusive historical prejudices: it is astonishing that after a connection which stretched back to the twelfth century only in 1980 did both governments sit down to examine the reasons for the mutual misperceptions that existed between both countries.

Whitehall's initial response to this latest example of crisis and redemption was to assume that it was purely a domestic problem that would be resolved by a little bit of tweaking of the Westminster model - hence four failed attempts at producing a successful internal initiative after 1972. By the 1980s it returned to the Anglo-Irish drawing board - as if accepting that the 1920 settlement needed to be revisited - and started a process which culminated in the signing of the Anglo-Irish agreement in November 1985, itself a blueprint for the 1998 agreement. In broadening the parameters of the problem the architects of the Anglo-Irish process were acknowledging changes in geo-politics: their continuing membership in the European Union, itself an experiment in transterritorial governance; the end of the 'external support system' through growing American interest in the Northern Ireland problem; the fall of the Berlin Wall and the collapse of communism as an aggressive international ideology; the removal of apartheid and South Africa's pariah status - all of these impacted on the nature of the conflict. Some of the actors (especially the republican and loyalist paramilitaries) began to look afresh at solutions which were not dependent on violence. When both made declarations on cessations of violence, in August and October 1994 respectively, they produced the conditions that allowed for intensive and inclusive negotiations, the outcome of which was the 1998 agreement. Bogdanor highlights the historic irony of the agreement which

> offers, in essence, a return to the past, a return to Gladstone's original conception of Home Rule in a form suited to modern

conditions ... the proposals for devolution, together with the North-South Council, giving institutional form to the Irish dimension, and the British-Irish Council offer a chance of realizing the underlying theme of Gladstonian thinking, i.e., recognition both of the various and distinctive national identities within these islands, and also of the close and complex links between them ... The British-Irish Council is an expression of the belief that the manifold links which exist between Britain and the Irish Republic can no longer be contained within a formal framework which, in theory at least, makes the two countries as foreign to each other as Russia and Brazil [288-9].

In practice the agreement made the connections and offers a putative solution to Northern Ireland's status within the archipelago.

References and Further Reading :

Paul Arthur, *Special Relationships: Britain, Ireland and the Northern Ireland Problem* (Belfast, 2000); Arthur Aughey, *Under Siege: Ulster Unionism and the Anglo-Irish Agreement* (London, 1989); Brian Barton, 'Relations between Westminster and Stormont during the Attlee Premiership', *Irish Political Studies*, 7 (1992), 1-20; J. Bowyer Bell, 'Aspects of the Dragonworld: Covert Communication and the Rebel Ecosystem', *Intelligence and Counterintelligence*, 3 (1990), 15-43; Derek Birrell and Alan Murie, *Policy and Government in Northern Ireland: Lessons of Devolution* (Dublin, 1980); Vernon Bogdanor, 'The British-Irish Council and devolution', *Government and Opposition*, 34 (1999), 287-98; Charles Brett, *Buildings of Belfast 1700-1914* (Belfast, 1985); Steve Bruce, *God Save Ulster: the religion and politics of Paisleyism* (Oxford, 1986); Steve Bruce, *The Edge of the Union: the Ulster loyalist political vision* (Oxford, 1994); James Bulpitt, *Territory and Power in the United Kingdom: An Interpretation* (Manchester, 1983); Patrick Buckland, *The Factory of Grievances: Devolved Government in Northern Ireland 1921-1939* (Dublin, 1979); Walker Connor, 'A Nation is a Nation, is a State, is and Ethnic Group, is a ...', *Ethnic and Racial Studies*, 1 (1978), 377-400; John Darby, *Intimidation and the Control of Conflict in Northern Ireland* (Dublin, 1986); John Dunlop, *A Precarious Belonging: Presbyterians and the conflict in Ireland* (Belfast, 1995); Ruth Dudley Edwards, *The Faithful Tribe* (London, 1999); Brian Faulkner, *Memoirs of a Statesman* (London, 1978); Michael Gallagher, *The Irish Labour Party in Transition, 1957-82* (Manchester, 1982); Peter Gibbon, *The Origins of Ulster Unionism: the formation of popular Protestant politics and ideology in nineteenth-century Ireland* (Manchester, 1975); David Harkness, *Northern Ireland since 1920* (Dublin, 1983); Simon Heffer, *Nor Shall My Sword: The Reinvention of England* (London, 2000); Deirdre McMahon, *Republicans and Imperialists: Anglo-Irish Relations in the 1930s* (London, 1984); Nicholas Mansergh, *The Government of Northern Ireland: A Study in Devolution* (London, 1936); Andrew Marr, *The Day Britain Died* (London, 2000); Keith Middlemass, *Politics in Industrial Society: the experience of the British since 1911* (London, 1979); David W. Miller, *Queen's Rebels: Ulster Loyalism in Historical Perspective* (Dublin, 1978); Janet Morgan, The Backbench Diaries of Richard Crossman (London, 1981); Tom Nairn, *The Break-up of Britain* (London: 1977); Sarah Nelson, *Ulster's Uncertain Defenders: Protestant political, paramilitary and community groups and the Northern Ireland conflict* (Belfast, 1984); Frank Newsam, *The Home Office* (London, 1955); Terence O'Neill, *The Autobiography of Terence O'Neill* (London, 1972); Claire Palley, *The Evolution, Disintegration and Possible Reconstruction of the Northern Ireland Constitution* (London, 1972); J.G.A. Pocock, 'The Limits and Divisions of British History: In Search of the Unknown Subject', *American History Review*, 87 (1982), 311-336; Norman Porter, *Rethinking Unionism: an attractive vision for Northern*

Ireland (Belfast, 1996); Richard Rose, *Governing Without Consensus: An Irish Perspective* (London, 1971); Charles Townshend, *Political Violence in Ireland: government and resistance since 1848* (Oxford, 1983); Frank Wright, *Northern Ireland: A Comparative Analysis* (Dublin, 1987).

16

From National Identity to Nationalism, 1945-99

JAMES MITCHELL

Three themes stand out in reviewing the history of the national movement in Scotland, by which is meant the broad movement which campaigned for a Scottish parliament whether within or outside the United Kingdom. First, in order to understand the movement, the major impediments that stood in its way and its position in modern Scotland, it is necessary to view it historically. Studies which focus on the immediate past are likely to ignore important features and are liable to make false assumptions. There was nothing inevitable about the establishment of a Scottish parliament. A number of alternative futures were on offer to Scots and the movement had to overcome formidable obstacles. Second, the success of the movement owed at least as much to the changing context of Scottish, British and, indeed, international politics and political economy. An argument presented here is that in the early post-war period, the movement had remarkable leadership. This leadership was energetic, imaginative and determined, though that did not prevent it from making some costly tactical and strategic errors. The context in which it operated however militated against its success. On the other hand, the much more positive context which was on offer in the 1960s and especially the 1970s was not enough to ensure success, in part, at least, due to the weaknesses in the national movement. Third, the relationship between the national movement and other social movements has been important. The labour movement was antagonistic for much of the post-war period, viewing class as the key cleavage in Scottish politics, but a more supportive relationship did develop after 1979.

I

A 'smouldering pile'
The Scottish National Party (SNP) won its first parliamentary seat in the dying days of the war. Dr Robert McIntyre was elected for Motherwell but the unusual circumstances of war, with a coalition in operation and each main party agreeing only to contest by-elections previously held, explain this result. McIntyre lost the seat at the subsequent general election but established himself as a key figure in the party in the post-war period. The party had split in 1942 with John MacCormick leading a dissident grouping to form the Scottish Convention, a cross-party/non-party campaign group. Prior to 1942 the SNP had been dogged by internal conflicts and the often unhelpful contributions of a number of colourful characters. Curiously, the split appears to have marginalised these elements in both organisations. In the period after 1945, under the often austere but always serious leadership of McIntyre and others such as Jimmy Halliday, the SNP contested elections, making little progress although a foundation, in terms of organisational and policy, was established which would later provide a launch-pad for electoral success from the 1960s.

The Scottish Convention engaged in standard pressure-group politics. During the 1945 general election campaign, questionnaires were sent to all candidates. Of those who replied, most stated that they favoured a Scottish parliament, especially Labour candidates including the three secretaries of state for Scotland during Attlee's premiership, Joseph Westwood, Arthur Woodburn and Hector McNeil. The main thrust of campaigning focused on the political parties at this time. Deputations met the Scottish leadership of the Labour and Unionist parties. Significantly, the British leadership of the parties refused to see the deputations and there was some cooperation between Labour and the Conservatives in agreeing to this. It soon became clear that, while polite, Labour and Tory leaders had no intention of pushing the issue of home rule and alternative approaches would be required. In 1947 a Scottish National Assembly was organised which purported to be representative of Scottish opinion but, as Jack Brand, has pointed out, this and subsequent assemblies were largely middle-class affairs. A number of significant figures and organisations attended but there was no official Labour or Conservative presence.

Once more, it became clear that this approach would not in itself work. A different strategy emerged attempting to harness what home rulers believed was the overwhelming support of the Scottish public for a separate parliament. A petition or national covenant as it was called was launched in October 1949 with the aim of pressuring the government into action. This shift of emphasis from an appeal to political elites towards a more popular appeal was the classic act of a group outside power. It was not that senior politicians ignored the movement, merely that they believed it could be contained. In a memorandum to his cabinet colleagues, Scottish secretary Arthur Woodburn's noted that the home rule movement was a smouldering pile that might suddenly break through the party loyalties and become a formidable national movement. He warned that this was more likely as Labour's programme was fulfilled, and the great dividing issues were settled, leaving the cleavages between the parties less deep and intense [PRO, Cabinet Papers (47) 323]. In fact, as the post-war consensus emerged, the home rule movement appeared more marginalised than at any stage in the period after 1945. In another cabinet memorandum Woodburn provided his colleagues with the results of an opinion poll which was largely in line with a previous poll conducted in November 1945:

Daily Express (2 July 1947) Gallup Poll on self-government for Scotland:
76% for
13% against
11% no views
Divided by party:
80% of Socialists
75% of Tories
70% of Liberals

All of this suggests that the national movement had considerable, perhaps overwhelming, support in Scotland. Campaigners were very active and generated much publicity and polls quoted privately by a decidedly unsympathetic Scottish secretary of state seemed to point to a movement about to make a break through. This presents a paradox. Theorists of nationalism and historians have long noted the unifying effects of winning a war (and the potential for break-up due to military defeat). Britain had come through a successful war and a welfare state was in the making - 'national unity' had been the great moral achievement of the war, according to William Beveridge, founder of the welfare state.

Two interpretations of the state of public opinion and the strength of the national movement at the end of the war are possible. First, the evidence suggests that there was a strong sense of Scottish national identity but not of Scottish nationalism. The second interpretation is that there is indeed ample evidence of support for a parliament, but that it was not felt strongly, other than by a small minority of campaigners.

Having a Scottish national identity was not only compatible with feeling pride in being British, being British at this time meant having a Scottish identity in Scotland.

This was reflected in the army where soldiers had fought for their country - Britain - but often in Scottish regiments. The United Kingdom had never been a state in which dual identities were seen as a problem. This was evident in the structures of the state: the United Kingdom had never been a unitary state. It had always been a union state. As Rokkan and Urwin noted, this was 'not the result of straightforward dynastic conquest. Incorporation of at least parts of its territory has been achieved through personal dynastic union, for example by treaty, marriage or inheritance. Integration is less than perfect. While administrative standardization prevails over most of the territory, the consequences of personal union entail the survival in some areas of pre-union rights and institutional infrastructures which preserve some degree of regional autonomy and serve as agencies of indigenous elite recruitment.' It was not a unitary state, 'built up around one unambiguous political centre which enjoys economic dominance and pursues a more or less undeviating policy of administrative standardization. All areas of the state are treated alike, and all institutions are directly under the control of the centre' [Rokkan and Urwin, 181].

From this perspective, the activities of the home rulers are viewed as those of a vociferous minority and the polls merely a manifestation of strong national identity masquerading as nationalism. This view was one which was to be found amongst many opponents of home rule. An alternative view is that there was broad support for a parliament but it was shallow and it was certainly not strong enough to overcome traditional party loyalties. This interpretation existed amongst opponents of home rule and, in time, also amongst home rulers themselves. In 1952 John MacCormick told the Scottish Covenant Association's national committee:

> Supposing five million people had signed the Covenant it was still
> open to the political parties to say that no matter how many people
> say they want home rule they do not want it so much as they want
> the Tory or Labour Party so we can ignore their expression of
> opinion. The only way in which the parties can be compelled to pay
> attention is by organising ourselves in some way as a political
> force [National Library of Scotland, Acc. 7505, no. 20].

If Scots at this time did want a parliament, then it was not very high on their agenda. Politics is not only about preferences but also priorities and a Scottish parliament was not a high priority.

II

A very British period
The decade after the Conservatives came to power in 1951 was a very British period in Scottish politics. Of course, that did not exclude the existence of a Scottish dimension and a strong sense of Scottish national identity. British state nationalism was strong for a variety of reasons. As argued above, it allowed for the incorporation and celebration of Scottish national identity within a wider loyalty to the state. The recent experience of war, pulling together to defeat a common enemy, was still important especially for the generations who had experienced it most directly. Notably, Scottish soldiers had fought for Britain within Scottish regiments, thus emphasising the existence of a Scottish national identity operating within British state nationalism. There was also a perception of economic success and social progress associated with state intervention and the welfare state. Much has been written about the post-war consensus but absent from most of this literature are references to the degree of consensus around territorial politics. In the 1950s there was no serious challenge to the territorial structures of government. Labour moved closer to the Unionist position on home rule and by the late 1950s it was officially opposed to a Scottish parliament being created. The Balfour royal commission on Scottish affairs made recommendations which were accepted by Labour and the

Conservatives. Only a few home rulers and nationalists on the fringe of politics complained about its proposals.

There was consensus on the need for state intervention and for support for welfare. Typical of this were decisions taken in the late 1950s by Harold Macmillan's cabinet on the future of the steel industry. A decision on the site for a new steel strip mill was, Macmillan informed his cabinet, a matter of broad national policy involving not merely economic factors but also social and political issues including sensitive questions of Scottish and Welsh sentiment. The decision to site steel plants in Scotland and Wales illustrates well the nature of the post-war politics. First, people looked to the government for jobs and economic security and government felt obliged to respond. Second, there was an expectation that special consideration should be had for the impact a policy had on Scotland.

The 1950s marked a period of relative tranquillity and consensus in British territorial politics. In retrospect, however, we can see that the seeds of later disillusionment with the state and planks in the campaign for a Scottish parliament were being laid. These were, for the most part, unintended and unforeseen consequences of public policy and the long-term effects of campaigns which had not been appreciated at the time. The royal commission recommended that a number of matters should be transferred to the Scottish Office - roads and bridges, electricity, food, and animal health - and made a plea to government departments to take account of Scottish national identity. Dismissed as insubstantial by home rulers, these transfers had a significance that only became clear a decade later. As Britain entered the era of economic planning from the late 1950s the country would be treated as a discreet unit for economic and planning purposes.

The national movement became more radical in its approach in the 1950s, largely because the appeal to the political parties and the Scottish elites had not been fruitful. The removal of the Stone of Destiny from Westminster Abbey, the election of John MacCormick as rector of Glasgow University and the EIIR case all had the hallmarks of student politics: unconventional with a stress on the symbolic but ultimately ineffective at the time. But each of these episodes played its part in keeping the movement alive. They entered nationalist mythology and, particularly in the case of EIIR, had very real repercussions in the long term.

The Stone of Destiny was symbolic in both Scottish and British nationalist politics. Reports of its removal to Scotland was generally greeted with amusement though a few of the movement's more conservative elements were far from impressed. In London there was less amusement at what was regarded as an act of vandalism. The Stone's symbolic significance for British nationalism became even more evident before the 1997 general election when the Conservatives made much of the decision to return it (officially this time) to Scotland. The EIIR case was to have far greater long-term implications. The announcement that the new queen would be officially designated Elizabeth the Second caused mild offence in Scotland. It seemed to confirm the view that the UK was merely a continuation of the England of old and not a new state. This was the basis for the legal challenge to the designation launched by MacCormick and Hamilton which once more provoked criticisms from conservative elements within the movement.

The myth of Scottish popular sovereignty was not born with this case but was given considerable legitimacy in Lord Cooper's famous ruling that, 'The principle of the unlimited Sovereignty of Parliament is a distinctively English principle which has no counterpart in Scottish Constitutional law' [MacCormick, 215-19]. It makes little difference that MacCormick and Hamilton actually lost the case, they created a weapon which would be used by the movement thirty years later. The notion of popular sovereignty was to be the basis of the 1988 Claim of Right and was supported by the Constitutional Convention. The 1950s may have been a barren time for the movement as measured by electoral progress and by efforts to convince the

elites to support a Scottish parliament, but there were unforeseen consequences of
the activities at this time.

III

Britain isn't working
In the lead up to the 1979 general election, Saatchi & Saatchi's advertising campaign
for the Conservatives included a famous poster in which a long line of people were
portrayed standing in a dole queue. The caption read 'LABOUR ISN'T
WORKING'. The *Economist* newspaper used that poster on one of its front covers
but scored out 'LABOUR' and replaced it with 'BRITAIN'. That headlined summed
up a feeling which had been developing from the 1960s. It was not a specifically
Scottish phenomenon. What was significant was the recognition that an alternative
future existed for Scotland outside Britain. This alternative did not exist elsewhere in
the UK to the same extent because there was not the same sense of national identity.

Governments struggled with economic difficulties and crises. These included
very real economic problems as well as some which were symbolically important but
all of which added to the perception that Britain was in decline. Sterling crises,
balance of payments problems, the end of empire, rising levels of unemployment,
and the rise of Europe all raised questions about the value of Britain as a polity. The
victory achieved in the war was receding in the memory. Expectations that the state
should provide welfare and protect jobs still existed but the state was less able to
deliver.

Problems in the 1970s were even greater than in the previous decade. The pound
sterling nearly died, as commentators later put it, at one point in the mid-1970s. The
Yom Kippur War led to the quadrupling of oil prices overnight and had a devastating
effect on national finances. Stagflation (inflation plus rising unemployment) hit the
British economy and Britain suffered from poor labour relations with strikes
apparently an endemic feature of British life. There was a clear sense amongst the
public that the government was losing control. Polls suggested that senior trade
unionists had more power than the British prime minister. Other states had similar
problems, though few were quite as acute as those that affected Britain. What was
significant about Britain was the damage done to the sense of British greatness and
the opportunity offered to Scottish nationalism, especially with the development of
North Sea oil in the context of the stridency of OPEC (Organisation of Petroleum
Exporting Countries). The context of Scottish politics had been changing and was
becoming much more conducive to the national movement's aims.

IV

Unfulfilled potential
James Porteous, a leading home ruler wrote in 1963 to Angus Gunn, secretary of the
Scottish Covenant Association, in telling him that he was

> reluctantly coming to the view that it is no use pretending we exist
> as an active body any longer. Perhaps we should, like the Scottish
> Parliament, adjourn *sine die*, and our members can support the
> SNP or Liberals as they feel disposed. It will be the end of another
> sang, but in this case we may perhaps sing a new one. ... Neither
> the Conservatives nor the Labour Party are any nearer supporting
> any measure of self-government for Scotland, and I cannot foresee
> a Liberal Government for many years at least. ... the SNP, which
> is both active and more rational than it used to be. It is benefiting
> now from some upsurge of national feeling in Scotland. The main
> points of difference which have divided Covenant from SNP

policy in the past seem to me to have lost much of their force owing to changes in world environment. Defence is very much a matter of NATO; Customs of GATT, EFTA, and perhaps the Common Market, with any other Commonwealth or international arrangements that may be made in the future [NLS, Acc. 5978, box 2, f. 3].

These comments were both shrewd and prescient. The SNP had been quietly working away during the 1950s though with little electoral impact. The party had lost its wilder elements and the basis of a serious political force had been established. The limits of the pressure group approach had become obvious. By the time Porteous was writing his letter, the SNP had achieved creditable results in two Scottish by-elections. In Bridgeton in Glasgow, in 1961, the SNP candidate had won 19 per cent of the votes cast, sufficient to convince him to give up his job and work full-time for the party. In 1962 Billy Wolfe won 23 per cent of the votes in West Lothian, though he was defeated by the Old Etonian baronet Tam Dalyell - the first of seven electoral confrontations between the two over the next two decades. The Tories lost their deposit in the by-election, the first such humiliation for the party in 40 years. New members started to join the SNP and new branches were set up across Scotland. The new wave of members often had no previous political experience, which was all too obvious at times, but these recruits did include a number of Labour Party members who were often as disillusioned with Labour's position on nuclear disarmament as they were with the perceived neglect of Scotland. The combination of a new context and a better organised, more mature SNP allowed the party to advance in the 1960s.

One of the most significant features of the national movement between the early 1960s and the late 1970s was the extent to which it became synonymous with the SNP. At no time before or after that time was this the case. This probably did damage to both the movement and the party. It harmed the movement as there was no cross- or non-party body arguing the case for a parliament and this allowed an impression to be left that support for a parliament was tied up with party politics. The SNP had the difficult task of representing a wide range of views, making it difficult to cut out a clear electoral profile and allowing it to be portrayed in a negative way by its opponents.

Circumstances may have changed to the advantage of home rulers but the movement was unable to take full advantage of the new situation. The SNP was not without blame. Poor leadership at crucial stages meant that opportunities were lost and strategic blunders were made. Divisions within the movement and within the party damaged the credibility of the cause and gave opponents opportunities to attack the idea of a Scottish parliament. Changed circumstances did not, of course, mean the removal of opposition to home rule. When pressure for change was at its most intense, opposition was at its most active. This opposition was formidable, had great experience and was extremely well funded.

As an organisation, the SNP was and remains remarkably open and democratic. Its leaders were often unable to provide leadership even if they had wanted to do so. Party members were determined to remain in control. The party had a collective leadership which was not a recipe for electoral success. It was not just leadership in terms of personnel that was confused but also in terms of direction. The SNP's strategy was to appeal to all voters and at times it appeared remarkably ill-informed as to the nature of its support and its potential support. As in the past history of the movement, the SNP wanted to appeal to the Scottish elites even though its greatest potential lay with the working class. Some in the party appreciated this but not all of the leadership did so.

Strategic and tactical confusion was most obvious in the late 1970s after the SNP had achieved its best electoral results. The parliamentary party and the SNP executive often disagreed. On key issues the party was indecisive or worse decisive but inconsistent. The debate on the Nationalisation of Aircraft- and Ship-building was the most obvious example. At different stages in the passage of the legislation, SNP MPs voted for, against and even abstained, while being urged to support the legislation by its executive and the shop stewards from the ship-building industry. The party never aligned itself successfully with the labour movement nor, at times, did it give any indication that it wanted to do so. The absence of a clear position on socio-economic issues was thought to broaden its appeal. In fact, it left it open to attack from all sides. Labour accused the SNP of being 'tartan Tories', while the Conservatives attacked the party as being too left-wing. The nationalisation of ship-building provided ammunition for both attacks. Of course, it should be remembered that the SNP MPs and its leaders were relatively inexperienced and faced determined opposition.

As the 1979 referendum approached, the crucial cleavage was not between supporters and opponents of a Scottish parliament but between supporters and opponents of independence. Even during the referendum campaign itself, this division was evident. Separate and contradictory campaigns were waged in favour of a YES vote. Labour's Scottish general secretary, Helen Liddell, remarked that her party would not soil its hands by campaigning with the Nationalists, while sections of the SNP treated the vote as a referendum on independence.

The No side was not only better financed but better organised and ran an altogether better campaign in 1979. The context was also important coming after the 'winter of discontent' of serious industrial action. Far from being associated with a bright new future, devolution became associated in the public's mind with a tired government which had run out of steam and with the bitter enmity between the two main parties supporting the measure. The No campaigners succeeded in associating constitutional change with the socio-economic *status quo* : labour unrest, high unemployment and inflation.

The result of the 1979 referendum was a slim victory for devolution: 51.6 per cent voted in favour of devolution. By any other measurement it was a victory for the No side. The supporters of devolution were defeated in 1979 in two important respects: the expectations they themselves had and which they had encouraged commentators to have were that they would win comfortably; and there was a clear in public opinion as support slipped away. Consequently, there was little enthusiasm for a campaign to demand a parliament on the basis of the results. A campaign of non-violent civil disobedience initiated by the SNP (around rising unemployment but in reality linked to the referendum result) took another two years to emerge. It is a statement on the nature of the national movement that it meekly accepted the result of the referendum in 1979.

V

Thatcherism

Many senior Conservatives took the view, not without some justification, that the Scots were not serious about devolution. A common interpretation of the state of Scottish public opinion in the late 1970s was that the Scots might say to pollsters that they wanted a parliament, but when it came to a serious vote on the issue they would back down. These polls were thought merely to be a way for the Scots to express dissatisfaction with the government. These expressions were no more serious than mid-term by-election results. In essence, nothing had really changed over the post-war period.

Events however soon altered matters dramatically. A firming up of attitudes occurred and the strong sense of Scottish national identity turned into a form of nationalism that eventually led to victory in the 1997 referendum. The explanation for this can best be summarised as 'Thatcherism'. Thatcherism was not just any form of unionism. There were two aspects of it which were significant and each related to how it was received in Scotland. First, it was perceived as neglecting the Scottish dimension. Second, it was perceived as the ideology of the minimal state. As we have seen, unionism had not meant uniformity and assimilation but support for a union state in which Scottish distinctiveness was welcomed. Under Mrs Thatcher, however, there was a growing perception that the Conservatives had no respect for the distinctive nature of Scottish politics. The Tory party allowed itself to be portrayed as assimilationist.

The Tory party's perceived support for the minimal state, contrary to what most Scots wanted, was evident on a number of issues during this period. The steel industry can once more be seen as illustrative of the changes in Conservative thinking. The closures of Gartcosh and later of Ravenscraig steel mills were perceived as direct attacks on an old order fondly remembered by Scots; and the steel industry took on symbolic importance for the national movement. The real conservatives of the 1980s were the majority of Scots who wanted to conserve the old order against the attacks of those assimilationist, anti-interventionist radicals who had taken control of the Conservative party. A new constitutional order increasingly became the way of preserving the old consensus. In this sense, the Scots have been entirely consistent in their support of the state over the post-war period. It has not been the British state or a putative Scottish state or some mixture of the two, but an interventionist, welfare state. Devolution became the vehicle for preserving this kind of state.

Not so much from its own efforts, but largely in reaction to Thatcherism, the national and labour movements became allied as never before. The Campaign for a Scottish Assembly (CSA), an all party pressure group, came into existence in 1980 and though its membership was small and its activities hardly noticed for a number of years, it provided a cross/non-party forum for supporters of home rule. The CSA was instrumental in the establishment of the Constitutional Convention which met for the first time in 1989. The convention's membership included the Labour Party and Liberal Democrats as well as the vast majority of local authorities (itself a major change from the a decade before when key figures in local government had been hostile to devolution), the churches, trade unions and other bodies representing 'civic Scotland'. The SNP and the Conservatives refused to participate. Crucially, the convention's founding document and the basis of its claim was popular sovereignty:

> We, gathered as the Scottish Constitutional Convention, do hereby
> acknowledge the sovereign right of the Scottish people to determine
> the form of Government best suited to their needs, and do hereby
> declare and pledge that in all our actions and deliberations their
> interests shall be paramount.

It was a radical statement and, notably, one accepted by both the Labour and Liberal Democrat parties. The 1950s EIIR case pursued by MacCormick had finally had a major impact. This marked a significant breakthrough for the movement. The SNP also changed. It had learned lessons from the 1970s and without needing to change its policies to any great extent it started to portray itself as a moderate left of centre party.

The post-Thatcher years saw the Conservatives attempt to inject a Scottish dimension to public policy. Secretary of state Ian Lang's 'taking stock exercise' was not taken seriously but his successor, Michael Forsyth, was more successful in attracting attention even though in many respects his approach was similar to that of Lang (and, indeed, that the post-war Attlee Government), but it was presented with more panache. After eleven years under Mrs Thatcher, the Conservatives were trying desperately to recover lost ground and to appeal to voters as a distinctly Scottish party. Forsyth engaged in symbolic gestures which might have succeeded in other circumstances. He literally put on a kilt to attend the Scottish premiere of the film

Braveheart and returned the Stone of Destiny to Scotland. But all of this was too
little, too late. It highlighted rather than reversed an image of the Conservatives as
anti-Scottish. It may have been an unfair description of the party but it was powerful
and had very real effect.

VI

The 1997 general election and referendum
The Conservatives lost all their parliamentary seats in Scotland in the general election
of 1997. It was a paradoxical election in that, although the establishment of the
Scottish parliament followed from the result, it had been a very British election
campaign during which 'New Labour' played down the distinctiveness of its
campaign in Scotland, at least as compared with previous elections. Tory leader John
Major seemed more intent on raising constitutional politics than Tony Blair. Major's
belief was that there were votes to be won, in England at least, in suggesting that
Labour would rip up the constitution. The loss of all the Tories' Scottish seats was
as much a result of British-wide issues as anything peculiarly Scottish.

The promised two question referendum was held in September 1997. In 1979 the
anti-devolution forces had been better organised and better financed, and had run a
more united and professional campaign than the devolutionists. The situation was
reversed in 1997, though the levels of spending were little different between the two
camps. With the virtual demise of the Conservative party in Scotland, morale inside
'Think Twice', the anti-devolution camp was very low, with few activists keen on
facing a hostile electorate so soon after the general election. Its campaign also lacked
leadership - 'All the generals had been lost', in the words of a senior figure in Think
Twice. The anti-devolutionists were also ill-prepared. The Tories among them could
not prepare for the referendum prior to the election as to do so would have been seen
as an admission of defeat in the forthcoming election.

The pro-devolution forces had been cooperating well in advance of the
referendum and a number of organisations had come into existence that established
contact between Labour and the SNP. An overwhelming majority was recorded for a
Scottish parliament and a convincing majority for it to have tax-varying powers. As
Alice Brown, David McCrone and colleagues have shown, electors voted for the
parliament not simply because they felt Scottish but because of the socio-economic
expectations they had of it. They believed that policies flowing from the new
parliament would improve the quality of public welfare in Scotland.

Studies of the referendum result suggest that the relationship between the national
movement and labour and other progressive movements in Scotland had become
mutually reinforcing rather than antagonistic. They also show that the movement had
achieved the required level of unity, without each of its parts having to abandon its
own identity. Labour and the SNP campaigned together, agreeing that a Scottish
parliament would mark an improvement in the government of Scotland without
agreeing on the final destination of the constitutional process. Their efforts also
suggest that the eighteen years of Conservative rule, particularly the experience of
Mrs Thatcher's premiership, had shaped public attitudes in Scotland.

Results of 1979 and 1997 devolution referendums:

	% of votes cast	% of electorate	% of adjusted electorate*
1979 Referendum			
Support a Scottish Parliament			
Yes	51.6	-	32.5
No	48.4	-	30.5

1997 Referendum
Q1: Support a Scottish Parliament
Yes   74.3   44.7   45.7
No   25.7   15.5   15.8
Q2: Support tax-varying powers
Yes   63.5   38.1   38.9
No   36.5   21.9   22.4
* *Figures were adjusted to take account of the estimated number of deaths since the compilation of the register and number of people double registered, etc.*

The first elections to the Scottish parliament took place in May 1999, using a new, more proportional voting system. These resulted in Labour becoming the largest party but without an overall majority. Labour formed a coalition with the Liberal Democrats. The SNP, as the second largest party in the parliament, formed the main opposition with the Conservatives and three others.

Results of first elections to Scottish Parliament, May 1999:

	Constituency % vote (no. of seats)	Regional List % vote (no. of seats)	Total no. of seats
Labour	38.8 (53)	34.0 (3)	56
SNP	28.7 (7)	27.6 (28)	35
Conservative	15.6 (0)	15.5 (18)	18
Liberal Democrat	14.2 (12)	12.6 (5)	17
Others	2.8 (1)	10.3 (2)	3

VI

Conclusion
There has been much debate and more assertion on whether Scotland will move towards complete independence or whether devolution represents the 'settled will of the Scottish people'. If the half century before its establishment is any guide, it would be rash to jump to conclusions. At various stages in post-war Scottish politics, there were few commentators who expected that a Scottish parliament of any kind would ever be established. Nothing can be taken for granted. It seems highly unlikely now but it is possible that the devolution experiment will be abandoned and the parliament be suspended.

Much that has shaped the debate and prospects of the national movement has lain beyond its control. Opposition to change has often been understated. The inter-play of context and political activity, among both proponents and opponents of change, were important factors in the establishment of the Scottish parliament and they will continue to contribute to the future constitutional development of Scotland. The base of a strong sense of Scottish national identity has been reinforced as a consequence of establishing the parliament but, as we have seen, national identity is not nationalism. One key may be the manner in which Scottish expectations develop. This is not likely to be straightforward however. If the parliament meets Scottish expectations, it is conceivable that electors will be hungry for it to have more power, but equally they may be satisfied. If the parliament proves a disappointment, this may provoke a demand for a better, more powerful parliament or perhaps for a reduction in its powers or simply for less politics. As scholars have long noted, central government concessions can satisfy or whet appetites.

References and Further Reading:
The Referendum Experience: Scotland 1979, ed. John Bochel, David Denver and Allan Macartney (Aberdeen, 1981); Jack Brand, *The National Movement in Scotland*

(London, 1978); Alice Brown, David McCrone, Lindsay Paterson and Paula Surridge (1999), *The Scottish Electorate* (Basingstoke, 1999); Sir Reginald Coupland, *Welsh and Scottish Nationalism* (London, 1954); David Denver, James Mitchell, and Charles Pattie, *Scotland Decides: The Devolution Issue and the 1997 Referendum* (London, 2000); Michael Keating and David Bleiman, *Labour and Scottish Nationalism* (London, 1979); John MacCormick, *The Flag in the Wind* (London, 1955); James Mitchell, *Conservatives and the Union* (Edinburgh, 1990); James Mitchell, *Strategies for Self-Government* (Edinburgh, 1996); Stein Rokkan and Derek Urwin, *Economy, Territory, Identity: Politics of West European Peripheries* (London, 1983); *Scotland and Wales: Nations Again?*, ed. Bridget Taylor and Katarina Thomson (Cardiff, 1999; Scottish Affairs Special Issue, *Understanding Constitutional Change* (Edinburgh, 1998).

Index

Aberdeen, 28, 73, 115, 117
Aberystwyth, 86, 87
Account of a Conversation, 36, 39
Act of Security, 31, 35, 72
Act of Settlement, 33
Adams, Sir Grantley, 97
Addison Act, 128
Agreement of the People, 15
Aikenhead, Thomas, 37, 38
Alaska, 94
Albania, 150
Albany, James, duke, 27
Albemarle, Arnold Joost van Keppel, 1st earl, 30
Albert, Prince, 87
Alien Act, 37
Alness, Robert Munro, baron, 138
American colonies, 9, 20, 21, 45, 50-57, 81
Anglesey, 86, 87
Anne, Queen, 30, 33, 73, 83
Anti-Corn Law League, 85
Antrim, 150
Arfon, 88
Argument on behalf of the Catholics of Ireland, 67
Argyll, 136
Argyll, George Douglas Campbell, 8th duke, 126
Argyll, John Campbell, 2nd duke, 5, 42, 44, 46, 47, 73
Armenia, 118
Arthur, King, 82
Articles of Confederation, 58
Ashmolean museum, 84
Asquith, Herbert H., 108, 109, 110
Assynt Crofters Trust Ltd, 130
Atlantic, 50, 52, 54, 55, 56, 57
Attlee, Clement, 138, 139, 149, 161
Austin, John, 18, 25
Australia, 8, 91, 92, 93, 94, 96, 98, 99, 100, 142
Austrian empire, 71, 109
Ayton, W. E., 119

Balfour, Arthur James, later earl, 94, 107. 108, 109
Balfour Commission, 7, 135, 136, 137, 138, 141, 156
Baliol, King John de, 33

Ballot Act, 103
Bannockburn, 121
Baptists, 75
Barbados, 20, 97
Barbour, Mary, 128
Barlow, Sir Arthur, 134
Barony Church, 77
Barrington, Sir Jonah, 61
Basilikon Doran, 82
Bastille, 67
Batoum, 144
Belfast, 8, 11, 67, 69, 106, 109, 143, 145, 149, 150
Belhaven, John Hamilton, 2nd baron, 30, 33
Bellamy's, 92
Bentham, Jeremy, 18, 56
Beresford, John, 64
Berlin, 126
Berlin Wall, 151
Bernera, 125
Berwick, 28
Bevan, Aneurin, 89, 139
Beveridge, William, 155
Bevin, Ernest, 149
Bew, Paul, 110
Biggar, Joseph, 103
Bill of Rights (USA), 59
Birmingham, 89
Birmingham Political Union, 85
Birrell, Augustine, 109
bishops, 22, 23, 72, 73, 103
Black Acts, 4
Black and Tans, 111
Blackstone, Sir William, 16, 17, 18
Blackwood's Magazine, 119
Blair, Tony, 11, 95, 142, 162
Blenheim, 98
Board of Agriculture, 128, 129
Board of Trade, 29
Bodin, Jean, 34
Boece, Hector, 34
Bogdanor, Vernon, 151
Bolingbroke, Henry St John, 1st viscount, 17
Bonar Law, Andrew, 144
Book of Common Prayer, 72, 73
Border Advertiser, 120
Boswell, Alexander, Lord Auchinleck, 45
Boswell, James, 45, 46

Braes, 125
Brand, Jack, 155
Brandon, duke of, *see* Hamilton
Braveheart, 162
Brazil, 152
Bridgeton, 159
Bristol, 84
British-Irish Council, 152
British North America Act, 91, 92, 95
Brooke, Sir Basil, 147
Brown, Alice, 162
Brown, Ernest, 138
Bryce, James, 105
Buccleuch, Henry Scott, 3rd duke, 47, 48
Buchanan, George, 3, 34, 36
Buckingham, George Villiers, 1st duke, 29
Buckingham Palace, 110
Bulkeley, 84
Bulpitt, Jim, 145
Burgh, James, 56
Burke, Edmund, 56
Burke, Richard, 68
Burke, Thomas Henry, 88
Burnet, Gilbert, 30
Burns, Robert, 75
Bustamente, Alexander, 97
Bute, John Stuart, 3rd earl, 46
Butler, R. A., 140
Butt, Isaac, 102, 103

Caernarfon, 87
Caernarfonshire, 83
Call to the Church, 78
Callaghan, James, 137, 142
Calton Hill, 93
Cambridge Union, 92
Camden, John Jeffreys Pratt, 2nd earl, 69
Cameronians, 77
Campaign for a Scottish Assembly, 161
Campbell, Sir George, 102, 106
Campbell interest, 5, 44-47
Canada, 8, 91-100, 103, 108
Canada Acts (1840, 1867), 115
Canadian Confederation, 91
Canberra, 91, 96, 100
Canterbury, 97, 99
Cape of Good Hope, 93
Cardiff, 2, 8, 11, 81, 82, 84, 86, 88, 89
Cardigan, 82
Cardiganshire, 86
Carleton, Sir Dudley, 22
Carlyle, Thomas, 119
Carmarthen, 84, 86, 89
Carron iron works, 47

Carson, Sir Edward, 98, 108, 109, 110, 111
Carstares, William, 39, 72, 73, 74, 80
Cartier, George, 95
Cartwright, John, 56
Case of the Church of Scotland, 39
Catholic Relief Acts, 64, 68
Catholic, 6, 10, 15, 26, 33, 63, 64, 67, 68, 69, 70, 71, 78, 79, 80, 88, 103, 106, 107, 148, 149
Cavendish, Lord Frederick Charles, 88
Cawdor, 84
Cecil, Robert, 82
Celtic, 87, 88, 89
Chalmers, Thomas, 74, 75, 78, 80
Chamberlain, Austen, 94, 109, 111
Chamberlian, Joseph, 105
Chamberlain, Neville, 129
Chamberlain Act, 128
Chambers, Sir Robert, 18
chancellor, lord, 42, 43, 44, 46
Channel Islands, 54, 118
Charest, Jean, 99
Charlemont, James Caulfield, 1st earl, 63
Charles I, 26, 29, 71, 82
Charles II, 23, 24, 26
Chartists, 84, 85
Cheshire, 29
Chester, 54, 84
Chile, 3
Christchurch, 98
Church and Nation Committee, 79
Church of England, 4, 13, 14, 71, 72, 75, 79, 87
Church of Scotland, 6, 29, 43, 44, 47, 49, 71-80, 123, 136
Chuter Ede, James, 149
Churchill, Lord Randolph, 106
Claim of Right, 3, 93, 157
Clarendon, Edward Hyde, 1st earl, 29
Clark, Andrew Inglis, 91
Clerk of Penicuik, Sir John, 4
Clyde, 127
Clydebank, 130
Clydeside, 127
Clydesmuir, David John Colville, baron, 138
Coercive Acts, 51, 52
Coke, Sir Edward, 15
Colonial Laws Validity Act, 93
Colwyn Committee, 146
Common Market, 159
Commons, House of, 1, 2, 5, 12, 13, 14, 16, 17, 18, 19, 20, 22, 30, 50, 54, 55, 57, 58, 63, 66, 69, 82, 83, 86, 88, 92, 99, 100, 103, 105, 106, 108, 109, 110, 114, 116,

117, 118, 119, 128, 133, 135, 140, 144, 149
Commonwealth, 159
Company of Scotland, 29, 31
Confederation of British Industries, 136
Congested Districts Board, 126
Congregationalists, 75, 76
Conservative government/party, 89, 103, 107, 108, 109, 124, 126, 130, 136, 137, 142, 148, 155, 156, 157, 158, 160, 161, 162, 163
Considerations upon the Union, 37
Constantinople, 144
Constitutional Convention, 3, 157, 161
Contemporary Review, 105
Continental Congress, 57, 58
Convention Act, 69
Convention parliament, 34
Convention of royal burghs, 99
Convention of Scottish Local Authorities, 99
Cooper, Thomas, Lord, 3, 137, 157
Cooperative Women's Guild, 135
Country party, 16
Covenant, 7, 71, 74, 76, 108, 135, 156
Covenanters, 24, 26, 28, 71, 72
Craig, Sir James, 145, 146
Craig, Sir Thomas, 33, 36
Craig, Sir William, 150
Crawford, Sharman, 102
Crawfurd, Helen, 128
Crimean war, 119
Crofters Acts, 6, 123, 124, 126, 128, 130, 131
Crofters Commission, 124, 130
Crofters war, 128
Cromarty, George Mackenzie, 1st earl, 36, 37, 38, 39
Cromwell, Oliver, 5, 26, 27, 30, 31, 38, 82
Cromwell, Thomas, 82
Crosland, Anthony, 135
Culloden, 121
Cumberland, 29
Cumberland, William Augustus, duke, 46
Cumbernauld, 130
Cumnock, 130
Curragh mutiny, 109
Curtis, Lionel, 109
Cymru Fydd, 88

Dail, 145
Daily Express, 155
Dalkeith, 115, 116
Dalmeny, 115
Dalyell, Tam, 159
Darien scheme, 4, 31, 33

Davies, Norman, 81
Davitt, Michael, 124
De Cive, 34
Declaratory Act (1720), 10, 61, 62
Declaratory Act (1766), 51
Declaration of Arbroath, 3, 96
Declaration of Independence, 58
Dee, John, 82
Defence of the Realm Act, 129
Defoe, Daniel, 17, 18, 37, 38, 39
Denbighshire, 83,84, 88
Derry, 62, 63, 149
Devine, Tom, 74
Devonport Dock, 118
Devonshire, 63
Diamond, Jack, 149
Dicey, A,V., 105, 106, 108, 119
Dickens, Charles, 92
Dillon, John, 107
Disarming Acts, 5, 46
Disruption, 76, 77
Dissenters, 6, 67, 75, 76, 78, 80, 85, 87, 119
Dollan, Patrick, 127
Doon, 130
Dover, duke of, *see* Queensberry
Dover House 133, 134
Dr Bonham's Case, 15
Drennan, William, 64, 67
Dublin, 10, 30, 44, 54, 61, 62, 63, 65, 67, 68, 69, 70, 88, 103, 106, 110, 111, 146
Dublin Evening Post, 62
Dumbarton Herald, 120
Dundas, Henry, 47, 48
Dundas, Robert, 47
Dunedin, 98
Dungannon, 62
Dunraven, Windham Thomas Wyndham-Quin, 4th earl, 107
Durban, 98
Durham, 54
Dutch, 30, 31, 34
Dynevore, 84

East India Company, 31
East Lothian, 42
Economist, 115, 158
Edge of the Union, 148
Edinburgh, 2, 3, 10, 11, 37, 42, 47, 72, 74, 75, 134, 135, 136, 137, 138, 140
Edward I, 81
EFTA, 159
Eglinton, Alexander Montgomerie, 6th earl, 136
Egypt, 118
Eikon Basilike, 82

Eire, 147
electorate, 1, 18, 81, 84, 109, 113, 116, 142
Elizabeth, Princess, 33
Elizabeth I, 82
Elizabeth II, 157
Ellis, Tom, 87
Ely, 63
Empire Settlement Act, 129
England, 1, 22, 42, 43, 49, 53, 62, 72, 79, 82, 83, 84, 85, 86, 87, 88, 91, 97, 100, 102, 103, 113, 115, 116, 117, 118, 119, 120, 121, 130, 133, 134, 157
England's Case against Home Rule, 106, 119
English Liberal Association, 117
Enlightenment, 45, 46, 47, 48
Essay at Removing National Prejudices, 38
Europe, 3, 7, 23, 25, 36, 71, 138, 150, 158
European Union, 2, 151
Evans, Gwynfor, 89
Evils of Centralisation and its Cure, 119
Ewing, Mrs Winnie, 141
exchequer, 28, 30, 133, 140, 147
Exclusion Act, 16
Exclusion crisis, 15, 16

Faithful Tribe, 148
Falkirk, 47
Fawcett, C.B., 117
Federal Constitution, 59-60
Fenians, 102
Ferguson, Adam, 47
Ferguson, John, 124
Fielding, W.S., 96
Fife, 75, 91
Findlater, earl of, *see* Seafield
Fitzgibbon, John, 66
Fitzwilliam, William Wentworth, 2nd earl, 69
Five Articles of Perth, 24
Fletcher, Andrew, Lord Milton, 44, 45, 46, 47, 48
Fletcher of Saltoun, Andrew, 24, 30, 35, 36, 37, 39, 40, 45
Flood, Henry, 61, 62, 63
Florida, 56
Follick, Mont, 89
Forbes, Duncan, 44, 45, 46
Forfar Herald, 113, 120
Forster, W.E., 104
Forsyth, Michael, 161
Forth road bridge, 135
Forth-Clyde canal, 47
Forward Movement, 78, 79
Foster, John, 64, 65
Fotheringay Castle, 121

Fox, Charles James, 18, 63, 66
France, 30, 31, 43, 46, 48, 67, 68
Franklin, Benjamin, 47
Free Church of Scotland, 77
Freeman, E.A., 105, 106
Freeman's Journal, 62
Frome, 117

Gaelic Athletic Association, 103
Galloway, Joseph, 56, 57
Gallup Poll, 155
Gartcosh, 161
Garvin, J.L., 108
GATT, 159
Geddes, Patrick, 119
General Assembly of the Church of Scotland, 3, 6, 25, 73, 75, 76, 77, 78, 79
George, Henry, 124
George, Prince of Wales, 66
George I, 83
George II, 83
George III, 46, 57, 66
Germany, 38
Gibbon, Peter, 149
Gilmour Report, 7, 134
Gladstone, Herbert, 108
Gladstone, William Ewart, 7, 87, 103, 104, 105, 106, 107, 114, 115, 116, 118, 120, 121, 125, 151
Glasgow, 44, 47, 75, 77, 78, 91, 98, 124, 126, 127, 128, 129, 130, 131, 159
Glasgow Herald, 136
Glyndwr, Owain, 81
God, 13, 14, 15, 17, 19, 35, 80
God Save Ulster!, 148
Godolphin, Sidney, 1st earl, 30, 38
Golden Acts, 4
Goschen formula, 137
Govan, 124, 127
Government of Ireland Act, 111, 144, 147
Government of Wales Act, 144
Grant, Francis, 38, 39, 40
Grant, James, 117
Grant, John, 117
Granville, George Granville Leveson-Gower, 2nd earl, 104
Grattan, Henry, 10, 61, 62, 63, 65, 66, 91, 103
Great Advantages by an Union with England, 39
Great Yarmouth, 93
Green Book, 151
Greenshields, James, 43, 72, 73
Grenville, George, 54
Grenville, William Wyndham, baron, 66, 67, 68
Griffithite (Arthur Griffith), 110

Grotius, Hugo, 34, 38, 39
Gunn, Angus, 158

Haddow, Sir Douglas, 139, 141
Haig, Field Marshal Sir Douglas, 77
Haldane Report, 134
Halliday, Jimmy, 154
Hamilton, 7, 141
Hamilton, Ian, 157
Hamilton, James Douglas, 4th duke, 43
Hanoverian succession, 30, 33, 38, 74, 83
Hansard, 92
Harcourt, William, 125
Hardwicke, Philip Yorke, 1st earl, 46
Harley, Robert, 30
Harrington, James, 15
Haverfordwest, 82
Heaney, Seamus, 150
Henry VIII, 26, 34, 82
Hervey, Frederick Augustus, earl bishop of
    Derry, 62, 63
Hibernian Journal, 62
Highland Land League, 135
Historical Account of ... Parliament of Scotland,
    35-36
History of Parliament, 4
History of the Union, 37
Hitler, Adolf, 94
Hobbes, Thomas, 34, 35, 38, 39
Hobhouse, L.T., 109
Hodge v. the Queen, 95
Hodges, James, 37, 39
Hohenzollerns, 36
Holland, 43, 72
Holyrood, 6, 11, 27, 93, 100
Home Government Association, 102, 103, 114
Home Office, 125, 138, 147
Home Rule for Scotland, 119
Home Rule movement, 6, 7, 8, 10, 88, 91, 92,
    96, 100, 102-122, 123, 134, 135, 136, 137,
    139, 149, 151, 155, 156, 159
Honyman, Bishop Andrew, 34
Housing Act (1923) 129
Housing Act (1924), 124, 129, 130, 131
Housing, Letting (Scotland) Act, 127
Housing and Town Planning (Scotland) Act, 129
Howth, 110
Huddersfield, 117
Huggins, Sir Godfrey, 99
Humber, 100
Hume, David, 48
Hume, John, 138, 140
Hunter-Scott Committee, 128
Hutcheson, Francis, 44

India, 135, 144
Interest of Scotland in Three Essays, 39
Inveraray, 46
International Scots Home Rule League, 114
Inverness, 125
Inverness-shire, 125
Ireland, 5, 6, 8, 9, 10, 20, 25, 26, 29, 30, 35,
    36, 44, 46, 48, 49, 61-70, 72, 79, 81, 84,
    87, 88, 89, 94, 100, 102-112, 114-121, 123-
    126, 128, 131, 141, 151, 152
Ireland Bill, 149
Irish Free State, 79
Irish Land Act (1881), 88, 123, 128
Irish Land Act (1903), 107
Irish Land War, 128
Irish Reform Association, 107
Irish Republican Army, 114, 149, 151
Islay, Archibald Campbell, earl (and later 3rd
    duke of Argyll), 5, 44, 45, 46, 47, 48
Isle of Man, 54, 118
Italy, 109
Ius Populi Vindicatum, 38

Jackson, William, 69
Jacobins, 69
Jacobites 5, 36, 43, 45, 46, 47, 72, 74, 80, 83,
    121, 133
Jamaica, 97, 98
James V, 34
James VI and I, 5, 15, 25, 29, 33, 82
James VII and II, 3, 15, 23, 24, 27, 33, 34, 83
Jansenists, 71
Jeffrey, Francis, 46
Jeffreys, Judge George, 83
Jesus College, 84
John, E.T., 88
Johnston, Tom, 134, 137, 138, 140

Kames, Henry Home, Lord, 45, 46, 49
keeper of the great seal, 42
Kent, 29
Kettle, Thomas, 110
Kidd, Colin, 23, 24
Kilbrandon Commission, 7, 90, 133, 139, 141,
    144
Kilmuir, 125
Kilsyth, 130
king, 12, 13, 14, 15, 16, 19, 20, 23, 24, 25, 26,
    30, 31, 33, 34, 35, 50, 54, 57, 58, 66, 82
King, William Lyon Mackenzie, 94, 96
Kinghorn, 91
Kitchener, Horatio Herbert, 1st earl, 127

Labour government/party, 7, 8, 89, 90, 114,

124, 127, 128, 129, 130, 131, 135, 137, 140, 142, 145, 147, 149, 155, 156, 158, 159, 190, 161, 162, 163
Lampeter, 86
Land League, 103
Land Reform Policy Group, 124
Land Settlement (Scotland) Act, 129
Lang, Ian, 161
Lansdowne, Henry Petty-Fitzmaurice, 5th marquess, 109, 110
Larne, 109
Lauderdale, John Maitland, 1st duke, 5, 23, 27, 30
Laws of Peace and War, 38
Leap in the Dark, 106
Leckmelm, 125
Lecky, W.E.H., 106
Leeds, 126
Legitimist Jacobite League, 121
Leighton, Archbishop Robert, 35
Leinster, 63
Levellers, 15
Leviathan, 34, 35
Lewis, 125, 129
Lhuyd, Edward, 84
Liberal Democrats, 161, 163
Liberal government/party, 8, 49, 85, 86, 87, 88, 90, 103, 104, 105, 107, 108, 109, 110, 114, 115, 116, 117, 119, 121, 126, 127, 131, 133, 135, 136, 155, 158
Liberal party (Canada), 95, 96, 99
Liddell, Helen, 160
Liverpool, 84, 85, 86
Liverpool Mercury, 86
Lleyn peninsula, 86
Lloyd George, David, 86, 87, 89, 109, 110, 111, 129
Local Government Board, 128
Locke, John, 4, 16, 17, 18, 38
London, 36, 42, 46, 63, 65, 66, 68, 72, 82, 83, 84, 86, 87, 118, 126, 133-38, 140, 144, 145, 146, 149, 157
London, Treaty of, 27
London Working Men's Association, 85
Long, Walter, 110-111, 128
Lords, House of, 1, 2, 13, 14, 16, 18, 19, 20, 22, 42, 43, 44, 46, 50, 58, 72, 73, 92, 93, 106, 107, 118, 119, 133
Lords of the Articles, 23, 24
Lossiemouth, 94
Lothian, 44
Lothian, earl of, 136
Lothian, Schomberg Henry Kerr, 9th marquess, 126, 133

Loughborough, 89
Louis XIV, 71
Lovat estates, 46

Macandrew, James, 98
MacCormick, John, 154, 156, 157, 161
MacDonald, James Ramsay, 89, 94
Macdonald, John A., 91, 95, 96, 106
MacDonnell, Alexander, 107
MacDonnell Report, 134
Macgill, Stevenson, 75
Machinery of Government Committee, 134, 139
Machynlleth, 81
Mackenzie, Sir George, 34, 35, 37, 38
Mackintosh, J.P., 141
Maclay, John, 140
Macmillan, Harold, 157
MacNeice, 151
Macpherson, Donald, 98
Macrae, David, 120
Madoc, Prince, 82
Madrid, 89
Major, John, 162
Making of the Future, 119
malt tax, 43-44
Maltese, 148
Manchester, 85, 86, 87, 126
Manley, Norman, 97
Mansergh, Nicholas, 145
Maori, 98
Mar, earl of, 136
Marjoribanks, Edward, 116
Marlborough, 98
Marlborough, John Churchill, 1st duke, 30
Mary, Queen of Scots, 3
Maryland, 54
Massachusetts, 58
Matthew, Colin, 104
Mazzini, Giuseppe, 108
McCarthy, Justin, 102
McCrone, David, 162
McHugh, Michael, 127
McIntyre, Robert, 154
McNeil, Hector, 155
Melbourne, 99, 100, 121
Melbourne, William Lamb, 2nd viscount, 76
Members of Parliament, 10, 16, 55, 62, 82, 83, 87, 88, 89, 92, 100, 105, 111, 114, 115, 116, 118, 134, 136, 137, 139, 140, 145, 148, 160
Merioneth, 82, 87
Merthyr Tydfil, 84, 85, 86
Mesopotamia, 144
Methodists, 85

Middlesbrough, 88
Midlothian, 7, 115, 116, 118
Millar, Ian, 141
Milton, John, 15
Mitchell, James, 119, 140, 141
Mitchell, William, 116
Moderate party, 6, 74
Moncrieff, Colin Scott, 121
Monklands, 130
Montagu, Edwin, 111
Montgomeryshire, 87
Montrose Review, 119, 120
Morgan, Kenneth, 88, 89
Morley, John, 107
Morocco, 89
Morrison, Herbert, 141
Morton, Graeme, 48
Mostyn, 84
Motherwell, 130, 140, 154
Mowat, Oliver, 95, 96
Muirhead, Roland, 114
Musgrave, Sir Christopher, 36

Nairn, Tom, 143, 149
Nantes, edict of, 71
Napier, Francis, 9th baron, 125
Napier, Theodore, 113, 117, 120, 121
Naples, 29
Natal, 98, 99
National Association for the Vindication of
    Scottish Rights, 7, 113, 116-21
National League, 103
National Party of Scotland, 114
nationalism, 6, 26, 30, 48, 88, 93, 94, 102,
    103, 105-111, 113, 115-121, 126, 133-
    141, 143, 149, 154-158, 160, 163
NATO, 159
Navigation Act, 31
Neath, 85
Nelson province, 99
Netherlands, 31
Newbattle, 116
Newcastle, Thomas Pelham-Holles, 1st duke,
    46
Newfoundland, 92, 94, 95, 98
Newport, 84
New South Wales, 92, 93
New York, 20
New Zealand, 8, 91, 93, 94, 97, 98, 99
Norfolk, 93
North, Frederick, Lord, 51, 52, 56, 63, 65
North Lochinver, 130
North Sea, 158
Northcote-Trevelyan reforms, 134

Northern Ireland, 2, 9, 10, 11, 92, 98, 108,
    110, 135, 137, 143-152
Northington, Robert Henley, 2nd earl, 63,
Northumberland, 29
Nova Scotia, 92, 95, 96

Observations on the Acts of Parliament, 37
O'Connell, Daniel, 102, 111, 119
Old Believers, 71
Oliver, F.S., 108, 109, 111
Ontario, 91, 93, 95, 99
OPEC, 158
Orange Free State, 98
Orde, Thomas, 63
Original Burgher Synod, 76
Otago, 97, 98
Ottawa, 91, 92, 94, 95, 96
Owen, Sir Hugh, 86
Oxford, 84, 87, 89

Pacific ocean, 94
Paisley, 75
Palestine, 144
Paris, 126
Parker, Henry, 15
parliamentarians, 14, 15, 82
Parnell, Charles Stewart, 87, 103, 105, 107,
    119
Partick, 124, 127
Paterson, W.P., 77
Patriot Resolved, 38, 40
Patronage Act, 6, 71, 73, 74, 75
Paulin, Tom, 150
Peace Society, 85, 86
Pearsean (Patrick Pearse), 150
Peel, Sir Robert, 84
Pembrokeshire, 84
Pennsylvania, 54
Persia, 144
Perth, 24, 46
Petyt, William, 16
Philadelphia, 55, 59
Phillips, Sir John, 84
Phoenix Park, 125
Picton, 98
Pitt, William, the Elder, 56
Pitt, William, the Younger, 61, 63, 64, 65,
    66, 69, 70
Plaid Cymru, 8, 89, 90
Plunkett, Horace, 109
Pocock, J.G.A., 144
Ponsonby family, 63, 66
Pope, 13, 25
Porteous, James, 158, 159

Porter, Norman, 150
Portland, William Bentinck, 1st earl, 30
Portland, William Bentinck, 3rd duke, 63
Portree, 125
Portuguese, 26
Post Office Act, 54
Pottinger, George, 138
Poulson, John, 138
Pownall, Thomas, 55
Poynings' Law, 10, 23, 29, 62
Precarious Belonging, 148
presbyterian, 4, 6, 35, 37, 38, 39, 43, 46,
    47, 67, 68, 71-80, 119, 123
Pretender, James Edward Stuart,the Old, 73
Pretoria, 199
Price, Richard, 19, 56
Priestley, Joseph, 19
Prince Edward Island, 92
privy council, 5, 10, 25, 26, 42, 43, 44
Prospectus, 117
Protestant, 10, 29, 33, 38, 62, 64, 65, 68,
    69, 71, 78, 79, 88, 102, 106, 108, 143,
    148, 149, 150
Provinces of England, 119
Prussia, 36
Pufendorf, Samuel, 34

Quakers, 85
Quebec, 56, 91, 95, 96, 97, 99
Queensberry, James Douglas, 2nd duke, 42, 43
Queensland, 91, 92

Rait, Robert, 4, 23
Ravenscraig, 161
Rebecca riots, 84, 87, 88
rebellion of 1798, 10
Redmond, John, 107, 110
referendum, 7, 18, 95, 96, 97, 141, 142, 160,
    162, 163
Reform Act (1832), 84
Reformation, 13, 25, 73, 82
reformers, 1, 2
regency crisis, 66
Rendel, Stuart, 87
Rent Restriction Act, 124, 128, 131
Renunciation Act, 62
Representatives, House of, 59
Rerum Scoticarum Historia, 3
Restoration (1660), 15, 26, 27, 35
Revolution, American, 50-60, 75
Revolution, French, 64, 67, 75
Revolution, Glorious, 1, 16, 27, 30, 34, 50
Rhine, 144
Rhuddlan, Statute of (1284), 81

Richard, Henry, 85, 86
Ridpath, George, 4, 33, 35, 36, 37, 39, 40
Riley, Patrick, 43
Rise and Fall of the Irish Nation, 61
Robertson, J.P., 116
Robertson, William, 47, 48, 74
Rogart, 135
Rokkan, Stein, 156
Romans, John, 116, 119
Rose, Richard, 145, 149
Rosebery, Archibald Philip Primrose, 5th earl,
    107, 114, 115, 120
Ross, Willie, 140
Roxburgh, John Ker, 1st duke, 44
Royal High School, 93
Royal Bank of Scotland, 44, 45
royalists, 14, 15
Rump parliament, 82
Russia, 71, 152
Rutherford, Samuel, 34

Saatchi & Saatchi, 158
St Andrews House, 134, 138, 139
Salisbury, Robert Cecil, 3rd marquess, 103,
    104, 107
Salmond, Alex, 96
Salzburg, 71
Samuel, Herbert, 108
Saxons, 88
Scandinavia, 93
Scotland, 2-11, 18, 22-49, 71-80, 81, 83, 87,
    88, 89, 90, 91, 93, 94, 96, 97, 98, 99,
    102, 113-142, 154-163
Scotland Act (1998), 91, 144
Scotland's Great Advantages, 39
Scotland's Grievances, 33
Scotland's Sovereignty asserted, 33
Scotsman, 116, 136
Scottish convention, 154
Scottish County Councils Bill, 118
Scottish Covenant Association, 135, 136,
    156, 158
Scottish Grand Committee, 135, 136, 139,
    140
Scottish Highlander, 120
Scottish Home Rule Association, 7, 113-121
Scottish National Assembly, 155
Scottish National Association of Victoria,
    120, 121
Scottish National League, 114
Scottish National Movement, 114, 120
Scottish National Party, 96, 114, 140, 141,
    154, 158, 159, 160, 161, 162, 163
Scottish Office, 5, 7, 29, 95, 114, 125, 133,

134, 135, 136, 138, 139, 140, 141, 157
Scottish Patriotic Association, 120
Scottish Toleration Truly Stated, 39
Scottish TUC, 136
Scottish secretary of state, 7, 42, 45, 114,
133, 134, 136, 137, 138, 139, 140,
155
Seafield, James Ogilvy, 1st earl, 42, 43
Seditious Meetings Act, 18
Senate (USA), 59
Seton of Pitmedden, William, 4, 37, 38,
39
Settlers, 150
Seymour, Sir Edward, 36
Shannon family, 63
Shettleston, 127
Shrewsbury, 84
Shropshire, 88
Sicily, 29
Sinclair, John (Lord Pentland), 133
Sinn Fein, 110
Skye, 125, 129
Small Landholders (Scotland) Act, 127, 128,
129
Smith, Adam, 47, 48, 55
Smith, Goldwin, 106
Smith, John, 11, 137
Smith, Sydney, 93
Smoaking Flax Unquenchable, 39
Snowdonia, 82
Social Services Agreement (1948), 148
Socialists, 155
Somerset House, 86
Somme, battle of, 77
South Africa, 91, 93, 98, 106, 118, 151
South Africa Act, 91
Southern Rhodesia, 99
Speaker (of parliament), 83, 92, 93, 98
Spectator, 105
Spence, Lewis, 120
Staffordshire, 84
Stamp Act (1765), 51, 52, 54
Steering Committee on Economic Policy,
149
Steuart of Goodtrees, James, 34, 38
Stirling Bridge, 119, 120
Stone of Destiny, 157, 162
Stormont, 2, 10, 11, 143, 145, 146, 147, 148
Stuart, James, 136
Supreme Court (USA), 60
Sutherland, earl of, 136
Swansea, 84
Sydney, 99, 100

Tarbat, George Mackenzie, 1st viscount, 37
Tasmania, 99
Tay bridge, 135
Tea Act, 51, 52
Thatcher, Margaret, 124, 161, 162
Thatcherism, 7, 160, 161
Thomas, Peter, 83
Thompson, F.M.L., 124
Thomson, Andrew, 75
Thomson, George, 137
Times, 11, 86, 103, 106
Tiree, 129
Toleration Act (1712), 6, 71, 73, 74, 79
Tone, Theobald Wolfe, 67
Toronto, 95
Tory, 16, 39, 43, 76, 83, 84, 99, 103, 104,
110, 111, 118, 133, 134, 135, 137, 140,
142, 155, 156, 159, 161, 162
Townshend duties, 51, 52
Transvaal, 98
Treasonable Practices Act, 18
Treasons Act, 20
Treasury, 28, 46, 56, 104, 129, 137, 139,
146, 147
Tredegar, 88
Trialogus, 40
Triennial Act (1641), 28
Trinidad, 97
Trinity College, Dublin, 110, 111
Trollope, Anthony, 99
Tucker, Josiah, 55
Tudor, Prince Arthur, 82
Tudor, Henry, 81
Tudor, Owen, 82
Tweeddale, John Hay, 4th marquess, 45
Tyrone, 62

Uist, 129
Ulster, 10, 11, 72, 103, 104, 106, 108, 109,
110, 111, 143-152
Ulster Twilight, 150
Ulster Unionist Council, 146
Ulster Volunteer Force, 108, 109, 150
Ulster's Uncertain Defenders, 148
Under Siege, 148
Unemployment Insurance Agreement, 146
Union of 1707, 2, 3, 4, 6, 7, 10, 18, 32, 33-
40, 42, 43, 45, 48, 49, 66, 71, 72, 73, 74,
77, 79, 80, 84, 91, 95, 113, 116, 117, 119,
120, 121, 123
Union of 1800, 9, 10, 48, 66, 69, 88, 102,
103, 106, 144
Unionist, 6, 10, 32, 37, 39, 48, 78, 79, 102,
78, 79, 102, 103, 104, 107, 110, 113, 117,

120, 135, 137, 143, 145-150, 155, 156, 160
United Free Church, 77, 78
United Irishmen, 67, 69
United Kingdom, 2, 4, 9, 10, 11, 20, 85, 87,
    91, 92, 100, 102, 105, 108, 115, 118, 119,
    120, 121, 130, 131, 144, 145, 147, 148,
    149, 151, 154, 156, 157, 158
United Presbyterians, 77
United States of America, 9, 47, 58, 94, 105,
    107, 119, 151
University of Edinburgh, 47, 75
University of Glasgow, 44, 157
University of Wales, 86
Urwin, Derek, 156

Vancouver, 92
Vanguard Unionist, 150
Vaughan, 84
Venezuela, 118
Veto Act, 76
viceroy of Ireland, 10, 25, 29, 63
Victoria, Queen, 84, 87, 95, 121
Virginia, 47
Volunteers, Irish, 10, 61, 62-65, 69, 110

Waddie, Charles, 117, 118, 119, 120
Waddie, James, 117
Waddie, John S., 117, 119, 120
Wade, General George, 44
Wales, 2, 6, 7, 9, 11, 29, 44, 49, 54, 81-90,
    95, 100, 118, 120, 130, 139, 141, 144,
    157
Wallace, William, 120
Walpole, Sir Robert, 43, 44, 45, 46
War of American Independence, 20, 52, 57
War, First World, 77, 86, 89, 94, 110, 126,
    127, 128, 129, 131, 135
War, Second World, 130, 134, 136, 138, 140,
    148, 156
Wealth of Nations, 47
Weber, Max, 148
Webster, James, 39
Weir family, 136
Wellington, 91, 92, 98
Welsh Language Society, 90
Welsh Nation, 87
Welsh Office, 139
West Indies, 97
West Lothian, 130, 159
Wester Ross, 125
Westminster, 1, 2, 3, 5-11, 25, 30, 39, 42,
    43, 46, 47, 54, 55, 74, 78, 82-87, 89-94,
    99, 100, 105, 106, 113, 114, 116, 118,
    120, 123, 131, 134, 136, 137, 138,

144-151
Werstminster, Statute of, 9, 94, 96
Westminster Abbey, 157
Westminster Confession of Faith, 75
Westmorland, John Fane, 10th earl, 67, 68
Westphalia, Treaty of, 38, 71
Westwood, Joseph, 155
Wheatley, John, 124, 127, 129, 130, 131
Whig, 16, 49, 76, 83
White, John, 77, 78, 79, 80
Whitehall, 94, 134, 137, 138, 139, 146, 151
Wick, 117
William III, 30, 33, 39, 72, 83
Williams, Gwynn, 86
Williams, Sir William, 83
Williams-Wynne, Sir Watkin, 83, 84
Wilson, J. Harold, 11
Wilson, President Woodrow, 151
Witherspoon, John, 47
Wolfe, Billy, 159
Woodburn, Arthur, 140, 141, 155
Wool Act, Irish (1662), 28
Wright, Frank, 149
Wylie, Robert, 37, 39
Wyndham, George, 107
Wynnstay, 83

Yom Kippur War, 158
Yorkshire, 43
Young Scots Society, 114, 136
Young Wales, 88

Zulu, 98